UNDERSTANDING PROPERTY LAW

Tim Murphy, Simon Roberts and Tatiana Flessas teach at the
London School of Economics and Political Science.

UNDERSTANDING LAW
Series Editor: Roger Brownsword

Understanding Contract Law
John Adams and Roger Brownsword

Understanding Law
John Adams and Roger Brownsword

Understanding Criminal Law
C.M.V. Clarkson

Understanding Public Law
Gabriele Ganz

Understanding Equity and Trusts
Jeffrey Hackney

Understanding Tort Law
Carol Harlow

Understanding Property Law
Tim Murphy, Simon Roberts and Tatiana Flessas

Tim Murphy,
Simon Roberts and Tatiana Flessas

UNDERSTANDING
PROPERTY LAW

Fourth Edition

LONDON
SWEET & MAXWELL
2004

Published by Sweet & Maxwell Limited
of 100 Avenue Road, Swiss Cottage, London NW3 3PF
(http://www.sweetandmaxwell.co.uk)

Tim Murphy, Simon Roberts and Tatiana Flessas assert the moral right to be
identified as the authors of this work

ISBN 0–421–82930–3

Typeset by LBJ Typesetting Ltd of Kingsclere
Printed and bound by TJ International Ltd, Padstow, Cornwall

Contents

AUTHORS' PREFACE TO THE FOURTH EDITION

Tim Murphy and Simon Roberts warmly welcome Tatiana Flessas as co-author of the Fourth Edition of *Understanding Property Law*; they are particularly grateful to her for taking responsibility for changes incidental to the introduction of the Land Registration Act 2002. We would like to thank Alain Pottage for his help with this edition.

WTM
SR
TF
May 2004

AUTHOR'S PREFACE TO THE FIRST EDITION

There is no single way of introducing the study of the English law of property. The approach adopted here, for good or bad, is "historical", in some sense. What follows is not, to be sure, a "narrative", but a selective "looking back" at aspects of the past which, in our view, shed light upon the present. Such an approach takes content, and the context of the content, seriously, if selectively, and places great stress on the concerns which underscored and motivated the generation of the materials which the student encounters. Of course an introduction of this kind involves the problem of presenting the subject in a way that led Milsom recently to observe that in parts of "our books on property law . . . the reader can sometimes wonder what century he is in" (1981, p.viii). But that is the point. It is not clear what century we are in, because the mind of the English property lawyer inhabits many centuries as if they were all part of the present. This is not a criticism: lawyers have a job to do and that job is not to write more history books but to get on and deal with what presses in the present. So this is an autocombustible text. It assumes that the student needs to know something of the past to get a grip on the present; but once that grip is reasonably secure, it assumes that he or she, in turning from contemplation (if student life can still be so described) to activity, to the work of the world, will forget these reminiscences in the course of getting on with the task in hand.

Much of this book owes its genesis to our experience of teaching property law to Intermediate students at the London School of Economics. Some of it derives from a handout for students prepared by the first-named author, who would also like to thank the participants in a research seminar at University College London for their comments on a paper dealing with "English Formalism". Pages 190–192 largely reproduce a section of a paper prepared for the Instituto di Diritto Comparato in Florence, "The Right to Housing and the English Legal Tradition".

We have run up many debts in the preparation of the present work. In particular, we would like to thank (without associating them with its many flaws) Stuart Anderson, Joe Jacob, Martin Loughlin, Martin Partington, Alison Real and Colin Scott.

WTM
SR
London
May 1987

THE IDEA OF PROPERTY

Relationship Between People + Things

Hunter-gatherers

If any social group is to exist, there have to be some understandings among the members as to how access to things in general, and to scarce valued resources in particular, is to be arranged. To use the lawyer's distinction, there is always a difference between a person's acquisition of physical control over resources and the common recognition, the shared understanding, that he or she rather than anyone else should control these resources. This much is true of even the most remote groups of hunter-gatherers, where relations between people and things are primarily geared towards consumption. Observers detect clear understandings how food, once gathered, should be consumed, about how the larger game animals should be divided up. Among the Hadza of what is now Tanzania, for example, only adult males may consume certain parts of game animals; and a hunter is expected to provide meat for the mother of the woman with whom he lives (Woodburn, 1972). In even the simplest societies, therefore, a set of norms surrounds the consumption of valued scarce resources, norms concerned not just with what kinds of things should or should not be consumed, but with who can consume particular things over which control has been assumed.

A general human and social condition, then, is being delineated. In any culture, there must be some conception of appropriate ways to allocate resources. There must be ideas about who can properly act in a given way in relation to a particular resource. In other words, there must be ideas about relations between persons, as well as ideas about the relations between persons and things, and these requirements tend to force other, sometimes very important, questions. Over which resources are persons to be permitted to assume control? In what sense, if any, are persons to count as or to be treated as resources? Perhaps most fundamental, if not always explicit, in any culture is the question of how the difference between a person and a thing is to be specified, which already presupposes that answers of some kind are available to the questions "What is a person?" and "What is a thing?".

Possession among hunter-gatherers of the most important resources—food—is of necessity transient and geared to regimes of consumption. In groups that are organised around stock-herding, the position is transformed. The accent is no longer confined to the distribution and closely connected consumption of valued things, but shifts to their conservation and management through time. The element of time is decisive here, since the time span over which people remain in control of certain things is greatly increased, and with it the degree of control which is required increases. The bush from which hunter-gatherers have picked today's nuts or berries can be forgotten until, with the cycle of the seasons, a new growth appears. A herd of goats, by contrast, demands closer and more constant attention. Assembling a herd of animals makes people think and reach understandings about what it means to have things in a way that a regime geared exclusively to distribution and consumption does not. Who shall assume managerial responsibility for the herd? Who should enjoy the resources which the herd represents? What should be done with the increased resources that become available if the herd expands? What should happen to the herd as contemporary managers grow old and die? All of these questions also point to the fact that the herd may represent a source of social power, more extensive in its contemporary implications, and more enduring in time, than the resources available to any hunter-gatherer.

The practice of agriculture, of settled cultivation of land, involves further changes in how it is possible to think. A particular tract of land, the fixed place of birth, living and death, may come to provide the ultimate anchor of both "individual" and "society" in such a way that the identity of person and group come to be constituted in terms of place. This link between person and place is strengthened by the processes of domestication which settlement involves. A home is built. Hedges, ditches and boundary walls at once intensify the relation between people and land, and provide the visible indications of inclusion and exclusion which fixed residence and settled cultivation inevitably come to involve. My goats cannot graze where you at the same time are trying to grow corn.

Settlement poses sharply and insistently other questions about the relationship between people and things. If you lose your ring or your cow, or have it taken from you, you may not be able to find it. Nor will it be obvious in most cases to someone encountering the thief that the thing in his possession is not his. Land stays put; most people remember where they were born and where they have lived. If someone takes your land, you must know unless you have moved on and abandoned it. So, settled cultivation forces people to think more intensely about what it means to have things, and about what things mean in terms of relations between human beings.

Land also permits almost infinite degrees of intensity of exploitation, depending upon the technological capacities of a society, whether for grazing, growing crops, or building. Land is also continuous: it raises the question of boundaries, of where my land begins and yours stops. And your use of your land or what you do on your land may interfere with my enjoyment of my land, or my ability to enjoy peace and quiet when I am at home. Even if these disturbances arise from your use of or failure to control an animal that belongs to you, it is our physical contiguity resulting from our respective occupancies of land which makes it possible for you to disturb me. If your music keeps me awake at night, or your goat eats my tomatoes, the conflict between us is not just a conflict between people but a conflict mediated by claims to land.

The need in any society for common understandings about management of and access to resources does not say anything about what those understandings might be. It does not mean that in any society there will be a conception of ownership in the sense that "This goat is mine" or "This is my field" means that I have exclusive access to it. It is possible for no one to think in terms of "my goat" or "my field" at all. But in all societies the different normative problems which the existence of the goat and the field presents for the members must be resolved. Who can manage the goat undisturbed, who can have its milk, its offspring, or the goat itself to eat, and what is to happen when the present holder dies? The same is true of land: who is responsible for its management, who may cultivate it, who can take the harvest and what difference will the death of human beings make to the answers to these questions? All of these questions flow from the very nature of the relation between people in society and goats or land, and answers to these questions are invariably found.

This general condition does not necessarily imply any explicit agreement, consciously arrived at, about these matters. Understandings about allocation may develop slowly over time, with their origins and content remaining unexamined by members of the group. Nor does anything that has been said require the presence of "government" in the sense of self-conscious efforts to provide rules about allocation or attempts to police those rules, let alone the presence of differentiated agencies established for that purpose. Ethnography abounds with examples of communities which clearly have shared ideas about how resources should be allocated, and where people appear to act regularly in conformity to those ideas, but where there are no specialised agencies to oversee how resources are managed or controlled.

While the presence of common understandings about management of, and access to, animals and land does not in any sense imply the need for government, the social power represented by the accumulation of a herd or the exercise of control over land does bring with it the possibility of sustained domination, and creates the conditions under which government may come into being. Stock-herding and settlement may provide both the resources on the basis of which it becomes possible to support a following and the means for rewarding loyal support.

Where the state does exist, this must have implications for the common understandings about resource management. First, these are likely to become progressively more articulate and explicit. Among the means through which sovereigns invariably seek to consolidate and extend control over their subjects are getting to know the local rules and offering facilities for dispute resolution. This necessarily implicates the state in recognising at least parts of the social repertoires of norms already in place, even in areas where the state does not actively become involved in rule-making. Where the state exists, the spontaneous, unconscious reproduction of norms within social groups will thus be supplemented by the conscious, often calculated, recognition and production of "law" within agencies of the state. So as the state assumes responsibility for handling disputes about resource allocation, at least some of the understandings relating to these matters are likely to be transformed into explicit, ultimately written, rules.

The evolution of specific royal or state machinery for dispute settlement is closely associated with taxation. This is perhaps the primordial form of the relation between a state and its citizens or subjects, in which resources are exacted for the waging of war or the staging of spectacles, or to pay for the costs of dispute settlement itself. Many of the earliest pressures to establish good government and to define property rights are rooted in royal searches for revenue and the resistance of loyal subjects. Some of the oldest conceptions of law and legality solidify around this set of problems. If the emergence of state-based adjudication presses in the direction of an ideal of judicial impartiality, how can that objective be sustained when the legal questions at stake concern the state's own rights to exact resources from its subjects? Institutional solutions adopted with varying degrees of success by different states—such as the separation of powers—went some way to managing this tension; the very recognition of property rights should also be seen as an outcome of the struggles and conflicts engendered in this situation.

A second major function assumed by states has been to police the circulation of things. Governments of the past often sought to control the movement of things within, or in and out of, the territories they claimed to control, to maximise the amount of wealth within the territory and thus the resources available for fighting wars. (For a different view, see Ekelund and Tollison, 1981.) Within this logic, the ideal of every state was to aim at a net inflow, through trade, of resources (and therefore the underlying assumption was that only some states could be winners in the game). For related reasons, governments in the past also sought to regulate consumption, by enacting "sumptuary legislation", to regulate, for example, the wearing of certain types of clothing (see Hunt, 1997). Such forms of regulation also sought to preserve gradations of rank in a stratified society, to regulate the signification or communication of status through things, through the clothes which people wore. Even the once common prohibition upon aliens owning land, which survives in some countries even today, has been a consequence of this way of thinking about the relation between people and things. Perhaps only the modern world has experienced a purely economic, rational approach to the planned regulation of consumption, in the form, for example, of war rationing.

Underlying almost all of these phenomena is the intricate and perplexing question of money. Perhaps what is most perplexing is the difficulty in identifying the basis of money— of working out what makes money "work". Is money itself a thing, or merely a conventional medium through which real things can circulate, merely a symbol the efficacy of which rests entirely upon habit, convention or law? None of these is a new problem (*cf.* Shell, 1993). What can perhaps be stressed is that it is the

duality of money which makes its role so difficult to understand. In many societies, it was both a thing and a medium. As a
medium, it posed the question of boundaries—are there social
exchanges in which money cannot or should not serve as a
medium (see Parry and Bloch, 1987)? Are there things money
cannot buy? Sumptuary legislation, for example, was a symp-
tom of the threat posed by money to the maintenance of social
status. Similar preoccupations about money attached in many
societies to the ownership of land. But, at the same time, money
was a thing with a value of its own. While money was closely
and explicitly tied to metal coin, the role of government in
relation to money was always prominent, in minting and issuing
coin and in seeking to regulate its circulation and use (and its
reconversion into metal). This ambivalence of money long
survived in the deep-seated reluctance of users of money to be
weaned from metal or the possibility of exchanging notes for
metal, and even today states hoard reserves of gold.

What emerges from this discussion is that the exploration of
the relationship between people and things requires the formulation of a number of precise questions. These are now listed,
though only some can be pursued in detail in this book.

(1) How far is the management or administration of a thing
    distinguished from its enjoyment such that the two are
    located in different groups or individuals?

(2) In what kind of units is management or enjoyment
    located?

(3) To what extent is enjoyment exclusive to a particular
    person, kinship group or territorial unit (to take the most
    obvious possibilities)?

(4) To what extent do those who manage or enjoy things
    have freedom of disposition over them?

(5) What are the principal means through which access to
    and control over things are acquired?

(6) What, if any, are the arrangements for intergenerational
    transmission of things?

(7) To what extent are there institutions within the group or
    external to it which are explicitly concerned with policing
    resource management and enjoyment?

Only close scrutiny of the arrangements and norms discernible
in a particular culture enables observers to answer these questions. It is simply wrong to suppose that they can usefully be

asked in general terms which transcend the particularities of different societies.

PROPERTY AND POLITICS

"... the power of a magistrate over a subject may be distinguished from that of a father over his children, a master over his servant, a husband over his wife, and a lord over his slave ... Political power ... I take to be a right of making laws, with penalties of death, and consequently all less penalties for the regulating and preserving of property, and of employing the force of the community in the execution of such laws, and in the defence of the commonwealth from foreign injury, and all this only for the public good" (Locke, 1924, p.118).

So far we have scarcely talked about the relations between people and between people and things in terms of "property" and "property rights", but these are the terms in which these matters have come to be spoken of in the West, among lay people and lawyers alike. What such ideas might involve has proved elusive, varying according to time and place. But at the most general level three core elements are brought together: some notion of an exclusive link between a resource and a particular individual or group ("This goat, this land, is 'mine/ ours'"); corresponding norms of transmission along lines of genealogy ("inheritance"); and readiness on the part of the state to recognise and underwrite such arrangements (the transformation of shared norms into "law").

Prominent in the contemporary West are two distinctive elements: a "possessive individualism" often traced back to John Locke, and what Arendt has labelled "the modern equation of property and wealth on one side and propertylessness and poverty on the other" (Arendt, 1958, p.61). This particular way of thinking about "property", "law" and "state" is specific to our time and place, putting us at risk of misunderstanding the resonance of property in earlier historical periods, and of overlooking some complex and entangled themes in political theory. These revolve around: an enduring notion that the domestication of land is the basis of civilisation; the conception of property as the foundation of political rights and social power; and an assumption that the institutions of government both emerge from and guarantee the enjoyment of property rights.

Land and citizenship

1. The concept of an individual capable of acting in society is constituted through the association of a person with a particular tract of land, where land is conceived as the fixed place of birth, living and death, in which individuals and society are rooted. The possession of property is thus linked to the possibility of citizenship and political participation.

This sense of birthplace as entwined with an almost primordial notion of property provides one indicator of how "property" contains elements which are not, as we would say, "economic" but which rather bear upon a conception of the political or public sphere. Looking back before "the modern age", Arendt notes that:

> ". . . property meant no more or less than to have one's location in a particular part of the world and therefore to belong to the body politic, that is, to be the head of one of the families which together constituted the public realm. This piece of privately owned world was so completely identical with the family who owned it that the expulsion of a citizen could mean not merely the confiscation of his estate but the actual destruction of the building itself. The wealth of a foreigner or a slave was under no circumstances a substitute for this property, and poverty did not deprive the head of the family of this location in the world and the citizenship resulting from it" (Arendt, 1958, pp.61–62).

As the twentieth century has vividly illustrated, those deprived of property are at the same time deprived of citizenship—the stateless have no place of their own. Private property can be seen as a basic human right, because it guarantees the reality of "place" which is necessary in order to ground the possibility of becoming a fully active citizen.

This sense of attachment of humans to land assumes or takes for granted the improvement of land through human labour, serving as the first hallmark of civilisation, as the sign of the transcendence of barbarism. It is the building, the cultivated estate, the estate with a wall around it, which expresses the humanisation or domestication of the land (see Wilson, 1988). Civilised man is born in a dwelling, in a house or a home; life will be lived around that place; to the natal earth the remains of the dead should be returned, and the place of the dead marked or even housed in a special building. This idea of a fundamental link between person and place retains resonance in, for example, nineteenth- and twentieth-century Germany and, more generally, in many traditional or ancestral modes of political thought, in which things—and especially land—link people across time or history and serve as a means of constituting a cultural identity and the possibility of a political community. Although it is common to attribute this idea of "belonging" to the Aboriginal peoples, there is in reality a strong current of thought within the Western tradition itself that people belong to the land.

In Western thought, however, belonging is often linked to the idea of property as either (or both) the source/basis of social power (especially in its landed form) and/or the source of independence and thus civic virtue (as well as *noblisse oblige*); in each case, participation in political life presupposes an idea of property that means possession of a relatively fixed and independent place in society. This is how Arendt discusses the classical period:

"Private wealth, therefore, became a condition for admission to public life not because its owner was engaged in accumulating it but, on the contrary, because it assured with reasonable certainty that its owner would not have to engage in providing for himself the means of use and consumption and was therefore free for public activity. Public life, obviously, was possible only after the much more urgent needs of life itself had been taken care of. The means to take care of them was labour, and the wealth of a person was therefore frequently counted in terms of the number of labourers, that is slaves, he owned" (Arendt, 1958, pp.64–65).

This way of thinking about property is often linked to land and agriculture. Civic virtue may be seen as potentially endangered by money or by the luxuries which money can buy, and this is an idea which has also sometimes been successfully transplanted to urban cultures as diverse in many respects as those of seventeenth-century Holland or Victorian provincial England (Davidoff and Hall, 1987; Schama, 1987). One of the conditions for successful transplantation of the scheme of civic virtue seems to be to attach to money many of the features associated with land: to insist upon its conservation and careful use, to save and accumulate it, or invest it; to guard against wasting it upon the consumption of luxuries (*cf.* Brewer and Porter, 1993).

MODERN:

The fundamental contrast here for Arendt is that the modern shift towards regarding all property as disposable or consumable leads to the disappearance of the idea of private property in the sense of a "tangible, worldly place of one's own" (1958, p.70) and therefore undermines simultaneously the traditional idea of private property and the traditional idea of the public sphere. For us, the argument goes, property is confused with wealth (or money), and propertylessness equated with poverty. Today we have very wealthy societies which are essentially propertyless "because the wealth of any single individual consists of his share of the annual income of a society as a whole" (1958, p.61). Mirroring this change in perceptions is the elimination of property qualifications from the formal criteria for citizenship or public participation. One result of this change is that it is often now thought wrong that wealth and politics should be closely associated. We think that, ideally, money should be kept out of politics. And it is also against this background that the periodic resurgence of themes such as a "property-owning democracy" need to be assessed (see Daunton, 1987). From Arendt's perspective at least, the slogan is nonsensical for the simple reason that there is no property left to be owned, only wealth to be allocated or distributed.

Government and the protection of property

Alongside these two themes are more recent strands in political theory which link property and political society together in a different way. In these, the sovereign is presented as coming into existence in order to provide protection for property. Here Locke, in his *Second Treatise of Government*, provides a particular account of the manner, and order, in which all this comes about. "The earth, and . . . all the fruits it naturally produces . . . being given for the use of men, there must of necessity be a means to appropriate them some way or other before they can be of any use, or at all beneficial to any particular man" (5.26). This is achieved through labour: whatever a man "removes out of the state that nature has provided and left it in, he has mixed his labour with, and joined to it something that is his own, and thereby makes it his property" (5.27). "It is plain that" this applies to "the earth itself", as well as to its fruits (5.32).

Government only develops later, under specific conditions, for the protection of the property that has been constituted in this way:

"Men at first, for the most part, contented themselves with what unassisted nature offered to their necessities; and . . .

afterwards, in some parts of the world (where the increase of people and stock, with the use of money, had made land scarce, and so of some value), the several communities settled the bounds of their distinct territories, and by law themselves regulated the properties of the private men of their society . . ." (5.45).

This is, of course, just one story. Earlier in the seventeenth century, Hobbes ordered things differently, placing the sovereign first, who then sets up a regulatory framework within which property is established. But in both cases government is conceived as set up contractually to remedy potential instability. This justificatory claim is explicit in Locke's characterisation of political power as "a right to make laws . . . for the regulation and preserving of property", and underlies the constitutional statements appearing at the end of the eighteenth century. But there is a paradox here as indicated above at p.5. On the one hand, the existence of sovereign power seems to be a precondition for the existence of property (as opposed to a vague set of normative understandings attached to things). On the other hand, the existence or protection of sovereign power has always been seen as presenting a problem for property. How can sovereign power be restrained from intruding upon the very property which it constituted?

The way Locke sets upon his argument had implications for the property regime under colonial expansion then taking place in the Americas. He was directly involved in these operations, holding a succession of public appointments relating to the colonies, and has been identified as one of the principal architects of the colonial system developed during the Restoration (see Tully, 1993). In this context his *Second Treatise*, which, as we have seen, forges an essential link between settled agriculture, property and government, can be read as an implicit justification of the expropriation of the North American Indian nations. The American Indians, by failing to settle and exploit the land in the European manner, by failing to assert mastery over the land, by restricting their activates to hunting, gathering and shifting cultivation left the land in a sense "untouched". It was therefore, within this scheme of thinking, *terra nullius*, the land of no one (a term which Hegel (tr. 1991, p.81) observed already anticipates a "relation to others"), and it belonged to no one precisely because human labour had not been deployed in cultivating and improving or shaping it (see further Williams,

1975; Tully, 1993). By the same token, the lack of institutions to protect and regulate human settlement was the index of a lack of government and thus the basis for calling into question the stance of the English Crown, which treated Indian leaders as sovereigns, and treaties as the means by which questions of title should be managed in the New World (for the international law issues, see Korman, 1996).

These issues are far from being merely historical ones. First, in Australia and Canada in particular, the question of Aboriginal or First Nation land rights (and political sovereignty) are today high on the legal and political agenda. During the 1980s and 1990s, representatives of "first nations" have gradually began to achieve reinstatement, through litigation, of the traditional regimes of land-holding engulfed during the eighteenth- and nineteenth-century colonial expansion. In Australia, for example, the High Court in 1992 recognised the survival of the system of "native title" followed by the Murray Islanders at the time of annexation.[1] In a quite fundamental way, these issues challenge the assumption, discussed above, that centred the "essence" of humanity in the conquest of nature and used the degree of domestication of space as an index of the degree of human self-development or progress. These transformations coincide, of course, with the then radical—but now almost traditional—reassessment of the importance of government or the state in the ordering of human affairs which took place in anthropology as better studies of hunter gather groups became available (Lee and Devore, 1968; Woodburn, 1972). Underlining this uncoupling of "order" and "domination", Clastres asks of the Yanamamo:

> "Why would a few members want to proclaim one day: this is mine, and how could the others allow the seeds of the thing primitive society knows nothing about—authority, oppression, the State—to take hold? . . . no one in such a society feels the quaint desire to do more, own more, or appear to be more than his neighbour . . . primitive society, the first society of abundance, leaves no room for overabundance" (1977, p.173).

Property and progress

The theme of progress and modernisation is also central to the treatment of property in the constitutional documents of the late eighteenth century. In 1789, the representatives of the French people resolved ". . . to set forth in a solemn declaration the natural, inalienable, and sacred rights of man . . .". These rights, the preservation of which was the "aim of every political association", were "liberty, property, security, and resistance to oppression".

These constitutional arrangements provided the basis for the debate about the merits and demerits of the accumulation of property and its unequal distribution. Marx complained that this based the right of man to liberty "not on the association of man with man, but of the separation of man from man" (tr. 1975, p.162). "None of the so-called rights of man . . . go beyond egoistic man . . . separated from the community. In the rights of man . . . society . . . appears as a framework external to the individuals, as a restriction of their original independence. The sole bond holding them together is natural necessity, need and private interest, the preservation of their property and their egoistic selves" (tr. 1975, p.164).

At this point there is a fairly fundamental shift or reversal in the way in which the relation between property and the political sphere is conceived. Instead of property being conceived as the precondition for political association—or even for civilisation rather than barbarism—it becomes, rather, an issue in itself for the political realm to address and concern itself with. The older themes do not disappear entirely, and some, such as civic virtue, are sufficiently pliant to be adapted, as we have seen, to a wide range of historical circumstances. But the essential inflection of this more modern way of thinking is to call into question the institution of property itself, and in the modern political arena, attitudes or policies regarding property become one of the ideological trademarks of political parties.

In part, this simply calls into question the distribution of property. Thus land reform, the break-up of large agricultural estates, as expressed in the demand for "three acres and a cow", became a major issue from the late eighteenth century through to the present day. Yet when the spotlight is turned on property as such, there are, Ryan (1984) suggests, two distinct inflections. In one, property is emblematic of self-development. In the other, property is conceived instrumentally. Instrumentalism justifies property in terms of efficiency. It links work and property in a particular way. Property is a means to an end, the efficient exploitation of the natural resources of the world. "It is the unnecessary employments", wrote Godwin at the end of the eighteenth century, "that . . . occupy the great mass of every civilised nation, while the peasant labours incessantly to maintain rich men in a state more pernicious than idleness" (1985, p.745). "The object, in the present state of society, is to multiply labour; in another state, it will be to simplify it" (1985, p.746).

The self-developmental perspective, by contrast, involved first, the idea that "there is, or can be, and certainly should be, something intrinsically satisfying about work; work is a characteristic form of human self-expression" (Ryan, 1984, p.11). Secondly, this tradition treats the relationship between people and what they own as intrinsically significant, as more than a mere instrumental means to an end. And it is this view of the significance of property which receives particular emphasis in Marx, who suggests that, beyond questions of allocation and distribution, property operates as a barrier to the realisation of true human existence as social being.

> ". . . the realm of freedom actually begins only where labour which is determined by necessity and mundane considerations ceases . . . Just as the savage must wrestle with Nature to satisfy his wants, to maintain and reproduce life, so must civilised man, and he must do so in all social formations and under all possible modes of production . . . Freedom in this field can only consist in socialised man, the associated producers, rationally regulating their interchange with Nature, bringing it under their common control, instead of being ruled by it as by the blind forces of Nature . . ." (tr. 1974, p.820).

All these strands had already converged in Godwin at the end of the eighteenth century:

> "There are many things, the fruit of human industry, which, though not to be classed among the necessities of life, are highly conducive to our well being. The criterion of these things will appear when we have ascertained what those accommodations are which will give us real pleasure, after the insinuations of vanity and ostentation shall have been dismissed . . . When it shall be rendered voluntary, when it shall cease to interfere with our improvement, and rather become a part of it, or at worst be converted into a source of amusement and variety, it may then be no longer a calamity, but a benefit. Thus . . . a state of equality need not be a state of Stoical simplicity, but is compatible with considerable accommodation, and even, in some sense, with splendour" (1985, p.753).

On the basis of these and many other critiques of property and inequality, a diversity of political projects have been constructed, from co-operatives to Soviet state socialism, which have aimed to speed up the pace of progress or to further human happiness through the redistribution or abolition of private property. In large measure, these aims and objectives were not achieved, and most projects of this kind have been abandoned, for the time being at least.

However, the eclipse or retreat of welfare socialism in Western Europe, and the collapse of state socialism in the East, leave behind them a confusion about the precise character of the present. Although many critiques of private property drew support from visions of "natural man" living in propertyless communities, the majority placed, as we have suggested, their principal accent upon progress. They would do better that which unadulterated capitalism did well (technology, exploitation of nature) but without the cost (unequal distribution of property, degradation of the working class). At the very least, then, their failure tends to foster a reactionary mode of thought, in which it is assumed that the clock is being turned back, and that politics is becoming less ambitious, emulating Victorian or even eighteenth-century styles of government, through deregulation, reduction of taxation, privatisation and so on. Correlatively, it may seem as if property is being liberated from the shackles of the state. This conjuncture enables Fukuyama to suggest that for many parts of the world liberal democracy is now the only universal ideology left in place, and that we have reached a position where "... we cannot picture to ourselves a world that is 'essentially' different from the present one, and at the same time better. Other, less reflective ages also thought of themselves as the best, but we arrive at this conclusion exhausted, as it were, from the pursuit of alternatives we felt had to be better than liberal democracy" (1992, p.46).

The basic problem with this view is that, as Lasch suggested:

"Right-wing economics conceives of the capitalist economy as it was in the time of Adam Smith, where property was still distributed fairly widely, businesses were individually owned, and commodities still retained something of the character of useful objects. The right's notion of free enterprise takes no account of the forces that have transformed capitalism from within: the rise of the corporation, the bureaucratisation of business, the increasing insignificance of private property, and the shift from a work ethic to a consumption ethic. When the right takes any note of these developments at all, it is only to attribute them to professional and governmental interference . . ." (1991, p.519).

In other words, at the very moment in history when the ideology of "possessive individualism" seems to triumph, other forces are at work in modern society which make this triumph a rather distorted way of representing the reality. Whatever our ideological commitments, these forces require that we look beyond individualism, and we will come back to this in the final section of this chapter. We must first turn to look more closely at inheritance.

INHERITANCE

In modern societies, a range of factors tend to combine to keep the question of property and the question of inheritance apart. Property is often justified as the "reward" for labour, thrift, saving; care for things is encouraged or valued. Inheritance, by contrast, seems like an accident of fortune, an unearned acquisition, an unfair advantage. "It is a gross imposition that men are accustomed to put upon themselves when they talk of the property bequeathed to them by their ancestors. The property is produced by the daily labour of men who are now in existence. All that their ancestors bequeathed to them was a mouldy patent which they show as a title to extort from their neighbours what the labour of those neighbours has produced" (Godwin, 1985, p.712). Inheritance is commonly seen as the key to the unequal distribution of property and changes in the laws of inheritance are seen as one of the key ways of securing a fairer, or more equal, or more just society. Inheritance is a key presupposition and a central source of inequality. Even Durkheim suggests that ". . . there can be no rich and poor by birth without there being unjust contracts" (1984, p.319).

As a result, the taxation of inherited wealth has featured prominently in the agenda of those committed to the redistribution of property. As projects of this sort have intensified in scope and complexity in England in this century, so the skills and expertise of lawyers which once extensively directed towards the legal framework for the preservation and distribution of property within families have been channelled towards the invention of increasingly sophisticated devices designed to minimise the impact of taxation regimes upon private wealth. Our focus here is on the earlier of these two stages—on the facilitation by lawyers of the inheritance of private wealth rather than the defence by lawyers of inherited wealth against the intrusion and depredations of the state.

From a wider perspective than that of modern society, property, and inheritance are closely woven together. The very idea of "property" suggests defined lines of intergenerational transmission. How these lines are defined is subject to considerable variation. The structure of any particular system of inheritance is largely shaped by the way in which it resolves two basic issues: the question of direction and the question of timing. In what direction—to which categories of heirs—is the property to devolve? At what point or points in the developmental cycle of the family is property to be transmitted from one generation to another?

Direction

Every inheritance system is inevitably grounded in the attempt to organise intergenerational transmission of things, since such systems are attempts to organise the property consequences of human mortality. This is not to say that horizontal systems are unknown: in some societies, things conventionally pass from elder brothers to younger brothers, as, in some instances, do thrones (the Saudi dynasty provides one of the most striking recent examples). This may especially be the case in polygamous cultures where brotherhood can span at least two generations, such that sibling succession can involve the succession to property—or power—by males who belong, in our terms, to the generation succeeding that of the brother from whom they inherit. In the most general terms, however, the proposition holds true: either things are destroyed on or before death, or some system must be developed for the passage across time through the generations of things which endure or are allowed to endure.

In England, as in the rest of Europe, the general direction of such transmission is vertical, and property devolves from parents to their children. So deeply rooted is this practice in Western culture that it needs to be stressed that this direction is not universal. Some African societies employ diagonal systems. One example is a "matrilineal" regime under which a man's property develops upon his sister's son. Such systems inevitably throw up their own, subsidiary, questions: how is the relevant sister to be identified; and which of her sons is to take the property? As the anthropologist Lévi-Strauss (1969) emphasised, there are a limited number of possible elements, of forms that these questions can take, but a vast range of possible ways in which these basic elements can be combined.

In England, as we shall see, diagonal systems have been subordinated to vertical ones. Vertical devolution itself permits a further choice: on the one hand, all the property devolves upon a single heir, such that no division of the estate takes place ("impartible inheritance"); on the other hand, the patrimony is split up among or shared between several heirs, usually the children ("partible inheritance"). Impartible inheritance most commonly involves preferential inheritance by the first born of the surviving males ("primogeniture"). Such a system poses the question of provision for the children who do not inherit. Must the heir maintain them, is alternative provision made for them, or must they make their own way in the world? We shall see that lawyers' attempts to accommodate these problems account for much of the complexity of English land law in the past and, as a result, for its rather contorted contemporary shape.

Partible inheritance involves the alternative of shared, simultaneous enjoyment of the property or its actual division or subparcellisation. Again, lawyers have had to accommodate this, and again we will see that it provides a further source of complexity. Finally, to anticipate what is discussed at length in Chapter 4, two points should be noted. First, among different social groups, both partible and impartible inheritance of land have long been practised in England, with the result that English lawyers have developed mechanisms to give legal effect to the whole range of possible directions outlined above. Fragmentation of title in English law is largely the result of attempts to accommodate this diversity of inheritance systems. But, secondly, we shall see that, while the distinction between partible and impartible inheritance accounts for the complex range of ways in which lawyers conceptualise what in practical terms is co-ownership of land within a family, the division between the two is blurred in practice, which is why, as we shall also see, the distinction between fragmentation of title and incumbrances upon title is in certain cases strained and awkward to maintain.

Timing: pre- and post-mortem inheritance

As we have said, the second crucial element of any system of inheritance is timing, and, in particular, the way in which inheritance and death are linked together or, for that matter, kept distinct. In some systems, the death of a senior member of the family is the moment at which his property passes to the next generation. In others, devolution is channelled away from death, in one of two ways. The most clear-cut method ("pre-mortem inheritance") is where devolution is completely detached from death so that most or all of the senior member's property has already passed on to the next generation when death occurs. In some societies, such a separation of death from devolution is taken very seriously. Members of such societies sometimes explain this by saying that devolution on death encourages disputes between members of a family at the very moment when the person best able to resolve them has gone. That is, if succession always engenders disputes, pre-mortem inheritance has the advantage of enabling elders who are "out of the fray" to assist in their resolution. Moreover, since where pre-mortem inheritance is practised, devolution of property through generations tends to be a drawn-out process phased over time in association with the important stages in the developmental cycle of the group—birth, puberty and marriage, as well as death—it avoids the potentially sharper or more intractable conflicts over property which an abrupt, total transition might seem to generate. More generally, this type of pre-mortem inheritance can be seen as a form of retirement on the part of senior members, which is sometimes kept separate from withdrawal from public or political life, as the indigenous observations about the dispute settlement function of such elders outlined above indicate. In Western Christendom, this form of inheritance was sometimes stylised into a more elaborate renunciation of the world: the retiring elder divested himself of all his worldly goods and withdrew to a monastery to contemplate his soul. More practical reasons might induce a peasant farmer grown infirm through age to hand over his holding to the next generation; in such circumstances, he might make his maintenance a condition of the transfer (*cf.* Macfarlane, 1978, pp.136–138, 141–143). In twentieth-century England, pre-mortem inheritance has been the central mode of intergenerational transmission only for the rich, as the principal means of avoiding or limiting the inroads of the Inland Revenue upon private wealth.

The second main form of pre-mortem inheritance involves determining the direction of devolution before death but making death the relevant time for devolution to occur. As we see in Chapter 4, the device invented by English lawyers which was known as the strict settlement, and which combined primogeniture with this intermediate form of pre-mortem inheritance, was one of the most important devices through which, by the

seventeenth century, landownership passed through the generations, and it is no exaggeration to say that this has left a decisive
mark upon English land law.

What has so far been outlined is not a set of legal rules, but
rather the range of preferred inheritance patterns inscribed
within particular cultures. Sometimes the English pattern was
absorbed directly into English law, as in the rule, now abolished, that the heir at law (who was ascertainable through the
principles of primogeniture) succeeded to the "realty" (the land)
of a deceased who left no valid will. Legal systems vary in the
degree to which they absorb and make mandatory certain
inheritance practices. English law has long given pride of place
to testamentary freedom, but this does not mean that the norms
which governed social practice encouraged people of property
to take advantage of the freedom which the law allowed them.

What has been outlined so far is also a set of preferred
patterns stretching over time. They are preferred patterns in that
they provide a grid of normative expectations, shape norms of
proper conduct across generations, and provide a frame of
reference for the resolution of disputes, whether or not the
society in question has a specialised system of adjudication. But
they are patterns of preference, encapsulating hopes and fears, a
way of envisaging how the future should be but also a way of
imagining bad futures, and thus, often again with the assistance
of lawyers in some societies, a source of pressures to invent
ways to make these undesirable possible outcomes at least
bearable. If the systematisation of inheritance is rooted in the
need to organise intergenerational transmission of property, it
has to take account of the absence of preferred heirs, especially
through infertility and infant mortality.

Where post-mortem inheritance is the norm, these possibilities
at least permit straightforward, if painful, choices for the childless person about to die in a society where transmission in a
vertical direction is the norm. As indicated above, the common
alterative in such situations is diagonal inheritance, though this
too can vary in the degree of precision which it assumes and the
precise form in which it is inscribed as a desirable, second-best
alternative. In Ancient Rome, for example, where infertility
among the upper classes was not uncommon, adoption—
usually, though not necessarily, of a blood relative—was one
preferred solution in this situation (Hopkins, 1983, pp.49–50,
194–195; Corbier, 1991). In England, this was not embraced,
principally because the combination of an elaborate system of

primogeniture and the intermediate form of pre-mortem inheritance which settled direction but not transmission before death was the dominant norm, and adoption in a full sense is most useful when you know that the possibility of a direct heir is no longer a practicable one. Roman adoption meant that your heir became, for all purposes, redesignated as if he were your direct heir; in England, with testamentary freedom, a pale imitation of this practice was followed in the face of infertility, when property was passed to a distant relative: he did not "become" your son but you might impose in your will the condition that he adopted your surname as a condition of the property passing to him.

Where full-scale pre-mortem inheritance is practised, this failure of preferred heirs is also relatively manageable in the majority of cases. When the time comes for the elder to retire (however the rightness of this time is arrived at), if he has no preferred successors, the property can be transferred to the second or third best, because the transmission occurs between living human beings. The accumulation of property in the Middle Ages by the Church of Rome is in part intelligible in this context. Someone retiring from the world preferred to give property to the Church rather than permit it to pass to distant relatives, who provided the only alternative destination (*cf.* Ariès, 1983; Goody, 1983).

It is the intermediate system, the combination of determining the direction of property before death while retaining the event of death as the trigger for transmission, which presented the greatest structural difficulties. A will, of course, can be made years before death, and thus pose a problem of a similar kind. But in English law, a will can always be updated; if you make a new will, it revokes its precursors. However long before the death of its maker a will is made, it is not a form of pre-mortem inheritance in legal or social terms, because of this quality of revocability. Heirs made by will, in English law, are always heirs-expectant or apparent; not only can they lose everything if the will is revoked, but, in addition, if they die before the maker of the will, their rights lapse automatically. This is not exactly the case with the intermediate form of pre-mortem inheritance which took the form of settlements of land (see Chapter 4). Here succession was made contingent upon the heir attaining his majority—conventionally, until 1969, the age of 21 for males, and now 18, and similarly for females unless they married below that age. Such a system threw up a simple problem which generated much legal complexity in order to accommodate it. When such a settlement was made, that is, when this type of pre-mortem inheritance was crystallised in legal, formal, terms, it would often be unclear who in the end would be the heir. This meant that such settlements had to provide for a range of possible alternatives, ranked in order of preference according to the normative framework within which members of the propertied classes, advised by their lawyers, worked. The legal complexities which this generated go some way to explaining the obscurity of some of the conceptual structure of English property law past and present.

The theme of inheritance may seem today to have diminished in significance. In practical terms, of course, inherited wealth remains an important factor in economic inequality. But conceptual schemes oriented to the management of inheritance no longer shape and configure the law of property to the same degree as in the past. Yet, curiously, a cognate version of the same core idea now seems to flourish in many parts of the modern world and especially, according to some observers and critics, in Britain. This is the notion and scheme of heritage or cultural property which is discussed below.

BEYOND INDIVIDUALISM: THE CHANGING SCOPE OF
PROPERTY RIGHTS

By the end of the nineteenth century, many commentators had come to see a threat to "individualism"—by which they meant primarily the sanctity of individually-owned private property and the closely related freedom of contract—posed by the "rise of collectivism". One of the most influential was the lawyer Albert Venn Dicey, and his arguments are still debated among modern historians (for discussion of Dicey and the historians, see Perkin, 1992). By the rise of collectivism, Dicey primarily had in mind the "spectre" of socialism, and many writers since (*cf.* especially Hayek, 1944) have followed this approach in setting the struggle of individualism and private property to survive against the collectivising and bureaucratising tendencies and imperatives of revolutionary or creeping socialism. What this perspective often tends to overlook is the problem raised by Lasch: how "private" and how tied to "individuals" is private property in the modern world? In this section we explore a number of areas where it is much less true than in the past to understand private property primarily in terms of individual ownership, and where it is essential to think rather in terms of units larger than the individual. But since such units are both more complex and more abstract than the old idea of the individual, it is sensible to think of them not as entities but as networks.

Economic networks: the rise of modern corporations

Corporate property is property "owned" by groups rather than individuals. Corporations are not new or specifically modern. Traditional corporations—the Stationers' Company, universities, cities—were incorporated under Royal Charter, and this form survives today. In relation to economic activity the corporate form was a device for pooling individual resources for undertaking large-scale economic ventures and the spreading of the risks attached to them. This is what is known as the joint-stock company; various legal mechanisms were available, including trusts and partnerships, for these purposes. Some of these companies became large and powerful: for example, until the middle of the nineteenth century, the creation of the Indian Empire was largely achieved by the East India Company.

The classical problem of corporate ownership was whether it could be said that the group as such had a legal identity. This mattered when things went wrong—when debts were owed and creditors moved in. For some quasi-corporate groups, like modern partnerships, this is still a real and pressing problem. Most solicitors' and accountancy firms are partnerships. In legal terms, this means that each partner is entitled, under the terms of the partnership agreement, to a share of the profits. That's the good side. But the flipside is that each partner is jointly and severally liable as an individual on the debts of the partnership, and no distinction is drawn here between his personal assets and his share in the partnership.

The historical basis of this was that partnership was a form of business association in which each partner could be expected to maintain a watching brief over the activities of the other partners and in that sense each partner served as a guarantor of the other partners so far as people dealing with the partnership were concerned. Such an assumption may work in the case of a small number of partners who can be expected to be in regular communication with each other so far as their joint affairs are concerned. But it becomes anachronistic or problematic in some modern large-scale partnerships which may comprise 100-plus partners.

The origins of the modern corporate form lie in the mid-nineteenth century. There are two key elements to this structure. First, a procedure called incorporation is now made available, which enables property to be pooled and owned by an artificial legal person: the corporation. This corporation can own land and other property, make contracts, sue and be sued, in its own right, under its own name, and not as the agent of real human beings. It is a legal entity in its own right. In its original form, such a company raised money—its start-up capital—by issuing shares either privately (*e.g.* to founder members) or publicly (on a stock exchange). The money paid for the shares now belongs to the company; in return, the shareholders have as securities their shares, and the expectation that they will receive dividends declared from the profits made by the company from its trading activities year by year. A stock market or stock exchange is simply a market in which the shares of publicly listed companies can be bought and sold; thus, profit announcements and anticipations of future dividend yields are one important factor influencing share prices at any one time. Companies raise the money they need through borrowing as well as share issues, and in modern conditions these are often regarded as tactical alternatives, depending on the financial and tax environment in which the company is operating.

The other key element in the modern corporate form is limited liability. Limited liability, put simply, means that the liability of shareholders for the debts of a company is limited to the value of the shares they have acquired. So where a company becomes insolvent and goes into liquidation, the shareholders can expect to lose the money they have invested in their shares, but the company's creditors will not be able to pursue the other assets owned by the shareholders in satisfaction of the debts owed to them by the company.

Early limited liability companies often took the form of family businesses in which the shareholders and the managers or directors of the company were the same people. Over time, starting in the United States, professional managers emerge, and displace family members (who may or may not remain as shareholders). One trigger for this is on the death or retirement of the founding entrepreneur. This trend, repeated more recently in some sectors of the British economy, is what Berle and Means (1932) famously called the separation of ownership and control. As companies expand their activities in scale and scope, so control of business decisions may pass to this cadre of professional managers and away from the "owners", *i.e.* the shareholders.

Not least because of the ability of companies both to borrow and to raise capital through further share issues, the corporate form involves the possibility of expansion in company size, which may be motivated by various factors, of which an important one is to obtain greater control over its markets. This is why business historians have taken such an interest in what they call vertical integration, the rise of multi-unit enterprises and the emergence of central controlling managerial hierarchies within large firms (Chandler and Drems, 1980). The separation of ownership and control (the development which most obviously affects the position of shareholders) tends to be accompanied by attempts by firms to replace market mechanisms in their environment with internal administrative mechanisms, so as to obtain better control over that environment. This means that vertical integration is often accompanied by what is termed backwards and/or forwards integration, a trend particularly pronounced in the United States. To illustrate, if we break down the commercial activities which lie behind the sale of baked beans in a shop, we can isolate at least the following stages: (a) the extraction or acquisition of raw materials—beans, etc., material for making cans; (b) the manufacturing stage, including food processing—cooking, preservation, canning, etc.; (c) distribution to retail outlets, local, national, or worldwide; (d) retailing (the consumer market). Any company operating anywhere along this chain may either rely on market mechanisms to move from the stage before it to the stage after it, or it may seek to absorb that prior or later stage into itself, integrating backwards and/or forwards, relying not on contracts but on central internal control for co-ordination of supply and of outlets.

As an alternative, companies in the same sector join together to control a market in their mutual interest, *e.g.* by regulating prices. These are called cartels and were outlawed in the United States by the anti-trust legislation contained in the Sherman Act 1890. Until the 1950s, however, cartels were common in the United Kingdom and encouraged by the government (see Freyer, 1992).

These are some of the factors underlying the growth in size of the large corporations. We should also note briefly the change in the character of share ownership. First, in the United Kingdom, the use of holding companies as an alternative to formal vertical integration became common. The shares of one company may be acquired in whole or in part by another, so that the former becomes a subsidiary of the latter. How closely integrated the operations of the companies will then become varies. Secondly, in modern stock markets (and Berle and Means had already spotted this trend 65 years ago), most shares are owned by large institutional investors—pension funds, insurance companies. In this sense, the ownership of the larger companies has already been socialised indirectly, not through the wide dispersion of individual share ownership, but through the holdings of these large fund-holders whose raison d'être is supposedly the financial welfare of large sections of society as a whole (a role which, to judge from current policy pronouncements, is, if anything, set to grow).

The legacy of these developments is a range of new regulatory problems for law and for government, domestic, transnational and international. There are two main issues. The first is economic. This is the broad domain of competition law. What experience of the modern corporate form has shown in a variety of ways is its anti-competitive potential. If traditional economic regulation by governments tended to stifle competition, as in the case of monopolies, so now governments are needed to promote competition and defend it against "private" monopoly, including predatory pricing, where one firm underprices its products in order to drive its rivals out of business. In these cases, it is said, consumers benefit in the short run but in the medium term lose out because they are deprived of choice as the weaker firms and their products go under.

The second issue follows from this but is broader and involves political and moral issues as well. This is the question of on whose behalf companies are run or for whose benefit they exist or with what goals in mind they should be regulated.

The traditional or first answer to these questions was the shareholders. They were and are the ultimate owners of the company; the directors of the company were in the end accountable to them and could be dismissed by them in the annual general meeting of the company required by law, if the shareholders so chose. But the concentration of share ownership in large institutional investors makes that traditional answer less satisfactory. And the decision-making processes of some of these institutions, *e.g.* pension funds, are hardly free from imperfection. In theory, these are funds which are merely professionally managed and held on trust for hundreds of thousands of individual beneficiaries. But these beneficiaries have little or no say in the decisions their fund managers make. So there is a certain harmony of interests between the senior management of firms and the senior management of the institutional investors, if only in terms of a shared interest in confining policy debates behind the closed doors of City and Wall Street boardrooms.

In any case, given the scale and scope of large vertically integrated or otherwise constructed corporate conglomerates, often directly responsible for hundreds of thousands of employees, and indirectly (through suppliers and subcontractors) able to exert a major, sometimes decisive, influence on the economic well-being of many others as well, many argue that a broader framework for evaluating corporate decision-making is required. This is what lies behind the rise of the term "stakeholders".

Within this perspective, it is said, corporations need to take account of the interests of all their stakeholders. Who these are is itself open to dispute: employees, consumers, the environment and environmental groups, peasants and farmers in LDCs, indigenous peoples and their claims to land, and so on.

So even if it is still true to say of the modern global "public" corporation that it is ultimately "owned" by shareholders, many of these are not individuals but pension funds or insurance companies, which are themselves owned by or operated for the benefit of large numbers of individual "ordinary" people, and its business decisions potentially affect not just the profits it makes and thereby the returns on their investments made to shareholders, but also the welfare of employees, suppliers, consumers, and even nations. What arises is a complex network of claims and obligations in relation to which the traditional language of individual property ownership is anachronistic, and where a more loose and open-ended terminology of powers, fiduciary obligations, and legitimate expectations is more serviceable. But it is not just a matter of the separation of ownership and control and the concentration of growing amounts of power into the hands of a relatively small group of professional managers; in the process, ownership is transformed into something more intangible, a loose set of financial entitlements whose realisability is heavily mediated by institutional relationships and structures. In this situation, the distinction between what is mine and what is yours becomes, in a sense, obscure. Put differently, private property has in many respects become socialised, not through the vehicle of the state but through the very logic of private property and the accumulation and concentration of wealth itself. All that then remains is to regulate these accumulations "in the public interest", to try to devise mechanisms, for example, to ensure that those who manage and control pension funds do not defraud present and future pensioners, in circumstances where the traditional rules are often inadequate.

This is, of course, socialisation without equalisation: the benefits are distributed unevenly. But little of the sanctity of private property—the exclusionary boundary which surrounds and marks off what is mine as opposed to yours—survives. But the main reason is the growth of complex networks rather than some simple shift from private to public. If a supermarket chain buys a plot of land in order to build an out-of-town super-market, all kinds of other "private" interests are potentially affected by the proposed development: neighbouring land-owners by the disturbances caused by the construction and by the subsequent influx of shoppers, shopkeepers in other loca-tions (such as the town-centre high street) who may lose trade, and so on. In addition, there are implications for the road system—are the existing roads adequate for the increase in traffic? There are also implications for the public transport system, whether publicly or privately owned.

Symbolic networks: cultural property

Quite apart from these kinds of interconnected practical matters, this example also points towards the increase in what might be called "symbolic networks", which again undermine the clarity of the distinction between what is mine and what is yours. This is that whole complex of environmental and cultural or heritage concerns which are so pronounced a feature of the modern age. The law may restrict a landowner's freedom of action with regard to trees standing on his land and he may be required to preserve them. Equally, you are not always free to demolish, or even replace the windows of, your house if it has been listed as being of historic interest (see Ross, 1996 for a useful summary). No doubt these symbolic or cultural concerns have an economic and material side which has long been recognised, specifically the economic value of tourism (see Mandler, 1997 and Boniface and Fowler, 1993). But they are also driven by something more diffuse, a redefinition of the relationship between past, present and future, a reconceptualisation of inheritance. What exists, tangibly, becomes important "in its own right" through the mere fact and longevity of its existence. And this process of thought now tends to extend beyond individuals, to embrace "cultures" and the "natural environment".

The term "cultural property" serves both to identify particular items or types of property and particular types of "owner" or "proprietor". What usually links the two together and tends to position debates about cultural property is "history", or a relation to the past which is established—or which groups and societies seek to establish—in the present (see generally Lowenthal, 1996). History tends to be important for cultural property debates in two ways. First, as a history of appropriation, seizure and removal of cultural items, or as a history of attempts to eradicate cultures and traditions, it serves as a mode of critique of the current placement and possession of cultural items, enabling distinctions to be drawn in debate between legitimate and illegitimate possession or retention. Secondly, history serves as a vehicle for recuperating and reconstructing (some would say inventing) cultural traditions in the present.

Take the still unresolved dispute between Britain and Greece over the Elgin Marbles (see Greenfield, 1996). These Marbles once sat on the Parthenon, temple of Athene, the patron goddess of Athens—a city which was itself the epicentre of the Ancient Greek civilisation from which modern Greeks claim descent. At the beginning of the nineteenth century, when Greece was under Turkish (Muslim, Ottoman) occupation, the British Ambassador to the Sublime Porte, Lord Elgin, obtained an authorisation from the Sultan which he claimed (and there is dispute about the evidence for the existence of this document) gave him permission to remove these Marbles. He did so, and in due course sold them to the British Museum, the money for this being voted by the British Parliament, and there they remain today. Greece has been claiming in every forum it can find that the Marbles should be returned.

This dispute is exemplary in many ways. Underpinning it is a history of imperialism (though, unusually, here it is primarily Turkish imperialism which stands accused, with Britain as a kind of indirect beneficiary). The claiming culture appeals both to its past violation—the act of removal—and to its present need for restitution so that the culture itself can be whole again. Moreover, the dispute is framed by a museum which has the item in dispute, and which inserts into the debate what we might call "museum values"—the values of professionalism in curatorship, display and access—values whose importance it asserts not so much on behalf of a particular culture but on behalf of the world or humanity as a whole (*cf.* Sherman and Rogoff, 1994; Walsh, 1992; Vergo, 1989; Lumley, 1988). In simple terms, the cultural importance of the Marbles is not denied by the British: far from it. The argument is that the items are too important to be returned, because they belong to European, Western or World civilisation as a whole.

The numerous claims made by Native Americans and others for the return from museums of cultural artefacts and human bones and skeletons are similar, except that often, unlike the Greek case, these groups do not have governments making the claim on behalf of their culture. In some cases, finally, such disputes can occur within a nation state, as in the rivalry between Quebec and the federal government in Ottawa over certain cultural items and their placement in federal museums on the one hand or Québécois locations on the other (Handler, 1988). Similar ideals underlie the return to Scotland of the Stone of Scone from Westminster Abbey.

What types of property constitute cultural property? In a sense, the answer is anything. What counts as cultural property is determined by political and other factors. Put differently, the term "culture" is inherently plastic and manipulable. We can single out three of four factors which have in reality been decisive.

First was the promotion by European governments, later emulated elsewhere, of national and/or imperial identity, involving the creation of state- or crown-sponsored museums and galleries, and from the second half of the nineteenth century onwards, the staging of international exhibitions in which trade and culture merge into each other. The establishment after the Revolution of the Louvre as a national museum probably gave the main lead to this process. This created the infrastructure for the accumulation, ordering and display of culture as a sort of national treasure. Societies varied in the extent to which this process was mirrored or even preceded by private collecting, and in the extent to which such private collections survived political upheavals.

What grows out of this largely Western practice is the institutionalisation, mainly during this century, of culture, in the creation of various cultural bureaucracies whose justification is supposedly both to identify cultural items and to protect them.

This occurs at the level of nations or states but also at transnational and international levels, especially via UNESCO and the concept of World Heritage sites. The definition of cultural property at this level is therefore largely determined by bureaucratic and political processes. In the United Kingdom, this takes the form of restrictions on freedom to export moveable property—pictures, statuary, etc.—and restrictions on the alteration, repair or demolition of designated ("listed") buildings and monuments. This process occurs whether or not the moveables or buildings or monuments are in private, charitable or public ownership. Also, in the United Kingdom the role of government in defining and preserving national culture or heritage is complemented by the work of the largest charity in the country—the National Trust, which is also involved in the business of evaluating what is worth preserving and in what form.

Finally, cultural property in this bureaucratic sense is a moving object because it is always adjusting to the passage of time. What is a new building at one point in time can become, as evaluations change, an object of outstanding architectural interest at another. Through the medium of art/architecture expertise, bureaucratic decision-making can require things to be preserved because of their representativeness, typicality or special qualities as so judged. At this point, what starts out as a largely high-art, elitist preoccupation conjoins with something somewhat different: factories, warehouses, signal boxes and office blocks join cathedrals and palaces as buildings requiring preservation orders.

From the early days of this kind of national heritage movement, a counter-movement was visible, which emphasised folk art, arts and crafts, cottages rather than palaces. This focus is in many ways the starting point for an approach to cultural property which identifies less with states and nations and their glories and more with the organic life of peoples. It therefore always tended to emphasise the local or regional rather than the national, the small scale rather than the grand, the natural rather than the artificial, the country rather than the city, the hues and tones of the earth rather than the gilt and glitz of the metropolis (see Samuel, 1994).

Ethnographic museums, now one focus of much contention, come somewhere in between these two movements. Museums of Man or Mankind, in metropolitan centres, sought both to exemplify the triumph of civilisation, if only by collecting and ordering scientifically these physical archives of what mankind is and was, and to draw upon a growing interest in low or "primitive" rather than high culture (see Coombes, 1991; Stocking, 1988). Paradoxically, perhaps, by collecting things in this way, albeit as species of primitivism, they unwittingly provided some of the seed-corn for the reassertion of cultural property and cultural identity by indigenous peoples who in the earlier part of the century were expected, by Europeans, largely to disappear through extermination, disease or assimilation.

What in many ways seems to have kick-started this resurgence of cultural identity among indigenous peoples throughout much of the world were the anti-colonial independence struggles in the Indian sub-continent and, later, in Africa during the 1950s, followed by the struggle in the United States in the 1960s over civil rights, which moved fairly rapidly from an agenda of non-discrimination to an emphasis on the history of slavery and the rediscovery of African cultural roots.

Along with these trends was the development in this century of social and cultural anthropology in Western and, later, worldwide universities, a discipline largely devoted to the reconstruction of cultural traditions, and through which, especially when the anthropologists began to be drawn from indigenous peoples themselves, combining science with a privileged voice, the search for cultural identity and thereby the identification of cultural property, could now be intensified.

But who owns cultural property? Some would claim that such a question already displays an ethnocentric bias or, specifically, a prejudice grounded in Western thinking. What if, for some groups who assert claims of cultural property, it is not a matter of ownership and control of things by people in a Western sense but rather, or also, a claim that a thing—whether natural or man-made, moveable or land—infects or invests a person or a group with its personality (or, if that is too anthropomorphic a way of putting it, invests a person or a group with its qualities and powers and "spirit") so that, deprived of it, the person or group is diminished? Or that, especially in the case of ancestral lands, whether used for hunting or for spiritual purposes, a people belong to those lands, or that what Westerners might recognise as dispossession of land is in reality a deprivation of cultural identity and therefore of authentic being—personhood and group-ness?

Perhaps even in a European case such as the Elgin Marbles, Greek identity—or is it Greek self-assertion and emancipation?

—is incomplete so long as a constitutive part of that identity remains elsewhere as a living mnemonic or memory of Greek subjection and exposure to oppression.

But for the most part, cultural property claims in the West assert something different from non-Western claims, though quite what is perhaps difficult to say. The identification of a thing as cultural property, even if it is in private ownership, is to assert some kind of public interest in the thing which justifies placing restrictions on its use, not for utilitarian reasons (this is in broad terms the justification for planning or zoning laws) but because that thing is thought to embody and/or exemplify a cultural tradition. The thing in some sense stands as a bridge between past, present and future. Its past serves to justify in the present its safeguarding for the future. In a legal sense, then, this public interest is in some way comparable to the notion of the "public" which we find in charity law. And indeed, those aristocrats who still own their country piles now embrace this theme with enthusiasm, relaunching themselves as guardians of a cultural tradition, of Britain's heritage.

At the same time, even in the West, the advent of multi-culturalism and its consequences following the movement of peoples in the age of imperialism and its aftermath, mean that the boundaries of cultural property are ever more contested, and that conflict over the definition and possession of cultural property becomes one important form of modern political and legal conflict between different social groups.

Persons as property

At the same time, a different dynamic needs to be noted. The process of modernisation, the triumph of liberalism and demo-cratisation, is often seen as involving a paradoxical shrinking in the scope of property. Perhaps the most prominent of these (with a number of persistent residues) is slavery. The institution of slavery always complicated the simple distinction between persons and things which organises the general structure of thinking about property. Conversely, its abolition can be read as the final triumph of the claim that people cannot be things. Equally, in many societies (including the United Kingdom), the character of the relationships between adult males and their wives, and between parents and their children, were once intelligible in part in terms of the language of property. The reason why a husband could not rape his wife was that they were of one body—in effect, one being— of which he was the substance and she the shadow, or to use a different analogy, he was the form and she was the substance (*i.e.* the raw material). Equally, adultery committed by another was an injury to the husband, for which he could sue the adulterer and claim financial compensation as, in effect, damage done to his property. Their children were the heirs of his body, and the wife was the lawful vehicle for this process of begetting. As such, the children belonged to their creator—the father. For these reasons—along with others, such as the lack of independence of mind or judgment, which applied to married women and children but also to servants and other dependants—property ownership and citizenship were closely connected. How much of this has changed is still open to debate (see Evans, 1993); but in most Western societies, the inappropriateness of the property model is widely recognised for conceptualising these relationships, just as in theory the institution of slavery is universally abhorred (even if the idea is sometimes transposed metaphorically into other, formally contractual domains, as in the expression "wage-slave"). Modern discourse tends to establish all humans as rights-bearing individuals and then to problematise the degree to which relationships between such beings should appropriately be treated in contractual terms or not.

Interestingly, however, this liberal vision is in one sense a triumph of private property. Marx (1975) foresaw this in the 1840s in his analysis of freedom of religion. Every individual owns himself or herself, and everyone has a claim to protection from the state as the guarantor of private property and as the mechanism for the enforcement of violations of such rights (*cf.* Glendon 1991). In so far as this model ousts its predecessor, in which some people more or less belonged to others, it introduces the potential for new sets of issues. On the one hand, rape within marriage can now be a criminal offence, and the possibility exists for a civil action brought by a wife against the husband for rape (wives are no longer the private property of their husbands). Children, too, have rights, and even, in some jurisdictions, so do the unborn (though the latter illustrates the persistence of older themes in changed conditions; the claims of the foetus almost turn the foetus-carrying mother into its, albeit temporary, property). Correlatively, what is at issue in the debate over abortion other than whether or not the woman owns her body?

Developments in biotechnology lead to questions of property rights being posed in new domains. What is sometimes called "technoscience" enables blood and bone marrow transfusions, egg and sperm "donation", organ transplants, and we now see the beginnings of gene therapy and transgenic medicine (see Jones, 1994; Russo and Cove, 1998). "It is easy to imagine a time when physicians know enough about the genome to say with confidence that one or other sequence would, if properly inserted in a fertilised egg, stop the recurrence of any one of a number of familial diseases" (Pollack, 1994, p.146). Biotechnology is itself increasingly part of the corporate, global business sector. Both in the United States and the United Kingdom, much of the research now done in this area, whether undertaken in universities or in private laboratories, is funded by the corporate sector from its R & D budget (see Rabinow, 1996), precisely to develop new drugs and new therapies which can be patented (*i.e.* made the object of intellectual property) and marketed. Most controversial of all is the patenting of gene sequences themselves. Shares of such companies rise and fall in the stockmarkets of the world depending on the latest news about drug therapies for AIDS, etc. The public may benefit from these new discoveries but so do companies and their shareholders.

These developments produce a situation in which intellectual property rights permeate every field of human endeavour. These bring into question again, if in a new way, how we should define what is a thing, and signal a partial collapse of the liberal paradigm of property as relations between people mediated by things.

But these developments also give rise to new questions concerning the rights of human beings who are the "source" of the human tissue needed for pharmaceutical research and gene-based therapies. The attempt, now successfully concluded, to compile a complete map of the Human Genome (see Bodmer and McKie, 1995; *cf.* Wilkie, 1994) has, as an unintended side-effect, drawn attention to the existence of rare gene pools among isolated, often small, human groups in various parts of the world. What rights, if any, should such groups, which have inherited some genetic material which may be of great potential value to the pharmaceutical industry, have over that material? Should they be able to benefit from its commercial exploitation?

A second issue returns us to the interlocking of biotechnology with the regime of private property in the more familiar sense. Various commercial organisations now offer the facility of long-term deep-frozen storage of body parts, such as umbilical cords, with a view to using some of this material in the future in medical interventions on the source patient and/or his family. What is interesting here, however speculative such developments may remain, is that they unfold the possibility of changing the relationship between the person and the body of the person, by permitting an explicitly proprietary relationship to be established between the person and an externalised body part. Egg and sperm banks raise similar issues.

In one sense, though, the commercialisation of the human body, often contrary to national or international law, is not new. Traditionally, in England, the law placed very severe restrictions on the ability to treat corpses as property. However, as late as the nineteenth century:

> "Outside of, and in opposition to, the law, a small but important sector of the population—anatomists, artists, physicians, surgeons, articulators, dentists and their suppliers— depended in varying degrees for their economic survival upon the ease with which the human corpse could be treated as a commodity.
>
> Corpses were bought and sold, they were touted, priced, haggled over, negotiated for, discussed in terms of supply and demand, delivered, imported, exported, transported. Human bodies were compressed into boxes, packed in sawdust, packed in hay, trussed up in sacks, roped up like hams, sewn in canvas, packed in cases, casks, barrels, crates and hampers; salted, pickled, or injected with preservative. They were carried in carts and waggons, in barrows and steam-boats; manhandled, damaged in transit, and hidden under loads of vegetables. They were stored in cellars and on quays. Human bodies were dismembered and sold in pieces, or measured and sold by the inch" (Richardson, 1989, pp.71–72).

What is new today is that a range of pressures push towards the development of trafficking in tissue or organs extracted from living human beings.

Chapter warns us as to the difficulties in
understanding the subject.

2

UNDERSTANDING AND MISUNDERSTANDING PROPERTY LAW

"Now if any the most refined Braine under heaven would goe about to Enquire by Speculation, or by reading of Plato or Aristotle, or by Considering the Laws of the Jewes, or other Nations, to find out how Landes descend in England, or how Estates are there transferred, or transmitted among us, he wou'd lose his Labour, and spend his Notions in vaine, till he acquainted himselfe with the Lawes of England, and the reason is because they are Institutions introduced by the will and Consent of others . . . the Positions and Conclusions in the Mathematicks have more Evidence in them, and are more Naturally Seated in the minde than Institutions of Laws, which in a greate measure depend upon the Consent and appointment of the first Institutors . . ." (Sir Matthew Hale, quoted in Pocock, 1989, p.219).

THE ABSENCE OF A GENERAL FRAMEWORK

Many law students believe that property law—and land law in particular—is difficult. It is seen as obscure, complicated, hard to grasp, resistant to all but the keenest (or most persevering) intelligence. The main objective of this book is to explore the reasons for this reputation and, in doing so, to try to make the subject more accessible.

Perhaps the first problem is that it is not clear where the boundaries of the subject are to be drawn. The boundaries of "contract", "tort", and "crime" are relatively clear, whether these boundaries are drawn by law teachers for pedagogical purposes or by practitioners as a means of describing and differentiating their own activities. Secondly, even if it is uncontentious to assert that property law is concerned with the way in which the enjoyment and management of things are regulated, no internally coherent conceptual framework exists in which such rules are to be found. There is, in fact, no such thing as "the law of property" in general. First and foremost, as we shall see, this is because the "law" regarding land and the "law" regarding other things have developed separately, and as a result, distinctive rules have grown up in regard to each. The legislature, the judiciary, lawyers in practice and academic lawyers all treat land as different from other things, so far as their respective engagements with or interests in the law of property are concerned. As we shall see, in "land law", the central focus is upon the major statutes of 1925; the law relating to moveables was largely codified in the Sale of Goods Act 1893 (now re-enacted in the SGA 1979); in addition there is "specialised" legislation dealing with areas such as corporations, patents and copyright.

Practitioners and academic lawyers work, for the most part, with a fragmented literature: there are books on land law and books on personal property (or the sale of goods) as well as the "modern" books on intellectual property, company law and so on. The labour of writing a book on "property law" is rarely undertaken.[2] And unsurprisingly—because law books have largely determined the "boundaries" of law courses—most law school curricula engage in a form of apartheid, keeping land law apart from what law there is relating to the ownership and disposal of other things. Indeed, the law relating to other things tends to appear interstitially, in commercial law courses for example, as principally a set of problems thrown up in the law of contract. It is not presented as something fundamental to the way English lawyers think about property and therefore as something essential to understanding what, for the English lawyer, property means. It is characteristic that the first textbooks on personal property, appearing in the mid-nineteenth century, were written as supplements for young barristers studying conveyancing by the authors of successful books on land law.[3]

These factors make it difficult to provide a coherent presentation of how English lawyers think about "property" in general. In this respect the common law stands in sharp contrast to the civil law jurisdictions of continental Europe, with their codified law modelled upon the example of Justinian.[4] Projects of codification pull in the direction of theorisation, completeness and logical arrangement. Codes also often state rules in very general terms, partly in the interests of logical coherence, partly for more practical reasons. (The Napoleonic Code was produced at great speed, so its generality and relative brevity was more or less inevitable.) English law has not grown up in this way, but rather in a piecemeal, particularistic and leisurely fashion. There are no clearly defined external boundaries between property and other institutions of English private law; nor are there any authoritatively arranged internal subdivisions of the subject. There is no one text which can serve as the starting-point for the lawyer or the student of law, that can be used in the way in which the *Institutes* of Justinian were used in the medieval universities.

The "rules" we are trying to understand in this book have emerged over a long period of time as a result of three inter-connected but distinct processes. First, the day-to-day activities of lawyers in their offices, devising mechanisms to give effect to the wishes of their clients; secondly, the "unplanned" accidents of litigation; thirdly, occasional legislative intervention, usually addressed to fairly narrowly defined problems which lawyers or judges have encountered in the course of their work. In addition, in recent years, the Law Commission has served as a limited channel for academic inputs into the legislative process. It follows that English law is often silent on matters which the professionals simply take for granted, and on matters of no practical importance which, if one was striving for completeness or logical arrangement, might need to be addressed.

So the upshot is that "property" has no single, simple meaning for English lawyers if and when they care to examine the concepts which they use. This fact is not in itself a problem, though one consequence of it is that what political theorists or economists have to say about property can often diverge from the way lawyers talk about it. For our purposes, the point which cannot be emphasised enough, and we return to it below, is that lawyers' conceptualisations of property grow out of the nature of lawyers' diverse involvements in the relation between people and things.

Lawyers encounter property in the following contexts. First, lawyers are involved in the preparation of written instruments dealing with title (essentially to do with questions of proof and mechanisms of transfer). As we shall see, the bulk of lawyers' work is of this character—providing the framework for trans-actions. Secondly, lawyers service and adjudicate upon disputes concerning property. There are two principal types of possible dispute in which lawyers get involved. First are those disputes which require the ascertainment of property rights, disputes concerned with fundamental questions of ownership. In these situations, one can see lawyers' "learning" as so many tools of the trade: as concepts and categories within which to present the argument and the decision. Here, it is important not to run together the tools with the uses to which they are put; a limited range of tools may be set to work in widely divergent dispute contexts. Secondly, there is a range of disputes concerning the use of property. Lawyers have come to elaborate a range of rights to property, and to land in particular, which provide a framework within which such disputes about land use can be processed.

Against this background, we have chosen to centre our discussion around land, and to deal much more briefly with property in other things, for several reasons. First, as already indicated, land law is conventionally taught and studied as a subject in its own right, and our principal task here is to assist the student embarking upon that rather arduous course of study. Secondly, as we have said, lawyers themselves have long treated land—and transactions involving land—as different from transactions involving other things. The legal regimes regarding other things are largely to be found in the law of contract, while the remedies for protecting or asserting claims to other things are largely a branch of the law of tort. Land has its own regime(s). It is obvious even to the layman that buying a house is a much more elaborate—and, again, arduous and stressful—affair than buying a car.

LAND LAW AND ITS PECULIARITIES

Considerable difficulties remain even if we abandon the attempt to deal with "property" in general and direct most of our energy to trying to understand land law. What is land law about? Most teachers would no doubt reply that it is about learning a set of rules, whether or not these rules should be set in their "context", whatever that means, and whether or not the exposition of these rules should be merely positive (just saying what they are), or evaluative (subjecting them to a critique developed from some perspective or other). But even if one accepts one of these versions of the pedagogical enterprise, at whom are these rules to be taken to be targeted? Are we concerned with what judges do in court, with what lawyers do in the office, or with what people do in life?

The absence, in England, of an established tradition of university legal education so far as the common law (as opposed to Roman law) is concerned, has meant that lawyers tended to learn what they really needed to know principally by sitting in courts, chambers and offices, listening, watching, helping out and, finally, by trial and error. Recent years have seen a rapid proliferation in the number of English law schools, in which land law is usually a compulsory part of the syllabus; yet even today, by contrast with continental Europe, academic institutions are largely peripheral to, or parasitic upon, the real business of law which is located somewhere else. The leading textbooks focus upon the decisions of the superior courts, as if they are enunciating a set of normative rules. This means that the practical character of land law is either ignored or taken for granted, and not made explicit for the reader. The heart of the matter—the work of conveyancers in their offices, preparing documents of transfer, drafting wills and so on—is largely treated as peripheral to the exposition of principle. This means that land law is presented in something of a vacuum, since its ground is the paper-work which takes place in the office and which is later worked over, in one way or another, by judges and legislators when problems emerge.

In the standard texts, as a result, it is sometimes hard for the student to tell what is a difficult question and what is not; what is a minor quirk of history which never posed any practical difficulty and so could be left undisturbed, and what is a major mess too complex for anyone adequately to resolve. However, even if the practical context, when supplied, can make some matters less mysterious, it is in and of itself insufficient. The closer one examines it, the more the highly instrumental character of land law comes into view. It then becomes necessary to ask to what ends the instruments are being put. This requires a much wider appreciation of the context of property law. Perhaps most important of all it requires one to explore the assumptions, the ideas which are taken for granted, the "unsaid" which makes what is said intelligible to the actors at the time—the owners of property, their lawyers and their judges—and which needs to be drawn out if we as observers are to understand what is going on. Without this "context of the obvious", a highly distorted reading of the legal material is likely to result.

This point is elaborated further below. Before doing so, we must note some more barriers to understanding which are at least relatively easy to state. The first is mainly of historical significance, but it remains fundamental to understanding the subject even today. This is what lawyers call the "1925 legislation". The study of land law in modern England very largely defines its scope and boundaries with reference to the matters at which this legislation was aimed. The study of land law today, in other words, is principally a gloss or commentary upon these statutory texts and the decisions which have interpreted them. For this reason, it will be necessary in certain parts of this book to discuss explicitly how judicial interpretation should proceed in the face of a body of statutory material of such length, complexity and, by the practical standards of English lawyers, longevity.

Given the centrality of this legislation to the study of land law, it is imperative for the student to grasp that much of its framework was constructed with the objective of simplifying certain aspects of the legal regimes governing the landed estates of the past, and specifically the various legal devices for creating and operating what were called "settlements" of land. This means that the problems to which the legislation was addressed have little direct relevance in the modern world of owner-occupation of houses and flats. A number of important difficulties flow from this fact of historical change.

The second barrier in the way of a coherent presentation, again principally of historical significance, is no less fundamental. This is the division between "law" and "equity". For much of the history of English law, there were, as again we shall see in more detail later, two types of courts proceeding in some measure independently, throwing up different guidelines, principles, rules and remedies, even if neither proceeded in a vacuum and each was, for many centuries, cognisant of the practices of the other. (The "trust" (see Chapter 5) is a good, and perhaps the most important, example of this jurisdictional divide.) It remains a fact that much legal energy was devoted to working out the relationship—largely in jurisdictional terms—between these two bodies of law, and that, even though these two streams of law, if they can be so described, are now administered in every court, history has left a deep imprint upon the contemporary fabric in this respect. As a result, any overall outline of the English law of property cannot but dart to and fro between law and equity, each with its own organising conceptual principles, at the expense of overall coherence.

The final, more technical, barrier to a coherent exposition of the land law is that the 1925 legislation left us with two distinct schemes regulating transfer of title to land. While one of these schemes—registered conveyancing—was, at least as it was publicly presented (*cf.* Offer, 1977), designed to replace the other—unregistered conveyancing—this process is still incomplete today. As a result, the student of land law has to master two different regimes of land law, which differ from each other, as we shall see in Chapter 10, in some important ways.

These problems from the past do not mean that property law must be studied as a branch of legal history. They do mean that some kind of understanding, however simplified, of the issues and problems which were regarded as important or difficult by owners of property and their lawyers in the past is still needed today in order to make the framework of property law more accessible. Such an understanding also helps to explain both the fact of and the need for "creative" interpretation by modern judges of the property legislation.

Which aspects of the past are more important is a matter of judgment in a general sense. In the chapters which follow, we have chosen to give the greatest emphasis to two broad areas in particular. First, we have tried to give some of the flavour of the practical logic which informed the development of settlements of land, because the problems generated by these practices formed an important target for the 1925 legislation. Secondly, and for similar reasons, we have tried to give some insights into the character of, and assumptions which pervaded, nineteenth-century conveyancing practice and the management by lawyers of the process of land transfer, because this provides a means of understanding the objectives behind the design of the scheme set up in 1925 to modify them.

Paying attention to the past in this way is also a way of encouraging renovation and innovation in the development of concepts and their application. Not everything is obsolete just because it is of nineteenth-century provenance: equally, not everything that seems to be modern is new in reality.

LAWYERS, JUDGES AND WORDS

The principal obstacles to the understanding of land law have been introduced. We must now examine more closely the central question outlined above: what is it all about? Is it about what judges do in court? Clearly, some of it is. Is it about what lawyers do in their offices? Clearly, some of it is about this as well. Such affirmative answers throw up another question. If different parts of what we classify as land law concern one or other of these activities, what is the relationship between these activities, and what does this mean for the study of land law? The standard textbooks give pride of place to the judges and treat them as if their principal concern is with the formulation or interpretation of rules, or the development of the law. One thing which this can obscure is the simple possibility that judges may often be indifferent to the outcome of the disputes upon which they have to decide.

Moreover, the construction of the pedagogical agenda around more or less heroic judges slotted in to a narrative of legal development can obscure the primacy of what lawyers do in their offices, preparing documents which serve as instruments to achieve a client's wishes, documents which, it is hoped, will not attract the scrutiny of a judge at some later time. These are the conveyances and deeds of transfer which move property around from one person to another and regulate its use, the wills and trusts which channel property through the generations within a family and are designed to preserve it from the depredations of the taxman. To prepare these documents, lawyers resort to verbal formulae—to forms of words—which have worked in the past, recycling and adapting them to meet the needs of the present, but with no particular concern to modernise the language or prune away the sometimes florid or redundant expressions inherited from the past.

This level of activity, which is so largely constitutive of what land law is, gives rise to a second point. When lawyers are trying to achieve a given result for their client, they often encounter a number of alternative ways of reaching it. Where a practical formula has proved reliable in the past, there is no reason not to use it again, and its use becomes a matter of routine. But if at some point it shows signs of running into difficulty, for example because of some judicial decision on the meaning of a word, phrase or formula which has arisen through an accident of litigation, it may well be discarded in favour of an alternative. The practice of law is about how to do things, how to achieve results. Where one formula appears problematic, you resort to a functional equivalent, to an alternative which will do the same job. We will need in due course to develop this theme.

The important point for now is that we should not exaggerate the importance of judges. The driving force in the history of land law has been the activity of conveyancers. Their expertise was essentially formulaic, and remains so in large measure today. The role of the judge must be seen against the background of this work of conveyancers. For the most part, the judge comes on the scene only in those relatively rare cases where things go wrong, and then as a reader of formulae, for the most part, rather than as an interpreter of rules. The judge's role is thus responsive; his principal task is to read the verbal formulae and say what their effect is in the event of a dispute. It is this relationship, too, which helps to explain why it was so frequently repeated that the Bench should defer to conveyancing opinion. If conveyancing practice has proceeded for a period of time on the basis that a particular formula has a particular legal effect, so that possibly hundreds of conveyances, wills or settlements have been drawn up on that basis, there is obviously strong pressure on a judge in the course of litigation to accept the interpretation of the conveyancers.

In the area of land law at least, these factors put in question the adequacy of viewing judges as "activists", whose role is to develop the law. The job of an English judge is to resolve disputes, in the particular sense of deciding, as between the contestants before him, who will win and who will lose. Once this is done, the judge then has to draw up orders so that everyone knows what they must do when they go away from court. Judges are not there primarily to develop the law. So there is a certain gap in a common law system between the primary concerns of academics, students and practitioners, even at the highest level. As Lord Goff has recently stated, in a case concerned in part with the law of restitution:

"... it is particularly desirable that your Lordships should, so far as possible, restrict the inquiry to the actual questions at issue in this appeal, and not be tempted into formulating general principles of a broader nature. If restitution lawyers are hoping to find in your Lordships' speeches broad statements of principle which may definitively establish the future shape of this part of the law, I fear that they may be disappointed".[5]

Judging in England is a practical activity. One of the most important aspects of that activity concerns keeping the litigation process under control. And more than anything, this means keeping control over the volume of private litigation. One consequence of this is that, however bizarre or obscure or antiquated a rule is, there is no incentive to change it unless it causes inconvenience in a practical sense. In other words, real, living law may diverge from what, in a theoretical sense, could be said to be the law. There are two basic, and irritating, points for the student of property law: lawyers work with what is to hand, however antique the materials may be; and some rules of law survive, remain part of the repertoire, long after they been used in any practical sense.

Judicial involvement in the development of land law thus takes place, for the most part, through the two-way communication of judges with lawyers. A lawyer tries to do something; in a dispute or a hearing, a judge says it has failed; the lawyers then look for another way of achieving the same result; and so on. Much the same can be said about the construction of pleadings and the business of oral argument by barristers before judges: the barrister searches for alternative ways of presenting the case; the judge chooses between them.

This opportunistic resort to functional equivalents can make matters seem more complicated than they really are. In the area of what is commonly called the "family home" or "home sharing", there are five or six ways of arguing and holding that a home owner will not be allowed to evict someone living in the home on an informal basis. From a conceptual point of view, some of these seem very different from the others; in a functional sense, they achieve the same result, and the choice between these concepts, for the purpose of giving a legal interpretation of everyday facts, seems arbitrary—a matter of personal preference or terminological fashion.

This suggests that the formalism of which judges are sometimes accused is somewhat different in character from the way it is commonly presented. What most English scholars mean by formalism goes something like this. Once upon a time, when faced with a dispute, judges evaluated the merits of the issues as they saw them. For example, where the argument was about whether an agreement for a sale should be enforced by the court, the judge would hear argument about whether the price was just and, if he concluded that it was not, would refuse to enforce it. Formalism is associated in most commentators' minds with a progressive refusal by judges to adopt this sort of attitude. Instead, the formalist judge asks simply whether certain general rules of contract formation have been complied with, and leaves it at that. The link between this alleged development and an ideology of legal certainty is also treated as obvious: the judge who evaluates is being "subjective" and therefore acting unpredictably. Even if barristers who appear before him regularly can predict how he is likely to respond in the event of a dispute, this kind of predictability falls far short, it is said, of the kind of certainty which a legal system must provide. First, because the predictions of counsel are necessarily based on their personal knowledge and practical experience of the individual judge in action. Secondly, because the sort of certainty which is expected is one that you can have irrespective of the particular judge you end up before if you have a dispute. If the consequences of a transaction are to be knowable in advance (which is what certainty is taken most of the time to mean), they must not depend on "subjective" factors but on "objective" ones that transcend individuals. From this it is a short step to saying that the fundamental characteristic of the judicial role is the negotiation of the tension between certainty and fairness.

Every received wisdom contains some grain of truth. But most of the time this so-called fundamental tension between certainty and fairness is not in issue. That is to say, most of the time judges are formalists, and for reasons connected with a need for certainty; but neither the formalism nor the idea of certainty are the ones we have so far described.

The formalism of the conventional wisdom is a formalism of rule-finding. This is true in two senses: first, to use the Weberian categories, that either a concrete balancing of the interests of contestants or a self-conscious evaluation of the merits with reference to some code of values is systematically excluded from the adjudicative process; secondly, and consequentially, that judicial decision-making is a matter of finding, following, or adapting rules, where the aims of consistency and logical coherence are paramount, and considerations of policy are not permitted to provide decision-making criteria. Judges themselves often play along with this caricature because it is convenient.

But the real formalism in play is not that of a rule-finder but that of a reader. The reading process, which lawyers call rather grandly "construction", lies at the heart of English formalism. The developmental dynamic of property law, viewed over time, is largely a tension between strategies of construction and the refinement of classificatory frameworks in or through which to fit interpretations.

This is revealed by the rather special meaning which the term "precedent" has long had for property lawyers. Usually, this term is taken to refer to the accumulation of binding judicial decisions over time and, as such, is regarded as a defining characteristic of the common law style. But property lawyers have long been familiar with a different kind of precedent. This is a model or specimen transaction—a model will, settlement, trust, lease—which sets out the recommended formulae and framework for designing a particular type of transaction. These "patterns" have always been prepared by practitioners and have served as an important reference point for lawyers in their day-to-day work. Such precedents were never binding, and depended in the end upon professional consensus for the influence which they had. In this sense, they served as an important source of professional opinion on the law of property and, given their practical importance, judges were expected— though could not of course be compelled—to afford them respect.

LANGUAGE AND THE PRESENT AND THE PAST

Since the middle of the eighteenth century, projects of legal codification have operated as an emblem of modernisation, seeking to embed in law an explicit break with the customs and practices of the past. Such projects continue to play a similar role today in the developing world. This feature of codification meant that, in nineteenth-century France and Germany, jurisprudence divided into two opposing camps: those championing codification as the expression of "reason", and those insisting that it must give expression to and embody the established customs and culture of the people or nation, which could only be known through "history" (*cf.* John, 1989; Honoré, 1982, pp.118–124). Property and, in particular, rules relating to the inheritance of property and its devolution through time, were often at the heart of this debate, because almost every society, however simple, has customary rules of some sort concerning these elementary questions, and the project of codification always poses the question of whether the code is to adopt or reject the traditional rules.

Property law in England underwent no such explicit break with the past of the kind generally associated with the project of codification. This is usually taken to be the principal reason why the study of property law is difficult. Even its language bears the imprint of the past, a rag-bag of Norman-French, ecclesiastical Latin and English archaisms. Property lawyers talk in an esoteric, peculiar language that seems radically divorced from the language of ordinary life.

This is indeed one reason why property law appears to be inaccessible, and it does have important, negative, practical consequences. It is not satisfactory, as we shall see, that the language used by lawyers to conceptualise home ownership today is as unintelligible as it is to the people who own them, or that people who own leases of flats do not understand what the words in the leases mean. But locating the difficulty of land law in its language can be misleading, or, at least, imprecise. If you read a legal decision, modern or not so modern, there are a number of reasons why you find it difficult to understand. Much of the time, what may seem to be a difficulty with the law is a difficulty getting to grips with the facts. This is because what underpins many, though not all, disputes about property is one or more property transactions, where the dispute is about some consequence or other of the transaction. It is the student's difficulty in understanding the transaction—its nature or its logic—which makes it difficult to understand the dispute, and it is this, in turn, which makes it difficult to understand the decision. Very often, at the level of language, a judge's decision is written in relatively non-esoteric, ordinary terms; but his account of the transaction is what is hard to follow. Why is this? Because commonly it is expressed in the language of the transaction itself. Much of property law, as we shall see in this book, is about what words mean, and the words in question are the words used by lawyers when they prepare transactions. And it is in the use by lawyers of words in transactions that the imprint of the past is most evident, and the barrier to understanding which flows from this fact most firmly in place. It follows from this that to understand the subject, you need to understand the kinds of property transactions with which lawyers have been principally concerned, past and present. And you need to understand typical transactions of the past because, as we shall see, they have left their mark upon the present not just in terms of the vocabulary we have inherited but in terms of the shape of the legal framework itself.

So far it has been suggested that the past impinges upon the present by shaping the language, the categories and some of the rules which lawyers use in property law. So we can understand the law better if we know something of this impinging past, of why people did the sorts of things they did, and of when they needed lawyers to facilitate them and when they did not. But one final point must be stressed in examining the impact of the past upon the fabric of English land law. Its impact has been on the terminology, the formulae, the organising structure of the rules, and to some extent the substantive content of particular settled rules. It does not follow from this that English property lawyers are interested in or concerned with the past as such, in the manner of an historian. Quite the opposite is the case, and even the studied antiquarianism of some of the standard textbooks is not an exception to this generalisation. Rather than, as with codification, the history of property law being sundered by a sudden break, English legal history is more a case of incremental drift, of changes which are often imperceptible precisely because English lawyers rarely take the past seriously, rarely approach it in its own terms. This means that change often appears as continuity.

To conclude, it must be emphasised that this blindness to history or this incrementalism of the common law cannot be attributed simply to the large space afforded by the English legal system for judge-made law. Exactly the same stance and drift can be observed in the approach of the judiciary to the interpretation of statutes. By contrast with, say, the law of contract or the law of tort, a considerable part of the land law has always been statutory. Like the documents used in private transactions, the statutes abound with formulaic expressions; they are written in the language of conveyancers of long ago. Secondly, the principal statutes themselves are now 80 years old. And so, with statutes as with conveyancing practice, the question arises of the nature of an English lawyer's attitude towards the past. Is English adjudication an historical inquiry? The answer is that sometimes it is and sometimes it is not. But "history" is just a method, a technique, which along with others enables counsel to formulate arguments and a judge to provide reasons for why he has resolved a dispute in the way he has. There is no normative hierarchy regulating judicial method. It is unsystematic, a matter of appropriateness, of practical experience. This has several consequences for the student of land law. First, since the shapes of the past are so deeply imprinted upon the fabric of the modern law of property, these shapes can be made more accessible by studying some of the practices of the past. But, secondly, since judicial resort to history is, so to speak, opportunistic, the reader of contemporary judicial decisions will find the past ignored as often as it is considered. Thirdly, the student encounters, in textbooks and in judgments, the assertion of long continuities, the removal of a judicial dictum from its (time-bound, historical) context and its insertion into a smooth plain of "fundamental principle" unmarked by time. The more sensitive to the particularities of historical context the student of the subject becomes, the more he or she is likely to encounter a peculiar kind of history in the pages of the law—a history which is not really interested in the past.

3

OWNERSHIP AND TITLE

Max Weber had the following to say about the practice of law in England:

> "English legal thought is essentially an empirical art . . . The legal thinking of the layman is . . . literalistic. He tends to be a definition-monger when he believes he is arguing 'legally'. Closely connected with this trait is the tendency to draw conclusions from individual case to individual case . . . In both respects . . . the art of empirical jurisprudence is cognate to him, although he may not like it. No country, indeed, has produced more bitter complaints and satires about the legal profession than England" (tr. 1978, pp.890–891).

An understanding of English property law requires close attention to this definition-mongering activity, to classificatory schemes which give shape and structure to the conceptual framework within which lawyers talk and think. These schemes are peculiar to lawyers and, in that sense, specialised. The distinctions contained in them, as we shall see, do not always correspond to the way people think about property in everyday life, or, indeed, to the way in which, in the modern world, other specialised ways of thinking, notably economics, define the nature of property. But the systems of classification within which lawyers work, like other systems of classification, rest on certain assumptions. These assumptions are not always made explicit in legal discourse, but when we examine them it becomes clear that they diverge less from those held in everyday life than do the classifications erected upon the ground of these assumptions.

The central assumption is that private ownership by individuals is the normal way in which things are held. This concept of ownership is made up from three elements: the right to manage things, the right to enjoy or consume them, and the right to

dispose of them during life or upon death. And the use of the
term "right" here indicates that, at its core, ownership is not a
way of conceptualising the relation between people and things
but the relation between people (between owners and non-
owners), a relation which is mediated by things. This last point
is elaborated below.

These elements of ownership, it is essential to grasp, are
treated by English lawyers as severable from each other. The
right to manage a thing may be held by one person, the right to
enjoy it by another, the right to dispose of it by a third. Equally,
each of these elements of ownership may itself be fragmented in
various ways. The right to manage, enjoy or dispose of a thing
may be shared concurrently between several persons, or it may
be split up over time, so that one or more persons has the right
at one time, another at a later time. As we shall see throughout
this chapter and the chapters which follow, this fragmentation
of elements of ownership and the internal fragmentation of each
element accounts for much of the complexity which the student
of property law encounters.

While the individual provides the model or paradigm of
ownership, an owner does not have to be an individual human
being or a group of them. Commercial organisations can own
property, as can public authorities. These are legal, non-natural
persons and are treated as if they were human beings for the
purpose of conceptualising their ownership of things: hence the
"trespassers will be prosecuted" signs commonly found outside
a block of council flats. Nor is this idea of "legal personality"
constructed by analogy with the human being a new concept;
centuries ago, when a bishop died, lawyers had to work out
what part of "his" property belonged to him personally and
what part belonged to the bishopric such that it would pass to
his successor in office. Equally, in this way, monasteries could
accumulate vast wealth through gifts while the monks who ran
them remained true to their vow of poverty. More recently, a
fire at Windsor Castle generated similar speculation about the
ownership of the assets of the English Crown.

English property law is permeated by a strong sense of
"individualism", and this is particularly true of the way it treats
the devolution of property on death. It starts from the position
that an individual owner has complete freedom to direct how
his property should be distributed after he is dead, by contrast
with most European systems, which start by guaranteeing
certain rights of succession to the next generation, constraining

freedom of testamentary disposition from the outset. Paradoxically, this testamentary freedom added to the complexity of ownership through devices such as dower (the common law's traditional provision for widows), which mitigated testamentary freedom, and leaves its mark even today, where disinherited widows and dependants must invoke a modern statutory jurisdiction which enables the court to make a discretionary award from the deceased's estate in such circumstances.

English lawyers are not much given to idle speculation, so these assumptions function for the most part as an implicit ideology rather than an explicit theory. Indeed, the term "owner", particularly in relation to land, is most likely to be encountered when it is not at issue. When it is, or when, for whatever reason, it is necessary to be more precise, lawyers are more inclined to use a different term: "title". In disputes concerning ownership they do not ask or seek to show who is the owner in any absolute sense, but rather which of the disputants has a better title to the thing at issue, ignoring the possibility that someone with an even better claim than anyone in court may come forward in the future. Again, there seems a marked contrast here between the English approach and that of the civilian systems modelled on Roman law. Roman law defined explicitly what ownership (*dominium*) was, and had a specific, general remedy (*vindicatio*) through which it could be asserted in court.

Two classificatory schemes, which provide the English law of property with such structure as it has, must now be singled out for discussion. The first concerns how lawyers classify things themselves, and the consequences which flow from this. The second concerns how lawyers classify the range of rights one may hold in respect of things. But we must first examine the distinction between these two focal points of classification, in which "rights" and "things" appear to belong to two different levels of legal experience. The term "property" is for the most part used by non-lawyers with unselfconscious ambiguity, its meaning slipping backwards and forwards between "the thing itself" and the "rights" a person has to the enjoyment of the thing. The difference between "your car" and "your rights" over it is not obvious to you most of the time as you go about your day-to-day affairs. You may never encounter the distinction at all unless someone steals the car and it finds its way through a chain of buyers and sellers into the hands of an innocent buyer who refuses to give it back when you trace the car to him.

The distinction is more obvious in other cases—for example, where you have an income interest in a capital fund. If you view the fund as the thing, then all you can say is that you have certain rights in respect of that fund—to be paid a certain percentage of its annual yield, for instance. But further, we must note that in such circumstances you can easily come to think of your rights in regard to the thing as a thing in itself, with which you can go to market, as it were, and trade. And if you think about debts or patents or copyright, "things" which have no tangible existence, the difference between the thing itself and the right to the thing becomes even more obscure. But for lawyers, this distinction is fundamental and needs to be maintained if the fabric of property law is to be grasped.

One further reason for the inaccessibility of property law to the student is that the distinction is not always clearly maintained in the words lawyers themselves use. For example, as we will see, lawyers often say "land" when strictly they mean "title to land". Because lawyers, like anyone else, know what they really mean from the context in which they use a word, they often use shorthand forms of this sort. For the non-initiate, this can cause confusion, since it seems to undermine what they are told is fundamental. So a commentator should often add a marginal note; we say "land" but strictly speaking we mean "title to land". *rights*

At any rate, it is much easier to grasp English property law if we always bear in mind that transactions involving things are, for lawyers, strictly speaking, transactions involving rights to things. For the lawyer, what you have is rights not things. From this base line, as we shall see, lawyers go on for the most part to talk about such rights as if they were the things in respect of which these rights are operative.

The things themselves:

THE CLASSIFICATION OF THINGS
How do lawyers classify things?
Real property and personal property

Originally, the emergence of property law was linked to the growth of remedial assistance from the royal courts in particular. The transformation of land law into essentially a body of professional know-how relating to land transfer—*i.e.* conveyancing—is consequent upon and not antecedent to the process of dispute settlement. This needs to be borne in mind as we turn to what is usually supposed to be a fundamental aspect of the English lawyer's way of thinking about property, namely the distinction between rights to land and rights to other things, or between real and personal property.

The terms "real" and "personal" come from the *Institutes* of Justinian, the most important textbook after the Bible in the medieval universities of Europe. The *Institutes* were divided into four parts: Persons, Things, Obligations and Actions. As Maitland tells the story, the distinction between persons and things was first appropriated by medieval English lawyers to distinguish two types of remedy or judgment, real remedies by which a successful plaintiff recovers the thing claimed, and personal remedies where the value of the thing may be all that can be recovered. By the mid-thirteenth century, real remedies were available for the recovery of land, but, according to Bracton, moveables could not be recovered through a real action: ". . . by merely paying [the defendant] is discharged whether the thing be forthcoming or no" (quoted in Maitland, 1909, p.368). This is not surprising for the Middle Ages, Maitland suggests, since most chattels were perishable and of a kind where it would be straightforward enough to assess the value of the thing; ". . . if the plaintiff got the [price] of his ox he got what would do as well as his ox" (*ibid*).

Maitland saw this as the ("much to be regretted") origin of "all our talk" about real and personal property. First, an action comes to be treated as "real" if you get possession of land from the court, as "personal" if you get damages and as "mixed" if you get both. This in turn led lawyers in time to distinguish "things real" from "things personal".

Whatever the historical origins of the distinction between real and personal property, and its consequences (good or bad) for analytical jurisprudence, it is worth recalling at this stage one central point made in the previous chapter. Lawyers' conceptualisations of property grow from the nature of lawyers' involvements in the relations between people and things. In the case of chattels, it is still the case today that their involvement is principally concerned with the litigation process. In the case of land, such involvement is subsidiary and subordinated to their involvement in the process of the management of land transfer. So the law of personal property remains primarily remedial in character, while land law is in essence structured around conveyancing.

Traditionally, if very long ago, the distinction between real and personal property did correspond to a fairly straightforward scheme of things, in particular to the distinction between immoveable and moveable property. In the modern law, however, perhaps the best we can suggest is that personal property means those rights which approximate to what lawyers mean by property which are not rights in land.

Choses in action

Alongside this distinction between the categories of "land" and "moveables" is a further distinction between rights in tangible and intangible property. Thus a right of way over land is intangible: you can touch your field but not your right to walk across someone else's. Rights in real property are thus internally divided into rights to corporeal (tangible) and incorporeal (intangible) things.

An analogous internal subdivision is made in the category of personal property, but its significance, as we shall now see, is slightly different. Things which have a tangible physical existence—cars, books, animals—comprise what lawyers mean much of the time by "personal property". But rights to intangible personal property have also come to be recognised, especially in modern times, by lawyers. They call such rights "choses in action". This means that these are things ("choses") whose ultimate "thingness" resides in the owner's ability to bring an action in court, rather than in a person's ability to take physical possession of the thing in which he has the right. You can reclaim a book or a cow that belongs to you by regaining physical control of it. But if someone interferes with intangible personal property, you can only bring a legal action to stop the interference and obtain financial compensation; you cannot take it back because it has no physical form. Examples of such intangibles are forms of industrial and intellectual property such as patents, trade marks and copyrights. Rights of this kind have the character of property in so far as they endure, within the limits laid down by law, against a wide range of people, and are capable of retaining their value and enforceability in the hands of the heirs of the initial holder, and can be passed on through sale or gift to others, who, through the transfer, acquire equal rights. These all provide examples, in the strongest sense, of rights which lawyers treat as things, where, by contrast with the ownership of tangibles, there is no thing which can serve as shorthand to describe the right to the thing in question (for the historical difficulties of conceptualising copyright, see Rose, 1993). As we suggested in Chapter 1, these rights to intangibles—what are now known generically as intellectual

property rights—have become of particular commercial importance and complexity in the era of global computer software
companies and the modern pharmaceutical industry (Haraway,
1997).

Certain types of debt or claims to money owed are also
classified as choses in action and thus as property rights. Here
the paradigm case is the right to repayment of borrowed money,
such as a bank loan. Also in this category are contractual
obligations to pay a fixed sum of money, as when you agree to
pay £90 to a garage to have a new clutch put in your car, or to
provide agreed quantities of specific goods, such as a case of a
particular claret. The duty of an executor to pay a sum of money
to a legatee is another example, the will endowing the legatee
on the death of the testator with rights conferring, *inter alia*, the
possibility of passing onto another what he or she has inherited.

The long-established recognition of the transmissibility of
rights to enforce debts makes the borderline between what
English lawyers treat as property and what they treat as contract
or as personal wrongs unclear. Some monetary claims, such as
damages for libel or for personal injuries, cannot be transferred,
cannot be brought within the scheme of choses in action. This is
sometimes said to be because of the indefinite and open-ended
nature of such monetary claims; that unliquidated damages are
"at large" until a compensatory figure is arrived at in the legal
process. But other jurisdictions manage such questions differently, and permit transferability in such contexts. Negotiable
instruments and money are also rights treated as things, and, as
a result, as property. As such, they differ from the older and
superficially analogous category of intangibles in land law,
which, as we see in Chapter 8, are largely property rights only
in so far as they can be annexed to tangible property, and are
not recognised as independently transmissible property rights.

PERSONAL RIGHTS AND PROPERTY RIGHTS

A further fundamental distinction embedded in the conceptual
framework of English property law, which, at the same time, is
only rarely articulated, comes to the surface when lawyers try to
conceptualise the enjoyment and management of things. This is
the distinction between those rights or interests which lawyers
treat as property from those which they do not. This distinction
too is not straightforward. What can be suggested is that, in so
far as English law does contain a core idea of what a "property

right" means, that idea involves the combination of two essential elements: durability and transmissibility. Property rights are durable in the sense that the present holder of the right can defend it over time against a range of other people, including the person from whom he obtained the right. They are transmissible in the sense that the holder can pass them on to other people. Either or both of these qualities may be considerably restricted (such restrictions are considered below), but the right is still conceptualised as a property right. Only if neither attribute is present will lawyers not speak of a property right.

There are two senses in which a right can be regarded as "personal" by lawyers. It may be personal in the sense that the right is held only against a particular person. So if such a right relates to the use of that person's land, it will not endure should the land pass into other hands. Traditionally, this was the case where a licence to enter and/or occupy land was enshrined in a contract. Secondly, a right may be personal in that it is exercisable only by the person who has the right, and is not transmissible by him to anyone else.

In the social world, this legal distinction is not always observable in the use which people make of things. Consider the following example. You see that a neighbour has begun to drive his cattle across a field, which you have always assumed does not belong to him, in order to graze them on common land which lies on the other side. To a lawyer, this observable fact drawn from everyday life might mean a number of different things. Your neighbour might simply be a trespasser; but if not, if his presence on the land was lawful, a lawyer could explain what you saw in several ways. Your neighbour might have a simple permission, a "licence", a personal right which operated in his favour and only in his favour, a right enforceable only against the present owner of the land, which the owner might be able to terminate or revoke at any time. Alternatively, a lawyer might say that your neighbour had a property right, an "easement", a right of way which he could pass on to anyone who bought his land in the future, a right which could be enforced against anyone who later bought the land over which the right of way operated. Yet again, of course, the explanation might be that your neighbour had bought or leased the stretch of land from the person you thought owned it. Exactly how a lawyer would arrive at one or other of these interpretations of what, for the non-lawyer, is one observable fact is examined later.

With some kinds of property rights, transmissibility appears to be the decisive element which distinguishes such rights from personal rights. This is the case with choses in action. A debt is classifiable as a property right in that it can be transferred by the creditor to someone else who is then the person to enforce the obligation. Such a right can be compared with the right to claim compensation for a personal injury, arising, say, from a car accident, which is not transferable. There is no magic in this distinction, and in some jurisdictions personal injuries claims are transferable.

Where there is a dispute arising out of observable facts of the kind in our example above, it is for judges to decide which legal category best expresses the true nature of the arrangement between the parties, to say what the transaction really means in legal terms. But the history of English property law can largely be read as an attempt to render this interpretative process unnecessary, pre-empting the need for interpretation by formalising the nature of the arrangement in advance. At worst, because no one likes litigation, this displaces the process of judicial interpretation from making legal sense of what people do in social life, of "facts", to making sense of words on the page which have been written by lawyers. At best, it renders disputes about "meaning" unnecessary or impossible, because lawyers have used verbal formulae which have become standard, the interpretation of which is beyond dispute in a court of law. We return to the significance of this in the final chapter.

OWNERSHIP AND ENGLISH LAW

Although, as we have seen, a concept of "ownership"—the idea that a person can acquire secure, exclusive enjoyment of a thing and transmit it to another—underpins the English law of property, lawyers rarely talk explicitly in these terms. Rarely in the literature do we encounter discussions which compare, in length or subtlety, with those of *dominium* in Roman law, nor does English legislation endow ownership with specific characteristics and consequences in the manner of the civilian codes. Instead, we must examine a cluster of techniques which English lawyers have developed over a long period of time for processing disputes concerning things. Some of these techniques can be presented as exemplifying a "principle", but even these "principles", as we shall see, are in fact abbreviated statements of how the business of litigation over things has been managed in the English courts.

[Really... process rather than principle]

Three central elements are combined here. First, "title" is treated as a relative notion, which is shorthand for saying that in a dispute over a thing, English courts confine themselves to asking who, as between the parties in court, has the better title. A further manifestation of this principle of relativity, as we shall see, is the effective absence of special remedies for owners as compared with those available to people with lesser claims to things. Relativity is complemented by two further principles. First, a time limit is placed on the availability of remedies for the recovery of things. Secondly, subject to these time limits, the logic of relativity of title has the effect of protecting the integrity of a good title against subsequent dealings with a thing inconsistent with that title. Each of these must now be examined.

Relativity of title

In Roman law, title and ownership were not distinguished. Rather, ownership and lesser rights were clearly differentiated. Separate remedies were available for the assertion before a tribunal of what were considered to be qualitatively different kinds of claims. As the English system developed, however, the distinction was blurred, as people who in practical terms were asserting ownership rights (and who presumably thought of themselves as the owner of the thing in question) made use, procedurally, of remedial avenues which were equally available to people making less ambitious claims.

The fulcrum of the English system of remedies is possession rather than ownership. If you pick up a jewel in the street, and someone takes it from you and will not give it back, you can take him to court and recover its full value, even though it is obvious that a third person has a better title to the jewel than either of you. The person who took the jewel from you cannot defeat your claim by pointing to the defects in your title. He must pay you the full value of the thing, not some lesser sum reflecting your merely possessory title. Your earlier possession suffices. The true owner asserts his rights in exactly the same way. In terms of the conceptual structure of English property law, the distinction between "true ownership" and merely possessory title is, at core, the difference between an earlier and a later taking of possession.

While the privileging of possession dates back to the very beginnings of the English polity, the concept of possession is a fluid one. The balance between possession as the basis for acquiring legal rights (including the informal acquisition of rights in the family home through "actual occupation", which is the possession requirement in other words), and other forms of acquisition, *i.e.*, the formal mechanisms of conveyancing (land transfer) and trusts, is constantly shifting. However, in the light of the new Land Registration Act 2002, which attempts to replace possession by registration as the *nec plus ultra* of title, the question of the foundation of land law on possession is reopened for further discussion by academics and practitioners (see Chapter 10 below).

The principal action available to protect interests in moveables was an action known as "trover" (now called "conversion"). One of the leading property lawyers of the nineteenth century, Joshua Williams, set out the basic rationale of the remedy in the following terms:

> "This action can be maintained only when the plaintiff has been in possession of the goods, or has such a property in them as draws to it the right to the possession. If the goods have been wrongfully converted by the defendant to his own use, the plaintiff will succeed, if he should prove either way his own right to the immediate possession of the goods; if he should not prove such right, he will fail. The property in the goods is that which most usually draws to it the right of possession; and the right to maintain an action of trover is therefore often said to depend on the plaintiff's property in the goods; the right of immediate possession is also sometimes called itself a special kind of property; but these expressions should not mislead the student, the action of trover tries only the right to the immediate possession, which, as we shall now see, may exist apart from the property in the goods.
>
> For let us suppose that the finder of the article lost, whilst ignorant of the true owner, should have been wrongfully deprived of it by a third person. In this case, the owner being absent, the finder is evidently entitled to the possession of the thing; and he will accordingly succeed in an action of trover brought by him against the wrong-doer. Here the property in the thing which was lost evidently belongs still to the original owner; but the right of possession is in the finder, until the owner makes his appearance. The owner's property then draws with it the right of possession; and should the finder convert the article found to his own use, he in his turn will be liable to an action of trover in respect of the owner's right of

possession. Thus, so far as we have already proceeded, we have found nothing more than a simple property in goods, existing with or without the right of possession. The action of trover tries the right of possession, and may or may not determine the property. For strange as it may appear, there is no action in the law of England by which the property in goods is alone decided." (Williams, 1856, p.24).

In the same way, if you hire someone's car, and a third person crashes into it and destroys it, you can recover its full value from him (or his insurance company), even though you have only hired it. Indeed, the logic of the English approach would seem to dictate—though there is no authority on the point—that the position would be the same even if the claimant were a thief. Thus, if you steal a car, and someone damages it, you could still recover in full against him. Your theft is no defence as far as he is concerned. The fact that you are a thief does mean that the person from whom you stole the car can claim its value from you if he catches up with you, and, of course, you might face criminal charges. But none of this helps the person who crashed into you.

In each of these examples, the earlier possession of the claimant enables him to succeed in court against the defendant. Even the true owner, when he claims, wins by virtue of his earlier possession or right to possession in a contest with a later comer. English law's conception of title is a relative one. The court listens to the claims of the parties who make an appearance and decides between them, according to which claim, compared or related to the other, is the better. The potential or hypothetical claims of others are not relevant and are excluded from the proceedings. In short, the outcome of a dispute about rights to things depends on who shows up in court. And this means the possibility—however hypothetical or unreal—of a series of law suits with different winners on each occasion, as people with successively better titles come forward and stake their claims.

Between the true owner and the finder, another possible claimant must be introduced. So far we have talked about finding things in the street, that is, as lawyers put it, on a highway dedicated to the public, on a piece of land which nobody really owns although over which, in the modern world, various agencies of government have a range of responsibilities. But suppose you find something in somebody's garden. What, in other words, is the position if you find something on land which belongs to someone else? In comparing the claims of finder and landowner in this situation, the general principle is that the claim of the landowner is preferred. The person in possession of the land is treated as being in possession of the moveables on it. (This needs to be distinguished from the superficially cognate proposition that whatever is attached to the land—a house or a fireplace in a house, for instance—forms part of it, a rule concerned with the transfer of a title rather than its nature.) But there is a complicating factor in disputes between finders and landowners. This flows from the fact that many privately owned places where people might find things are places to which the public has access, such as shops, garage forecourts and airport lounges. In such places, the thing which is found may only recently have been left there, and the landowner may be unaware of its existence. Until recently, the better view seemed to be that even in these circumstances the landowner would succeed against the finder, since his possession of the land was deemed to carry with it possession of things on it, so that, logically, his possession of the thing was earlier than that of the finder. However, a recent decision has held that where the public is permitted access to land, the occupier must take positive steps (*e.g.* posting notices) to assert title over moveables left or lost by others on that land if he wishes to succeed against a finder.[6]

Behind the landowner, of course, is the true owner of the thing. As long as his claim is not barred by lapse of time, he will be able to recover his possession, or the value of the thing. But even longer chains of potential claimants can be imagined. You own a car; someone steals it and then sells it to an honest buyer; he lends it to a friend and yet another person crashes into it and writes it off. Ownership of things can generate complex chains of legal as well as social relations between people.

This approach to title brings with it not only the possibility of a multiplicity of actions but also the possibility that a wrongdoer risks paying the full value of the thing to successive claimants. The Torts (Interference with Goods) Act 1977 addresses both problems. First, it requires plaintiffs to identify third parties who they believe may have an interest in the thing at issue. Such persons then have an opportunity to appear, and if, having been given the chance, they fail to do so, the court may deprive them of any claim against the defendant, to that extent preventing litigation arising in the future. Secondly, the Act requires anyone who is unjustly enriched through a chain of actions to reimburse someone who has paid out the value of the thing more than once. If, for example, I sell a ring which a finder has brought to me for valuation, the finder can recover in full against me, and I may have to pay again if the true owner later appears. The Act requires that the finder, in these circumstances, must account to the true owner, who, in turn, becomes liable to reimburse me.

The same general approach has historically been followed in relation to titles to land. Here, as we shall see, there are far more elaborate steps involved in its transfer than applies to most moveables, and, as a result, a sense of ownership which seems more absolute than relative. But the documentary evidence of title to land which is normally required on a transfer of title has, in principle, been seen as irrelevant in a dispute where a plaintiff asserts an earlier possession against a later comer. So if a landowner who had acquired his title by transfer wishes to proceed against a squatter, his earlier possession is in principle a sufficient foundation for his claim, which does not need to be bolstered by his documents of title. Similarly, if one person enters land as a squatter and is then displaced by another, new, squatter, the first squatter has the same recourse against the second as would the true owner.

So how can a purchaser be sure that a claimant with a superior title will not emerge in the future?

Limitation of actions

Fundamentally, this problem is contained by limiting access to the courts and the remedies they provide through placing time limits on the commencement of actions. Access to the legal process is limited in an arbitrary way by statute, in terms of certain fixed periods of years, which, in brief, give you six years to claim a chattel or its value and 12 to claim for land. Given these statutory periods, the crucial question, obviously, is when does time begin to run against the owner? In the case of moveable things, the answers are, from a legal point of view, relatively straightforward. If you lose something, time does not begin running, nor does time begin to run automatically if someone picks it up. It begins to run only when the finder does something inconsistent with your own title, such as using the thing as his own. So it follows that time does not begin to run if an honest finder makes an attempt to trace the owner, but it begins to run at once in favour of a dishonest taker. Again, if you lend someone something, time starts from the moment he refuses to return it on request.

Land admits of finer shades of "taking" (*i.e.* of occupancy). If you park your car on a piece of waste land, have you taken possession of it or do you have to build a fence around it before you can be said to possess it? The courts have, even in recent years, encountered some difficulty in defining what needs to have occurred before time starts to run against the landowner. What exactly must someone do if his possession of the land is to count as adverse? The courts have insisted that a claimant must show both factual possession and an intention to possess in order to succeed against the owner. What will satisfy either of these requirements inevitably depends upon the particular facts. These requirements themselves are placed in doubt by the Land Registration Act 2002, discussed in Chapter 10.

Nemo dat quod non habet

We should now have a fairly clear idea about what lawyers mean when they talk about the quality of a given title. A title's quality is not something to be thought of in the abstract, but relatively, in relation to other possible titles to the same thing. The quality of a title is judged by reference to its point of origin in time relative to that of others. The starting point is captured in a Latin maxim ("*Prior tempore potior jure*") which can be paraphrased as "The earlier in time, the stronger the right". In theory, then, to investigate the quality of a title when a transfer is contemplated, you must look back and see how it first came about. This is often unnecessary in practice, but it underpins how English lawyers think about the nature of title.

At this point we must introduce the third and final element of the conceptual structure, which expresses precisely this need to investigate back to the origin. It is expressed in a Latin tag: "*Nemo dat quod non habet*"—"No one gives what he does not have". What this means is that you cannot transfer—by gift, sale, or on your death—better (which primarily means "stronger", but which has a loose moral resonance as well) rights to a thing than you yourself have.

> "The general rule of the common law is that if a man dispose of a chattel, whether for value or otherwise, he can confer no better title thereto than he has himself. Thus if any one obtain possession of a watch, for instance, by theft or finding, and then sell it, . . . the buyer will not be entitled to retain it as

against the owner. Nor can the buyer require payment of the price paid by him before delivering up the watch to its owner; for a refusal to give it up, except on such conditions, would be a conversion of the chattel to the buyer's own use, and would render him liable to be sued for its recovery or value. And it makes no difference that the buyer purchased the watch in good faith without notice of any defect of title in the person from whom he took it" (Williams, 1926, p.666).

We shall see that there are some exceptions to this principle. Like most exceptions to the rather exiguous number of general principles in this area, they arise because of practical convenience. Finally, we should note that, once again, we see, in this principle, the lawyer's overwhelming preoccupation with transfer. One might say that if "relativity of title" is the slogan which encapsulates how courts go about their business, *nemo dat* sums up what happens in the lawyer's office.

If you find a jewel in the street and sell it, the buyer is as vulnerable to a claim from the true owner as you are yourself. Your title is no better than that of the person from whom you bought, and, as we have seen, that title originates in the taking of the thing itself.

The combination of relativity of title, the limitation of actions and *nemo dat* also means that, viewed strictly from the point of view of title rather than encumbrances on title (see below) there is no exact distinction between good and defective title in English law, although again, the new land registration regime (discussed in Chapter 10), attempts to clarify the status of all registered titles. Once again, we are back to the question of transfer of title. *Nemo dat* means that a squatter on land can pass on, by a will, what rights he has established just as the true owner can. The same transfer mechanisms are open to both. A daughter who takes under a will has as good a title as the original squatter who made the will. Even if she herself has never been present on the land, the will, coupled with the earlier possession, will enable her to succeed on the squatter's death against a later squatter who has taken over the land, provided she acts in time.[7]

If a squatter wants to sell his title, matters are more complicated, but, as usual, for practical reasons. In accordance with *nemo dat*, a will simply involves passing on to successors whatever you have got. A lawyer is likely to enter the picture if buying and selling is involved, not because a lawyer must but because most people suppose it to be sensible to have a lawyer (or at least someone skilled in the technicalities of transfer management) to act for them in such transactions. Of course it is sensible to have a lawyer as well if you want to make a will; but it is not essential, and if a layman makes a will, that fact is taken into account in its construction where appropriate. By contrast, if you buy land and later get into dispute with your vendor, the courts will expect you to have taken the care expected of a land transfer specialist in investigating the quality of the title at your leisure. Traditionally, this is what distinguished land transactions from commercial transactions, where speed not leisure was crucial.

With selling a title to land, what is decisive is the state of professional opinion concerning the prerequisites of a safe or good title and it is this which can make a squatter's title difficult to sell. More generally, lawyers' predominant concern in relation to sale of land has been with encumbrances upon the title rather than the quality of the title itself, with one important exception, namely fragmented title. Here, the focus is less upon the relative merits of a particular title *vis-à-vis* possible contenders, much more upon whether all the relevant interested parties who need to put their signatures to the documents of transfer have been ascertained and gathered in. As we shall also see, the differences at this point between title and encumbrance upon title become, or at least became, blurred for the English lawyer.

We have treated *nemo dat* as the working through of the logic of relativity of title in the context of the transfer of title. One can conclude by noting that its effects can be looked at from another point of view. *Nemo dat* can be seen as a principle which ensures the integrity and durability of an earlier title when the thing to which the title relates has passed into the hands of innocent later-comers who know nothing of the earlier title. Overall, its main significance is to highlight how fundamental to English law's conceptual scheme is the idea of relativity of title.

4

THE FRAGMENTATION OF TITLE
TO LAND

We must now outline the framework which English land lawyers created and within which they worked. We then look more closely at the goals which it came to be used to promote. We are going to examine, in some detail, the ways in which English law permitted title to land to be fragmented; a later chapter considers how the principal problems from the point of view of the management of transfers of title to land were addressed and in large measure overcome in a substantial body of legislation produced in the 1920s (usually called, in short-hand, "the 1925 legislation"). Before tackling these matters, however, some clarification of a contextual kind is needed, without which some of the processes of fragmentation presented here may seem more mysterious than they were in reality.

RENT

A full overview of the legal framework of the ownership and enjoyment of land would, until recent times, have required extensive discussion of the law of landlord and tenant as well as that concerning fragmentation of title. We have hived off most matters concerning landlord and tenant to other parts of this book, for the sake of convenience. But having said in earlier passages that lawyers have treated land as something special, it must now be said, with no less insistence, that land, and the legal arrangements for it, meant for many generations principally "rents". As we shall see, urban land ownership meant in many cities—and still does in parts of some today—the ownership either of ground rents issuing from the land on which residential properties stood, or rental income from ownership of houses or flats. In the agrarian context, land ownership also meant ownership of a revenue-generating asset. A landed estate, large or small, commonly comprised a number of farms, each of which was normally rented out to tenants. This legal relationship too is considered below (see pp.141–143). All that needs emphasis now is that fragmentation of title meant, in sociological terms, the carving up of rental income, whether the source be ground rents, building rents or agricultural rents. What we are examining at this stage did not mean the carving up of the use of land as such but of the revenue which it could be made to produce through time. Land is treated as special by lawyers; but what was really treated as special was land as a particular kind of source of revenue. Although we no longer, especially in the urban or residential context, talk in these terms, this is clearly expressed in the way in which economic historians talk about land prices in the past: they calculate their ups and downs, as people did at the time, in terms of so many "years' purchase"— the capital value of land at any time with reference to the amount of annual income which it yields. Forty years' purchase means the price of land is high; 25 years' purchase means it is on the decline. Unless we keep firmly in mind that fragmentation of title meant fragmentation of rights to rental income, stretching over time, we will find land law and the reforms of 1925 unnecessarily mysterious and obscure.

There was a downside: someone had to pay these rents (*cf.* Barrell, 1980). The social and the economic histories of England until the twentieth century largely converge around, or could be written in terms of, this rent relation. In theory, "rent" could take the form of the payment of money or the rendering of services. The fact that from quite early times the rent relation assumed the form of payments of money is one fundamental reason why it is so difficult to pinpoint the moment when England can usefully be said to have undergone the transition from feudalism to capitalism (see further pp.94–95, below).

In the modern world, of course, the majority of people spend most of their lives paying rent for the house or flat where they live. But for us, this is principally an economic relation: the rent due to the council, the mortgage repayments due to the building society, weekly or monthly monetary outgoings barely distinct from the quarterly electricity bill. In the past, by contrast, the rent relation was intertwined with a whole set of social relations of hierarchy and subordination. Rent bound people together socially and politically, as well as economically, in a fairly direct way.

In the past, rent took many forms, and the conceptualisation of these differences was the province of lawyers. Rent divided society into two classes of people: those who owed something to others in the form of rent, and those to whom something was owed. The latter were the freeholders, the men and the women who were free and therefore, in the case of men, claimed the right to participate in the business of rule, although not, except in a few cases, in the affairs of state. Social function, economic status and political rule are interconnected within this scheme of things. Only rights in common stood apart, in a certain way, from these representations of reality, for example, the right to pasture your sheep on common land (see Thompson, 1991, pp.1–15, 97–184). Such rights in common were all but eliminated, over a long period of time, by a complex historical process, largely complete by the middle of the nineteenth century, whereby land was enclosed.

As Yelling has emphasised, the term "enclosure" covers three distinct processes. First, the "laying together of scattered properties and consequent abolition of intermixture of properties and holdings". Secondly, "the abolition of common rights". Thirdly, "the hedging and ditching of the separate properties" whereby parcels of land, grouped together, are physically "enclosed" (1977, p.7). Enclosure tended to sharpen the exclusive nature of the rent relation, partly because it eliminated common land, and partly because it destroyed some traditional forms of rent relations. And enclosure was an occasion for lawyers to come upon the scene because it involved the close scrutiny of occupiers' legal rights to the land that gave them their livelihood. In its earlier forms enclosure of land came about by "agreement", sometimes approved by the Court of Chancery (see pp.99–101, below), and later it took place through parliamentary processes. "It was . . . an occasion when the legal title to common rights was closely scrutinised, and it is certain that throughout the country numerous claims for cottage common rights were rejected" (Yelling, 1977, p.230; see also Neeson, 1993).

Rent was central to the structure of the polity in matters of religion too. The Church of England was an "established Church" in several senses. It operated as an official ideological system so that membership of the Church was necessary in order to hold various kinds of public office. In addition, Church finances, from which the "livings" of the clergy were provided, were secured not by voluntary contributions from the membership but by a compulsory and increasingly contentious levy or tax on the income from land known as the "tithe" (for this see

Evans, 1976). While the tithe endured, it operated as a distinctive type of rent being drawn from land. Enclosure had transformative effects here too, by commuting the tithes and transforming them into the ownership of a defined parcel of land. Again, the variegated nature of traditional rent was homogenised into one general form. This general form was what lawyers call the "tenancy", and is examined below in Chapter 7.

For present purposes, three points need to be drawn out from the complex history of the rent relation. The first is that the imprint of the past upon the present has been most pronounced in terms of the schemes devised by lawyers to orchestrate over time the receipt of rents. This is the theme of the present chapter. The second point is that, of the multitude of rent relations which existed in the past and to which lawyers directed their attention when necessary, the only survivor today of any importance, if we ignore mortgages, is the tenancy. Finally, the centrality of rent in English society brings us to the core of what English lawyers mean by "land". It steers us, as it were, towards their metaphysics, to the ground of the way things are thought about rather than the way in which they can be said actually to exist (see further pp.137–138 below).

In this chapter we outline the basic building blocks used in the past to conceptualise land ownership, concepts such as the "life estate", the "entail" and the "fee simple absolute". The sketch of these concepts is supplemented by discussion of the practical uses to which these concepts were put, and in particular by an outline of one of the most important and distinctive practical methods of landowning in England—the device commonly known as the "strict settlement". The reader should be warned at the outset that many of these practices have become obsolete in the years since 1945 (for the reasons, see pp.229–231, below). The conceptual building blocks have also undergone various kinds of modification (see Chapters 5 and 6, below). Since the beginning of 1997, it has even become impossible by statute to create an "entail", which, as we see in this chapter, was the pivot on which the device of the strict settlement turned.

It follows that concern for the often very technical details of this body of law can increasingly be left to specialist legal and social historians. But a broad grasp of this field is necessary in order to provide perspective on the development of property law during this century by Parliament and by the courts. It helps us to understand why the law had to change, and in what respects. It makes it easier to see why it was that, despite a major statutory overhaul in the 1920s, a land law which had been adjusted to take care of the defects which had been thrown up by its past was not always well adjusted to meeting the challenges of the future. Specifically, the patently ad hoc way in which the law still handles the ownership and occupation claims of homesharers (see Chapter 6) can only be understood when it is remembered that these arrangements had to be improvised within a framework of legislation and legal practice which grew up to accommodate something quite different.

There is also a simpler reason for not forgetting the past entirely. Milsom (1996, p.247) refers sardonically to the use of the bland term "the history of property law" as "a puny name for the social and economic core of things", and this is true of what follows in this chapter. Legal change is social change, as well as a reflection of it. To know only the end result, with no understanding of the starting points, is to have less than half of the picture.

ESTATES IN LAND BEFORE 1926

Today, there are only two legal estates which can exist in land: the "fee simple absolute in possession" and the " term of years absolute". When a house is advertised as freehold, it is the former estate in land which is offered, and when it is described as leasehold, it is the latter. Leases are examined below in Chapter 7.

The simplicity of this position is now complicated by the emergence of a new form of land ownership called "commonhold". This is introduced by the Commonhold and Lease-hold Reform Act 2002, which became law May 1, 2002 and will fully come into effect by the end of 2004. In so far as commonhold can be conceptualised at this time, it is a hybrid form of land ownership that sits somewhere between Australian "strata" title and the structure used in North America to regulate condominiums. Commonhold consists of a community of freeholders bound together by the "commonhold community statement" or CCS. Each unit in the community is a freehold, and each is held by a freehold registered proprietor. The common parts of the community constitute the remainder of the commonhold, which is vested in the commonhold association. The only members of the association are the freehold registered proprietors of the commonhold units. The commonhold title arises as a matter of second registration: the CCS document is registered on the standard freehold registered with absolute title. This document is the heart of commonhold. As Clarke (2002, p.351) states, ". . . the CCS is a single document, on the registered title, containing the fundamental rules of the community . . . The special statutory attributes of this form of freehold ensure that a commonhold unit will be quite unlike a standard freehold. A purchaser buys into a community, its culture, regulations, duties and benefits."

Commonhold is both a species of freehold estate and, putatively, an entirely new form of landholding in England and Wales. Unlike the case in a leasehold community, the shareholders in each scheme will be able to change the community statement, and each community will be controlled by its members through general meetings and under directors that may be members of the community or professional outsiders. To a great extent, commonhold is the formalisation of a right to manage. Rather than a freeholder and leaseholders, the Act contemplates freeholders subject to a CCS and with the right to manage their own community. Further discussion of the Act should wait until it comes into effect and until practitioners and academics can assess its utility and the extent to which it gives rise to new forms of community. The questions that might arise in the future include the appeal of commonhold for increasingly urban communal living (*i.e.*, loft developments) and the linkages between commonhold tenancies and the appeal (or otherwise) of "gated communities". As the housing shortage in the United Kingdom forces the re-utilisation of commercial urban spaces and brownfield sites as the locales of residential homes, commonhold may emerge as the predominant form of urban and suburban land holding. However, it is too early to do more than ask questions. At this point, it is only possible to speculate on the outcome(s) of the Act or the extent to which CCS documents will redefine the nature of land ownership.

For the present, we can begin by noting that before 1926, the position regarding freehold estates in land was very different. There were then three principal legal estates in land which could be created, each with its own distinctive character. The fee simple was the biggest right—the whole interest in the land. But there were two lesser rights: the life estate and the fee tail or entail. The differences between the three relate to the possible duration of the interest created.

If X, the owner of land in fee simple, granted to A a life estate, A had a legal estate in that land for his lifetime. On A's death, his estate came to an end because its duration had been limited to A's life. This meant that on A's death, he had no interest in the land which he could leave to his heirs, because his interest terminated on his death.

Equally, the *nemo dat* rule applied. If A sold his life estate to B, B acquired an estate which would come to an end on A's death, not on B's death, because the estate which A sold was limited by reference to the duration of A's life in the original grant. Lawyers said that in this situation B acquired an estate "*pur autre vie*" (that is, for the life of another (A)).

If X, the owner of land in fee simple, granted to A a fee tail, what happened? The entail was an estate whose duration was limited to the continued existence of a particular class of heirs. A grant of an entail was often expressed as follows: "To A and the heirs of his body". This created a succession of interests which would endure as long as the lineage founded by A. As long as there were descendants of A, the estate would continue, but if the position was reached when there was no one left alive who could trace his descent back to A, the estate came to an end. So if A only had one child, B, and B had three children, C, D and E, but all three died childless, the estate would end on the death of the last of the three. It did not survive through the descendants of A's collaterals, or through descendants of collaterals of A's ancestors.

If X, owner in fee simple granted to A a fee simple, the position was different. Whereas the possible maximum duration of the entail is limited to the continued existence of a particular class of heirs, the possible maximum duration of the fee simple is not so limited, but can continue indefinitely until it comes into the hands of someone who dies leaving no heirs at all.

So, if A sells to B, the fee simple in the hands of B and his successors is not affected by the failure of A's lineage. And the same applies if B sells to C. A particular fee simple to land will only terminate if the person into whose hands it has come dies without heirs. So, if C, who buys from B, dies (i) with no will and (ii) with no living relatives who can succeed to his property under the intestacy rules, the estate comes to an end. Even if he died with no relatives, C could have "made an heir" by making a will. It is the fact that he has died leaving neither a will nor any relatives that brings the estate to an end.

In each of the three examples, we have defined the nature of the respective estates in land with reference to the circumstances in which, at some date in the future, they might terminate. We stressed above the importance of the practice of inheritance; we have now seen how the idea of inheritance was built into the basic ownership concepts of English land law. The next question is: what happens when these estates terminate? Who then owns the land? In relation to the life estate and the entail, the answer is found by looking at an additional feature of the doctrine of estates, the distinction between present and future interests. In the case of the fee simple, the answer is found by considering the consequences of another doctrine—the doctrine of tenures—which provides the starting point for the role of equity in land law and is thus outlined in the next chapter.

THE DOCTRINE OF ESTATES—PRESENT AND FUTURE INTERESTS

Since the fee simple is the biggest right to land it follows that

(i) if X grants A a life estate, or

(i) if X grants A a fee tail,

then in either case X has not divested himself of (parted with) his entire interest in the land. He has carved out of his greater estate a lesser estate. So when these lesser estates "determine" at some date in the future, X or his successors will get back the fee simple. When the grant is made, X is no longer entitled to current enjoyment of the land. He has a future interest, that is, a right to enjoyment at some time in the future, even though at the time of the grant it is not possible to say exactly when if ever the right to enjoyment will materialise.

When someone has a present right to enjoyment, lawyers say that the person has an estate or interest in possession. This does not mean that the person is in fact in physical possession of the property (because he may, for example, have leased it). It means that the person is entitled to present enjoyment of the land (one form of which is receiving rent from a tenant).

Where X has carved out a lesser estate from his fee simple, lawyers say that he retains a reversion of the fee simple. This describes the fact that (i) he has parted with the present right of enjoyment, but (ii) he has not parted with his entire bundle of rights in the land, because he has only created out of his fee simple a lesser estate. At some indeterminate date in the future, the lesser estates will determine, and then the reversion in fee simple will come into possession.

Before continuing, we should draw attention to a slipperiness in lawyers' terminology which can confuse the student coming to the subject for the first time. We have stressed so far the contextual importance of land as rent-yielding, or, in other words, that many occupiers of land were and are tenants paying rent to landlords. As we see in more detail in Chapter 7, one defining feature of a tenancy is that it gives the right to "exclusive possession" of the land, "exclusive" meaning, in particular, exclusive of the landlord. A tenancy is, in effect, the exchange of a right to receive payment of rent for a right to exclusive possession. Because, where there is a tenancy, the landlord is "excluded", as just explained, for the duration of the tenancy, the landlord's interest (the right to receive the rent) is commonly described as the landlord's "reversion" on the lease.

It is important not to confuse this with the distinction between present and future interests—between interests in possession and interests in reversion—which we are exploring in this chapter. The reversion on a lease, that is, can itself either be an interest in possession or an interest in reversion, a present right to receive the rents or a future right to receive them which is postponed to a present right.

Subject to these qualifications, we can now return to the distinction between present and future interests, and consider some examples of how the distinction worked.

EXAMPLE

If X, owner in fee simple, grants a life estate to A, A has a life estate in possession, X retains a reversion in fee simple. When A dies, X will have a fee simple in possession again. If during A's life, X sold his property rights—his reversion—to P, then, applying the *nemo dat* rule, P could be in no better position than X. When A died, P's fee simple would then fall into possession.

From this it follows that it was possible before 1926 to split the legal fee simple into a number of lesser estates, which could come into possession at different times. Thus in a grant it was possible not only to grant estates in possession, but also to create estates in the grant which would only take effect in the future. This enabled owners of property to create a whole series of successive interests in the same piece of land.

EXAMPLE

X, owner in fee simple, grants to A a life estate. On A's death, B was to have a life estate. On B's death, C was to have an entail (*i.e.* an estate whose duration was limited to the continued existence of C's descendants). The future interests created here were called by lawyers *remainders*. So at the time of the grant:

A would have a life estate in possession;
B would have a life estate in remainder;
C would have an entail in remainder.

But even though X had carved out three interests from his fee simple, he still had not disposed of his whole bundle of rights because he never granted the fee simple to anyone. Therefore after C's death, X has a reversion in fee simple.

On A's death:

(a) if B is still alive:

B has a life estate in possession;
C has a remainder in tail;
X has a reversion in fee simple;

(b) if B is dead (so that his life interest has already determined):

C has an entail in possession;
X has a reversion in fee simple.

In these examples, X could of course have created a remainder in fee simple in favour of D to take effect when C's entail came to an end. If he had done that, then X would have granted away his entire interest in the land, and no reversion in his favour would arise on the grant.

THE LOGIC OF ENTAILS

We have focused so far on the core distinction between entails and fee simples in terms of the possible duration of the two types of interest. We need now to look a little more closely at how entails worked in practice. As we shall see, the inheritance of property held under this type of interest closely resembles the rules governing succession to hereditary peerages and to the English Crown.

Entails, like peerages and the Crown, were subject to the two core principles of primogeniture: (i) that the timing of your birth relative to your siblings determined your priority in the order of inheritance and succession; and (ii) that that matter of timing was subject, in turn, to an overriding priority accorded to males over females. Put simply, the first-born male succeeds before the second-born male, but a male born after any number of females succeeds ahead of all of them.

So an entail granted to A, who had one heir (B), who left three children (C, D, E), the last of whom died without direct heirs, would devolve as follows:

(i)   on A's death, B, if still living, would hold the estate;

(i)   on B's death, the first-born surviving child (subject to the gender rule) would succeed.

We must now add one more detail to complete the picture:

(iii) Suppose C is the first-born surviving child (etc.) referred to in (ii). On C's death, the estate will devolve to his first-born surviving child (etc.). In the absence of such children, it moves across to the next sibling of C, subject, as always, to the general rule of the priority of males over females.

One further point about this practical logic needs to be made. The devolution of entailed estates involved the priority in the order of devolution of males over females but not necessarily the exclusion of females. However, it was possible to exclude females entirely and confine, on creation of the entail, its devolution through a direct male order of succession (so that a female heir would breach a particular line of succession).

Today, the legacy of these schemes of ownership is more salient on the margins of politics than of property. The Hundred Years' War between England and France had as one of its pretexts a dispute about the possibility of succession to the throne of France through the female line (the so-called Salic Law—see Beaune, 1991, pp.245–246). More recently, the exclusion of females enabled Mrs Thatcher to create two hereditary peerages which would lapse on the death of their recipients (Viscounts Whitelaw and Tonypandy, as they became) since the succession to them was limited to male heirs (*i.e.* to A and the heirs male of his body) and neither had such an heir or was expected, subsequent to the creation of the peerage, to produce one. Still more recently, there have been discussions about the discrimination involved in the priority accorded to males over females so far as succession to the peerage and the Crown are concerned.

Barring entails

The entail was a natural device for the lineage-oriented families of the medieval period, and the basic device of the perpetual entail was to be found throughout Western Europe, enduring largely unchanged in some countries until the era of codification (when it became one of codification's principal targets). In England, however, desire to tie lineage to land and land to lineage through the entail came, quite early, to be subject to pressure in the opposite direction which centred upon the *transferability* of entails. We do not know exactly why and perhaps we never will. One reason might be that land owner-ship in England was much more dispersed and fragmented than in many countries on the continent, and that this fact alone encouraged a more "economic" orientation to land ownership among the English landed classes than prevailed abroad. In any event, it is clear that lawyers were under pressure to find ways of making it possible for entailed estates to be bought and sold. Here we will simply note that the ways which were invented were exceedingly complicated, involving a cluster of fictitious formal transactions and fictitious court procedures. But it must be stressed that lawyers faced two distinct problems in trying to facilitate the transfer of entailed estates.

The entail was principally a means of providing for the descent of rents through a lineage across time. It was not difficult for lawyers to invent mechanisms by which the person presently entitled to these rents could transfer his entitlement to a purchaser for the duration of his life. The difficulties were, first, could the claims of the heirs under the entail be barred and, secondly, could ways be found for a purchaser from the present holder to acquire a title which was not put in jeopardy if the lineage to which the entail related failed? The first hurdle was the first to be overcome: fictitious mechanisms were invented which barred the claims of the lineage—and of the "next in line", in particular—against the purchaser when the seller died. A modern analogy is what happened on the abdica-tion of Edward VIII. Since the English Crown is in effect entailed, and any particular incumbent of the throne essentially only a tenant in tail in possession, it was necessary to exclude the claim of any possible heirs which he might conceive with "the woman he loved" in order to secure the succession subsequent to his own death to his brother (who became George VI after the abdication) and his own heirs (*i.e.* Elizabeth II and her own heirs). Otherwise, on Edward's death, his heir could have claimed the throne from its then occupant. (Given the nature of the issue, the position was resolved by a customised Act of Parliament, the Declaration of Abdication Act 1936, which excluded any claims from heirs of Edward. As it happened, these measures were unnecessary, since he died childless.)

Even if the claims of "the heirs of the body" could be excluded, a purchaser of an entail would only acquire a "base fee", that is, a title which would terminate on the failure of the lineage, when there was no living person who could trace his descent directly to "A and the heirs of his body". By the late fifteenth century, this too was overcome, through more conveyancing ingenuity and this is what is meant by "barring" an entail, which can be regarded as the ability to convert it into a fee simple for all practical purposes. Allowing this to happen is sometimes attributed to the common law's inherent bias in favour of free alienability of land; an alternative view is that this bias "is a grossly over-worked explanation of oddities in medieval land law" and that "it is much more likely that the judges were not so much influenced by views of policy, as by the difficulty of finding any technical flaws in a very ingenious device" (Simpson, 1961, p.126). We are not concerned with the details of this device but only with its basic structure, which was put on a statutory footing in the Fines and Recoveries Act of 1833, and with the uses to which it was in fact put.

Once it became established that entails could be barred, one response might have been to try to block that possibility by creating a string of successive life estates spanning several generations (to A for life, remainder to A's son for life, remainder to A's grandson for life, etc.). Such an evasion of barrability was blocked by a number of common law rules, developed over a long period of time. These rules were of immense complexity, and many of them are now obsolete. In broad terms, they were directed against the remoteness of vesting of absolute interests. The most important of the rules that survive today are known as the rules against perpetuities. These too are very convoluted, though they have been simplified somewhat for practical purposes by the Perpetuities and

Accumulations Act 1964 and further reform of these rules remains on the agenda. All that can usefully be said, for present purposes, about this body of rules is that, in different ways and for different reasons, they restricted the range of unborn persons (for example, A's grandson where A is a child) in favour of whom interests in property could be created. In particular, they precluded the possibility of a string of estates operating in favour of unborn generations of descendants.

When an entail was barred, the owner in tail would from that time be able to deal with the land as if he was an owner in fee simple. Importantly, this meant that, after barring the entail, he could sell the land to a purchaser as an owner in fee simple. The effect of barring the entail was to shut out the remainderman or reversioner, destroying their rights. So if land was granted to A for life, remainder to B in tail, remainder to C in fee simple, B could bar the entail, thereby converting it into a fee simple, thus destroying C's rights. This requires A's participation during his lifetime, but B could do this on his own after A's death, when the entail fell into possession.

At this point, the student coming to the subject for the first time is usually baffled, or convinced of the irrationality of the English law of property. How, the cry goes, could the law permit, in so blatant a way, the remainderman in fee to be robbed of what was his by right? Before answering this question, this problem needs to be distinguished from a different problem with which it can be confused. It should be obvious from what has already been said that a system or property ownership of the kind described above, which placed such a central emphasis upon inheritance, would not only run up against (and need to anticipate) the foreseeable absence of heirs at any stage in a family's history, but also need to anticipate (and, if possible, devise mechanisms for managing) devolution from adults to children or infants.

Again, political history provides well-known examples of the problem of infants. When Richard the Lionheart died in 1199, he left no direct heirs. But his "next-in-line" male sibling (already dead) had left a son, Arthur, who was still a child. Richard's youngest surviving brother, John, who was already an adult, possessed a following, successfully seized the throne, eliminated Arthur, and established the subsequent succession in favour of his own children. On the death of Edward IV in 1483, his direct male heirs (the so-called "Princes in the Tower") were eliminated by Edward's brother, who became Richard III. Retrospectively at least, the unlawfulness of the act of usurpation received recognition in the fact that the elder of Edward IV's two sons was designated by posterity Edward V, so that the next King Edward to ascend to the throne was designated Edward VI (on the death of his father, Henry VIII, in 1547).

In the conditions of the Middle Ages, where the inheritance of property and the succession to (hereditary) political office were somewhat jumbled together, the prevalence of such *real politik*—less-entitled adults with supporters ousting more-entitled infants on the death of the prior incumbent—is not surprising. However, a comparable problem arose in the seventeenth century, when political, religious and, ultimately military opposition to the then monarch, James II, led to his flight from his kingdom. James was a Catholic, had two grown-up Protestant daughters by his first marriage, and a son by his second, who was brought up as a Catholic (known as Charles James Stewart, the Old Pretender). Following James's flight, Parliament offered the Crown to a childless couple comprising his elder daughter and her husband, and when they were dead ensured that it passed to the second daughter.

The son, and his son after him (Bonnie Prince Charlie), were both excluded, and both launched unsuccessful invasions of Britain. In these extended conflicts (which lasted from 1688 to at least 1745) we can observe a certain prising apart of schemes of succession to office and inheritance of property. But the very fact that there were doubts about the legitimacy of the succession to the throne, imposed as it was, in effect, by Parliament, highlights the enduring—and seemingly fundamental—character of the scheme of inheritance discussed here.

Just as in politics, the inheritance of entails was not unproblematic, because the claims of infant heirs could be excluded in practice by less entitled but more powerful adults. The obvious way to avoid this was to develop viable devices to protect the longer-term interests of infant inheritors and this, in essence, was achieved in English property law by the mechanisms known by the technical name of the "trust to preserve contingent remainders". We touch on this in the next chapter; here we return to the more basic issue: how did it ever make sense for the law to recognise the barring of entails, *i.e.* to give and take away in conceptual terms at the same time? The answer is that the practical logic of barring entails was rather different from what its formal logic might suggest.

At first, the device of barring the entail arose out of the search for mechanisms to sell or transfer entailed estates. This in turn generated a new set of practices, which seem to have been fairly well defined by the late seventeenth century, which both made use of the device of barring the entail while, perhaps paradoxically, deploying the device so as to keep land in the family rather than alienate (sell) it. The practical effect, it was widely believed as late as the nineteenth century, was to tie up land over many generations within a particular lineage, despite the barrability of entails. This was achieved by adopting a device known as the strict settlement, and land was kept within the family by a process known as settlement and resettlement.

What made all this possible was that the entail could only be barred by B:

(i) if the entail had come into possession, *i.e.* the life interests had determined; or

(i) if, the entail still being in remainder, B had the consent of the person with the prior estate.

This enabled land to stay in a particular family over many generations, although, as we shall shortly see when we examine it more closely, it did not guarantee such an outcome, however desirable that might have seemed to the people of the time.

STRICT SETTLEMENTS: LEGAL AND PRACTICAL ASPECTS OF DYNASTIC STRATEGIES

The device of the strict settlement was perfected by conveyancers towards the end of the seventeenth century. We explain its rationale in a moment; we must first outline its formal structure. The central structural features of its mechanisms were as follows.

X grants land to A for life, remainder to B in tail, with remainders in fee simple over. (The remainders over—*i.e.*, behind the entail—are not important, because A and B are going to bar the entail.) It is this grant of successive interests which is called a settlement.

A and B agree to bar the entail. A's agreement is necessary because, as we have seen, B cannot bar the entail on his own because it is still in remainder. A and B therefore, acting together, now have control over the fee simple in the land. But the object of the exercise is to keep the land within the family. Therefore, having broken the settlement, they then proceed to resettle the land as follows: to A for life, remainder to B for life, remainder to B's eldest son in tail, with remainders over.

The settlement illustrates the way in which English lawyers subordinate elegance or simplicity to the achievement of practical objectives. The strict settlement had one overriding objective, to ensure the passage of whatever lands were to be settled in such a manner as to maximise the possibility, from a legal point of view, that an identical passage could occur in the next generation.

Suppose you are a landed nobleman in your late fifties. Your eldest son and heir-presumptive (in English law, only God can make a heir) has just reached 21 (today, it would be 18) or, at perhaps a slightly older age, is about to marry. Suppose, further, that the principal family estates are already settled. You have a life estate in possession—you are what lawyers call the "tenant for life". You draw the rental income from the estate. Next in line is your eldest son who has, at the moment, a remainder in tail. As always, there are remainders over, people further down the queue. (We can leave over for the moment the question of who they are.) If your son outlives you, he will, on your death, become a tenant in tail in possession and be able, as already seen, to bar the entail on his own and deal with the land on the basis that he is entitled in fee simple. You might feel sure that he would not, if that happened, rush off and sell or mortgage the ancestral estates; but your legal adviser would almost certainly tell you that it was best to leave nothing to chance. Much better for you and your son to get together, bar the entail while you are still around, and resettle the estates in such a way that the entail is pushed back a generation, with your son, under the new settlement, taking only a life estate in remainder which would fall into possession on the "dropping" of your life.

Why should the son agree to the resettlement? No doubt, in the majority of cases, the question hardly arose: it was the done thing. And if the resettlement was to take place on the marriage of the son, the prospective wife's family might well insist upon it taking place as a condition of providing the dowry. Indeed, in the normal case of a settlement on marriage, the settlement would make specific provision for the dowry and who was to be entitled to what from it (on which more later). But apart from these factors, which probably explain why resettlement occurred in the majority of cases, there were ways in which parents could coerce their more recalcitrant heirs.

Because the resettlement could occur only when the son was of age, he would need cash in order to have fun in town or undertake a "Grand Tour". How could he raise the money? If he and his father came to an arrangement whereby if the son agreed to the resettlement, an income would be raised for the son out of the estate. The only other way the son could raise money would be by mortgaging or selling his entail, but that would be like selling his inheritance for a bowl of soup, and would cause a scandal in society. Some did (see, *e.g.* Sykes, 1982); the balance of advantage for most lay in acquiescing in the wishes of their parents.

This pattern could be, and often was, repeated every generation. When A died, after the resettlement, his son would have only a life estate in possession, and A's grandson would now have the entail in remainder. When the grandson reached his majority, the same thing would happen all over again.

The central object of this settlement-resettlement device, then, was to prevent the entail from ever coming into possession. Once that happened, the tenant in tail could bar the entail as we have seen. That would mean that he now had a fee simple, and, subject to details which can be ignored for the present, would be able to alienate (sell) the land away from the family. But we still have not penetrated the mystery of why the law colluded in shutting out the claims of the remaindermen behind the entail being barred. We can see the practical logic underpinning this now if we look more closely at a typical settlement.

Suppose the new settlement, made on the heir-presumptive's marriage, looks something like this:

(1) To A for life. A is the head of the family and under the new settlement remains entitled, by virtue of the life estate in possession, to the rental income from the family estates.

(2) To B (the heir-presumptive) for life.

(3) Then to the first son of B on the body of B's first wife and the heirs male of the body of such first son lawfully to be begotten (*i.e.* excluding bastards).

(4) Then to the second son of B on the body of B's first wife and the heirs male of his body, etc.

(5) Then to the third son, etc. down to the tenth son of B.

If the settlement stopped here, it would fail to provide for the devolution of the estates in the event of the marriage which occasioned the settlement in our example producing no male children who survived. And the whole point of the exercise was to think about such possibilities in advance. Two principal choices presented themselves in the event of a failure in the direct male line. Either the estates could pass on to the daughters of B or, as readers of *Pride and Prejudice* should recall, they could move collaterally, following the same pattern, to the junior male line. To simplify, if B had one brother, C, at the time of the settlement, and succession through males was the preferred family choice, we would have:

(6) To B's brother C for life.

(7) Then to C's first son and the heirs male of his body, etc. down to C's tenth son lawfully begotten, etc.

In such cases, only then would we find:

(8) To the daughter or daughters of B for life, etc.

The order could, of course, be reversed, with B's daughter or daughters taking in preference to the male heirs of the younger son. And, further, female succession could be organised in a number of ways. Daughters could take in order of seniority or in equal shares. If the former, it would be essential to spell out what should happen if a daughter died without issue. If, as was probably usual, she took in tail male, the estate would pass to a collateral male on her death (*i.e.* one or more daughters of B would be preferred over B's collaterals (C); but on such a daughter dying without a direct male heir, the estate would devolve to C or his (male) heirs). Obviously all manner of further permutations and refinements of the basic model were possible.

Writing in the nineteenth century, Sugden advised that, in the event of failure in the direct male line, there should be partible inheritance by the daughters, rather than succession in tail male in order of seniority, because of the inconvenience of the estate passing backwards and forwards from one branch of the family to another if collateral male descent was consistently followed (1858, p.113).

For the sake of completeness, there will be a remainder in fee simple in the settlement. But this remainder was, for all concerned, something remote. The classical settlement meant that someone would, short of genealogical catastrophe, inherit the estates long before the ultimate remainderman was reached, preferably as a tenant for life (inheritance by the next generation); more risky, especially from a legal point of view, succession by a tenant in tail from the second generation, (namely one of A's male grandchildren); failing that, succession by the women of the family.

Wives and dependent children in the primogeniture regime

The discussion so far has centred around the structural consequences for English land law of the practice of impartible inheritance—and of primogeniture in particular—among certain strata of the English landed classes in the past. This has left open the question of what provision was made for people other than the emergent heir, such as the widow of the tenant for life and the younger brothers and sisters of his successor. An examination of this dimension of the strict settlement reveals further sources of complexity, and should help us to understand better the rationale which underpinned the precise shape of the framework adopted in 1925, as well as why more recent reforms have been felt necessary.

Provision in strict settlements for wives and anticipated dependent children could be secured in a number of ways. For children, the most flexible device was to convey a lease to trustees on trust to "raise portions" (for trusts, see Chapter 5), but it was often the case that this device, or a rent charge, was attached to some of the family estates only, and the main estates, with which the family was most closely associated (which, again, might mean those which had descended through the male line rather than come to the family through marriage), might be kept free of such charges. The aim was to provide a capital sum for use as a dowry by the daughters and a provision for the younger sons, though these capital sums might not be paid over for many years, and the sons and daughters receive only interest on the capital, which, in legal terms, belonged to them.

Much was, no doubt, left to private negotiation and family consensus, when the portions were due but the capital unavailable. Unmarried daughters may have been especially vulnerable to postponement of the capital sum in the interests of the family at large, at various times hedged in by agricultural depressions and galloping charges. The formal legal rights must often have constituted merely a backdrop against which this informal negotiation and compromise occurred. An unmarried daughter might thus defer calling for her portion, and instead remain effectively dependent on receiving interest payments from her family. For a daughter who married, her portion, whether realisable on marriage or, through interfamilial negotiation, only later, in some sense represented the basis for calculating her "jointure", the provision for her widowhood.

What is significant about the strict settlement method of accommodating widowhood is the temporary nature of the property provision, a provision for widowhood only, after which the estate of the husband's family would be discharged of a liability. The jointress of such a dynastic settlement generally had very little formal say in the transmission of property to the next generation, unless, as seems to have occurred only rarely, significant property had been settled upon her, at the time of or after her marriage, to what came to be called her "separate use". This seems from the available evidence to have been relatively uncommon in the case of dynastic families.

It might not be too far-fetched to suggest that women who belonged to or married into dynastic families were marginal in terms of the control which they had over the family property. This point is highlighted not only by the absence of control over intergenerational transmission, but by the very nature of the jointure, which effectively, in its developed form, left the widow in the position of a mere passive recipient of an income secured upon some or all of the family estates, with no formal control over the management of the property (though she could obstruct a sale, such that the "problem" of jointresses loomed large in the conveyancing reforms initiated from the beginning of the 1880s).

The jointure can be compared with the medieval modes of provision for widows, which survived in some agricultural communities until at least the eighteenth century. Under medieval common law, a widow had a right of dower over all the freehold estates of which her husband had been seised at any time during the marriage, even if he had alienated them before his death. Under the common law, she had a right to a third of the rents and profits from the land during her widowhood at the expense of the husband's heir. The husband had a similar right over this wife's estates, called a "tenancy by courtesy". "Freebench", the equivalent provision where the land was held by customary tenure, variously gave the widow a third or a half of the rents and profits, according to the custom of the manor. For the propertied classes, such an automatic, status-based means of securing provision came, quite early on, to be regarded as inconvenient. They interfered with any form of planning. The jointure was evolved as a device for planning and calculating the provision; what is significant is the transformation in the nature of the jointure itself, in its increasing subordination to primogeniture and intergenerational transmission.

Originally, in Tudor times, jointure involved conveying certain lands to husband and wife as joint tenants (see further below). On the death of one spouse, the survivor would be exclusively entitled to the rents and profits, and would further be exercising powers of control and management over this portion of the family estates. "Joint tenancy" was the origin of jointure, but denoted a more active, more participatory role for a woman during widowhood. It denotes a form of planning, but not necessarily intergenerational planning. If made by way of dower, it would exclude the common law rights which would arise in default of such provision. Elaborate devices were conceived by conveyancers to exclude dower, culminating in the Dower Act 1833, which effectively abolished the right to dower, if not the problem it addressed. But during the same period, jointure was attenuated to a mere right to receive a certain revenue and open to criticism, at that, for burdening the rent rolls at the expense of agricultural improvement.

Clay (1968) has suggested that in the eighteenth century, a failure of direct males was often followed by the *paterfamilias* making an increased, perhaps extravagant, provision for the daughters. This could well have endured into the nineteenth century, though the Victorian enthusiasm for agricultural improvement may have tempered such practices. More recently, Spring (1993) has argued that most historians have neglected the steady shift which occurred away from female inheritance of land and the way in which the principal function of the strict settlement was to exclude dower and to redefine the terms of the portion/jointure ratio. The strict settlement, she argues, was in reality a marriage settlement which was, at the same time, a disinheritance settlement.

ALTERNATIVES TO DYNASTIC SETTLEMENT:
LEGAL ASPECTS OF PARTIBLE INHERITANCE

The dynastic ambition which fuelled the strict settlement was not, as indicated above (see pp.17–18), universal among the landowning classes of England in past times. Lawyers had to accommodate pressures from urban elites in particular and to some extent from those with more modest agricultural holdings which pushed further in the direction of partible inheritance. By its very nature, partible inheritance always poses a basic choice between actual division of the inheritance—what lawyers came to call "partition"—and concurrent enjoyment by the inheritors of the patrimony.

Joint tenancy and tenancy in common

Concurrent enjoyment of the patrimony by its inheritors was stylised by lawyers into something called the "tenancy in common". Tenants in common had "undivided shares" in land. No such co-owner could point to a particular room in a house or a field in a farm and call it his or her own. Rather, he or she shared generally with the other co-owners in the enjoyment of the land. This is not mysterious if we remember that enjoyment was primarily geared to the receipt of rents, and the tenancy in common was thus a mechanism for sharing out a rental income among members of a family over time directly, rather than indirectly through the more contorted mechanisms of the dynastic settlement discussed above, in which, in legal terms, the income from the estate "belonged" to the tenant for life, but was overlaid with a multiplicity of claims from the widows, daughters and younger sons.

The tenancy in common stood in contrast to another form of co-ownership called the joint tenancy. The difference is tied up with the consequences of the death of a co-owner. Someone who died a joint tenant had nothing which could pass, through will or intestacy, to his or her heirs. The "share" of such a person in the enjoyment of the land simply added to that of the surviving joint tenants. Lawyers called this the operation of "survivorship". In other words, if there were three joint tenants, each would be entitled, while they lived, to a third of the income arising from the land. If one of them died, the survivors would take one half of the rents each. By contrast, the death of a tenant in common would lead to his own entitlement passing on to his heirs. "Survivorship" did not operate here. And in so far as it involved a share in a rental income, a tenancy in common could over time become extensively fragmented, with the consequence, that, in due course, as we shall see, transfer of a title held in common in this way could become an extremely complex affair.

So far, we have presented fragmentation of title as principally a consequence of the circulation of land through time, of lawyers' attempts to accommodate a diverse range of strategies geared to pre- and post-mortem inheritance. As long as people settled their land in the way described above, conveyancing was a slow and complex process and the complexities gave rise to many risks of defective title. The 1925 legislation, therefore, attempted to facilitate the conveyancing process itself, and to simplify the character of title and the mode of its proof. It achieved these two related objectives by making it impossible after 1925 to split the fee simple into successive lesser legal estates. This was brought about by saying that, after 1925, the entail and the life estate could only exist in equity, and a modified terminology was adopted to reflect this change. The language of "estates" was abandoned, leaving lawyers to speak of "entailed interests" and "life interests". Because they can only exist today in equity, they can only exist behind some form of trust. We must now consider what it means to speak of "trusts" and "equitable interests". In a later chapter (pp.229–231, below) we outline the recent (prospective) abolition of the entail as an equitable interest by the Trusts of Land and Appointment of Trustees Act 1996, and the reasons which lie behind its abolition.

5

EQUITY: ORIGINS AND RATIONALE

"Equity" has had a long innings in the history of philosophy. What exactly it meant or means today as a philosophical theme is as elusive as attempting to define "justice". One aspect of the difficulty is the same in each case: each idea has something to do with the way in which we think about what law is, or claims to be or to provide. In each case too, it is generally recognised that no actual legal system can provide perfect equity or perfect justice. Perhaps Kant is the most blunt when he calls equity "a silent goddess who cannot be heard" (1797; tr. 1965, p.40).

The other way of embarking upon the study of equity is to follow the example of an historian such as Maitland, who saw equity as a body of doctrines, rules and practices which has arisen out of the work of a distinct set of courts. These courts did not spring up fully armed at some moment in time; they did not emerge as the result of some plan, but gradually over time as English monarchs reacted to the demands placed upon them. So intimate was the connection between monarch and the principal court that emerged—the Court of Chancery—that during the interregnum many sought, unsuccessfully, its abolition. The weakening of this intimate link between monarch and chancery was a precondition for equity to "settle down" and become a set of rules administered by a set of courts more or less like any other, albeit with a distinctive character.

The King's Courts of the Middle Ages (King's Bench, Common Pleas, Exchequer, and the Assize Courts) were particularly concerned with resolving disputes which today we would describe as involving the criminal law, land law and tort. Access to these courts depended principally upon obtaining the appropriate "Writ" from the King's Chancellor, that is, from the Keeper of his Great Seal, the fixing of which to a document impressed it with the royal authority. To seek redress for any wrong in the courts, a complainant had to bring his case within one of the writs available. Over time, this system became increasingly elaborate, and a central concern of the royal courts became whether the pleadings (the plaintiff's statement of the wrong complained of in the writ) were correct in every detail. If some mistake had been made in the pleadings, the plaintiff would often be denied his remedy. This led to dissatisfaction among litigants, and an increasing volume of petitions began to come before the King requesting that he should give redress and do justice where his courts had not done so and these petitions, increasingly, were handled by the King's Chancellor. In its essentials, this is the origin of what became the Court of Chancery.

MEDIEVAL TENURES AND THE EMERGENCE OF THE EQUITY JURISDICTION

One particular way in which the common law courts of the Middle Ages failed to respond to the demands placed upon them concerns us here. This is what became known as the "use". In order to understand this, we must consider briefly one of the cornerstones of medieval land law, the doctrines of tenures. Leaving aside his claim to be entitled by right of blood, William the Conqueror held England from 1066 by right of conquest. He acquired the kingdom of England; he did not inherit it, as he did his duchy of Normandy. (This is why the kingdom could devolve on his death to his second son, though the duchy went to his eldest.) As a result, all land in England was held, directly or indirectly, of the King. In legal theory at least, as a result, all "allodial" land claims—claims to ownership independent of and prior to the rights of the sovereign—were denied. In its place arose the feudal maxim *"Nul terre sans seigneur"*—no land without a lord. (See Gurevich, 1985, pp.47–48, 254–255; Reynolds, 1994, pp.48–74). The "doctrine of tenures" was the elaboration by medieval lawyers of the range of conditions upon which land was so held. At various times from 1066 onwards, this land had been granted to barons, who held as tenants of the Crown. All grants were conditional (see Milsom 1996, pp.247 *et seq.*)—that is, land was granted in return for certain kinds of services. These might involve the provision of knights (knight tenure) or agricultural produce (socage), etc. We will concentrate on knight tenure here. Someone who held land of the King in knight tenure might himself grant some of that land to others. In early feudalism, this would usually be done by subinfeudating, that is, by the tenant creating his own tenant and becoming himself a lord as well as a tenant of the Crown. This second grant would also be conditional, and might well in this example have been itself a grant in knight tenure. This process could continue, with a whole chain of lords and tenants, each tenant, within such a hierarchy, owing loyalty expressed through homage and the provision of services to his immediate lord, each lord, in return, owing protection to his subordinate. The history of this system, royal efforts to stop subinfeudation, the later disintegration into what is sometimes called "bastard" feudalism, even the adequacy of the term "feudalism" itself for understanding the character of medieval social and political relations, need not concern us here.[8] The military tenures, which we use here for illustrative purposes, were abolished in 1660. Most vestigial remains of the doctrine were removed by 1925, but still today all land is held of the Crown by virtue of this doctrine. This is why the term "tenant" is so widely used in the language of property lawyers (as in "tenant for life") to describe the position of people who are not in the narrow modern sense tenants of landlords. Even fee simples are, in theory, held of the Crown and so, strictly speaking, such an owner is a "tenant in fee simple". In Britain today, the precise nature of the Crown's right in relation to land rarely requires close attention. But in some post-colonial societies, the "feudal" theory has required careful and critical scrutiny in the context of modern disputes concerning Aboriginal land claims.[9]

As we have seen, tenurial relationships meant that most people holding land owed services to their immediate lord. These services became less significant over time, especially in relation to military tenures. This was because they began to be commuted to fixed money rents. Instead of providing a knight, the tenant just paid a fixed sum of money. With inflation in the late Middle Ages, these fixed payments became less significant.

But, in addition, lords had other important rights over the land of their tenants. These were known as the "incidents" of feudal tenure, and here, once again, we encounter the importance of the problem of inheritance for understanding how property law developed. If a knight died, his heir had to pay to the lord a relief before he could enter into his inheritance. If, on the death of his father, the son was still a minor, the lord had a right of wardship, which meant that the lord could take whatever produce or rent the land yielded until the son came of age. These rights were inflation-proof, and so became of great value to lords, and especially to the Crown, as the value of the services declined. Not unnaturally, wardship was resented, and people began to seek ways of minimising its effects.

Military tenures were connected, both in their origin and their supposed function, with fighting. Suppose, then, that such a tenant went off to war, from a sense of duty either to his King or to his God, or in the hope of booty, not knowing if and when he would return. What provision could he make for his family during his absence? One scheme was to transfer his estate to a relative or friend who was staying behind, who could look after it and administer it until he returned, or who, should the knight die abroad, could take care of it until the knight's son reached his majority and could take it over himself.

So the tenant transferred his estate but did not intend to allow the grantee to benefit from the land personally. Rather, he was to look after it on behalf of the grantor's family. The grantee was morally a custodian of the land, and not entitled to use it for his own purposes. But if the grantor died in the Crusades, was there any way in which his family could prevent the grantee from taking the benefit for himself? If they went to the common law courts, they would be told that the legal estate in the land was vested in the grantee, and that he was entitled to the benefit himself. The family was not recognised by the common law as having any rights in the land.

So the family might petition the King, arguing that although the strict legal rights in the land were vested in the grantee, nevertheless, his conscience was bound by the circumstances in which he had acquired that estate. It was wrong for the grantee to be able to assert his legal rights against the family.

These appeals to the King came to be delegated to his Chancellor, the keeper of the King's conscience as well as his seal. The Chancellor was usually a man of the Church. Around him grew up what became an early form of bureaucracy—the Chancery. Appeals against the injustices of the common law came to be taken to the Chancery, and the basis of its jurisdiction to "mitigate the rigour of the common law" had its origin in medieval notions of conscience.

When petitions from such families found their way into the Chancery with some frequency, the Chancellor came to recognise that the conscience of the grantee was bound. His authority proceeded against the person, *i.e.* the Chancellor would forbid the grantee to take the benefit himself, under threat of imprisonment. By doing this, the Chancellor was beginning to recognise the rights of the family against the grantee as something more than personal. They were beginning to have what could be regarded as property rights of some kind, because by preventing the grantee from asserting his legal rights to enjoyment of the land, the Chancellor was in effect saying that those rights belonged to the family. And so in the course of time, we come to speak of these rights as "equitable rights" (because they have their origin in the protection of Equity or the Court of Chancery) or equally we refer to them as "beneficial rights" (because they tell you not who has the legal title (the legal estate) but who is entitled to enjoyment or the benefit of the land). In other words, these early inventions by the Chancellor marked the beginning of what is today a commonplace of English jurisprudence—the splitting of rights of ownership into legal rights (title) and equitable rights (the right to enjoyment).

USES AND TRUSTS

This device, of granting land to X for the benefit of Y, became known as the "use". X held the title "to the use of" Y. It became used in the late Middle Ages as a way of circumventing the problems caused by the incidents of feudalism.

As explained above, these became due on the death of the tenant. So, if someone was old or thought he was about to die, and his heir was a young boy, the dreadful prospect of a long wardship looked inevitable. But the use provided a way of avoiding the incidents. The tenant could grant his estate to a younger man "to uses" (for the benefit of his heir). If he did this then, when he died, the incidents would not arise, because he had not died as a tenant, and the incidents only arose on the death of someone who died as a tenant of his lord. When the heir was of age, the grantee could then transfer the estate to him, having administered the land in the meantime for the benefit of the family, and the arduous wardship would have been avoided.

In Tudor times, the Crown became particularly concerned about the loss of revenue which resulted from resort to such uses, and in 1536 Henry VIII forced through a reluctant Parliament the Statute of Uses, which abolished many of the uses discussed above. Popular discontent at this statute led Henry to give ground four years later, and allow uses of a part of a man's land to be created in a will (Statute of Wills 1540).[10]

The effect of the Statute of Uses was that for some time uses ceased, with limited exceptions, to be recognised if created *inter vivos* ("between living people"). But in the late seventeenth century, the use effectively reappeared in what has become its contemporary form: the trust. Like the use, the trust permits obligations to be attached to property of any kind, requiring it to be applied in a particular way, and such obligations are enforceable in a court of equity. Trusts of property were not confined to trusts of land, even if, as we have seen, their precursor, the use, did originate in the context of land and the tenurial relationships of the Middle Ages. Much of the "learning" of the law of trusts, indeed, is concerned with trusts of funds rather than with trusts of land. Because, however, we are concerned here with trusts of land, our central focus is upon the more limited notion of the trust as involving a splitting of ownership rather than upon the more diffuse idea of the trust as a form of equitable obligation attached to property. And it must suffice for the moment to note that while English law permitted the fragmentation of the fee simple "at law" into life estates and entails, the importance of trusts of land was less than it now is.

As outlined above, one lynchpin of the 1925 reforms was the abolition of the life estate and entail as legal estates in land. The reasons for this were embedded in the difficulties that such fragmentation generated for the management of the process of land transfer by lawyers, which is why the details of these reforms are considered in later chapters of this book. For the moment, what matters is that the life estate and entail were not abolished as such: the strategy of reform proceeded on the basis that the substance of these devices should be preserved, but that, for conveyancing reasons, they could only "subsist" behind a trust.

In simple terms, the 1925 legislation made trusts of land much more important, and equity much more significant in terms of the manner in which disputes in the courts arising out of the ownership and occupation of land could be framed. Many more questions to do with the enjoyment of land now rest within the province of equity than was the case in the past. Ownership of the fee simple has been reduced, conceptually, to a matter of the ability to give good title, to the capacity to engage in exchange. Use rights which approximate to the incidents of ownership are issues for equity: an absolute owner of land is now called the sole beneficial owner, the term "beneficial" indicating the interposition of equity in conceptualising rights. This leads to some curious reversals at the conceptual level. Lesser use rights, like easements, were permitted in 1925 to continue to function as legal interests, and a leasehold interest in land remained, along with the fee simple, the only legal estate capable of existing in land after 1925. There is no underlying logic to this scheme of things; it is intelligible only in terms of practical convenience, and in terms of how, given such a legislative framework, it is possible to frame a dispute or pose a question in the courtroom. The conceptual scheme of English land law is as it is for practical reasons; in no way is it sensibly regarded as the product of "reason" in some larger sense. In this way, the artificial character of English law, as opposed to the natural reason of the civilian lawyer, which continental codification was meant to embody, persists through the ambitious English codification of 1925.

THE REGULARISATION OF EQUITY

The development of the rules of equity was dependent upon the gradual transformation of the royal secretariat into part of the judicial apparatus of England. At first, the Chancellor intervened on an ad hoc, case-by-case basis, deciding petitions in terms of what conscience required. There was, at this stage, no clear sense of the application of rules and therefore no significant conception of precedent or rule-following. Rules began to emerge in so far as typical fact-situations came to be seen as being appropriate occasions for the intervention of equity and granting of an equitable remedy. But until the conflicts between King and Parliament which led to the Civil War and the execution of the King in 1649, no clear boundaries or limits were recognised by the Chancery to its jurisdiction. This became especially pronounced during the reign of James I (1603–1625). It led to a collision between equity and the common law courts over the limits of the equitable jurisdiction. Problems arose for example over equity's use of a remedy known as the "injunction". Equity might forbid someone from bringing an action in the common law courts. Could it also forbid a successful plaintiff in the common law courts from enforcing his judgment against a defendant who had petitioned the Chancery to intervene? In this conflict, equity justified its activity in the same way as James I explained his notion of kingship in relation to Parliament and the common law. James argued that God's law was above secular or "ordinary" law (*i.e.* the common law). It was the King who "knew" God's law because the King's conscience was a faculty bestowed by God enabling him to discern God's law. For James, indeed, kings were gods (Oakley, 1984, pp.93 *et seq.*). The absolute power of kings could not be discussed by their subjects, just as it was blasphemy to discuss whether there were limits upon God's omnipotence. The Chancellor was the keeper of the King's conscience. When the conflict between the common lawyers, led by Sir Edward Coke C.J., and the Chancery under Lord Ellesmere came to a head, James consequently resolved the problem in favour of the Chancery. Ellesmere explained the decision of the King as: "The Chancellor sits in Chancery according to an absolute and uncontrollable Power, and is to judge according to that which is alleged and proved; but the judges of the common law are to judge according to strict and ordinary (or limited) powers".[11]

Thus, during this period leading up to the Civil War, the position of equity was very much tied up with the position of the King within the polity. While this was later transformed, James's decision is carried through to the modern law in the maxim "Equity prevails over law".

We cannot elaborate here upon what this notion of "absolute" power meant to political theorists of the time. It must suffice to observe that this way of thinking about royal power had a long ancestry and was a centrepiece of medieval ideas about the nature of government (*cf.* Pennington, 1993, pp.54–75, 106–118). It was only loosely connected with the idea of "absolute" royal power which came to prominence in France much later in the seventeenth century, was visualised in the construction of Versailles, and was carried through to its logical conclusion in Prussia and later in Austria-Hungary in the eighteenth century. How and to what extent English governmental arrangements changed during this period are matters of considerable dispute. Quite undue prominence has been given to the writings on government of John Locke and to the ideology of the social contract (see Clark, 1985 and 1986). But for our purposes the most significant change was perhaps the incorporation of the Court of Chancery into the regular judicial apparatus of the polity, and thus the removal of the monarch from any direct input into the judicial process apart from the retention of the prerogative of mercy in relation to punishment (Gatrell, 1994, pp.197–221). Thus Lord Nottingham, Lord Chancellor after the Restoration, said that the conscience which should guide the Chancellor was not "*naturalis et interna*" but "*civilis et politica*". What this meant was, quite simply, that the Chancery had become a court like any other, part of the ordinary power of government—*i.e.* subject to law—and not part of the absolute, uncontrollable, undiscussable power of the sovereign. And in 1734, Jekyll M.R. described the basis of equitable remedies as being *"secundum discretionem boni viri"*, a *"bonus vir"* being someone *"qui consulta patrum, qui leges juraque servat"*. (Equity was to be dispensed "according to the judgment of a man of virtue", such a man being one who "upheld the decrees of Parliament and the law".)

One anomaly did remain, though it perhaps seemed less odd in the past than it does today. As long as the Chancellor presided over Chancery— which he continued to do until the Judicature Acts of the 1870s—his office uniquely contradicted whatever tenuous version of the separation of powers emerged in eighteenth-century political theory in England. He was an officer of state, and when the cabinet system developed, he was—and remains—a member of the executive and the ministerial head of a government department. He was, and is, a member of the legislature as a peer of the realm. Whether this "anomalous" position still makes sense in the light of world wide democratic practice, is, at the time of writing, under discussion. The Government would like to abolish the position (and convert it into a regular Secretary of Stateship, and has already renamed the Lord Chancellor's Department as the Department for Constitutional Affairs). But influential figures in the judiciary are anxious about the diminution of influence of the judiciary on matters relevant to them that this would involve.

But for a long time this was not anomalous: the position was part of the constitutional framework—a monarchical constitution that was unwritten. That these arrangements were tolerated tells us something about how people of the time understood the character of the "merely civil" law, the work of the Chancery in supervising the administration of trusts, settlements and wills. It was part of the business of government but not, in our terms, part of the political process or that part of the judicial process which bore upon the liberties of the subject. The idea of the Lord Chief Justice sitting in the cabinet was, by contrast, much more controversial and a very rare occurrence. Such an arrangement was not illegal or unconstitutional, but many thought it inexpedient "because it tended to excite a suspicion of political partiality in the administration of justice". "It would not be proper", said Lord Eldon in the House of Lords, "that the same individual should act, first as a minister to institute prosecutions

for treason and sedition, and afterwards as the judge to preside
at the trials" (Twiss, 1846, p.352). The origins and subsequent
history of equity can be said to lie in the nature of the remedial
assistance it came to afford. The systematised form of this
assistance must serve as our point of departure.

The two principal remedies are specific performance and the
injunction. Both reflect the once intimate association of Chancery with the absolute power of the King. A decree of specific
performance is an order by the court requiring someone to do
something (*e.g.* to perform a contract), and the injunction is an
order by the court forbidding someone to do something. Both
issue against the person (they are called remedies *in personam*).
Today this means that if the person against whom they are
issued disobeys the order, he will be in contempt of court and
may face imprisonment. Both remedies can be seen as the
marshalling of the power of what today we call the British state
behind "private" transactions concluded by people with the
help of their lawyers. As we shall see, from the perspective of
courts rather than conveyancers, the role of specific performance
of the contract for the sale of land was pivotal for the way in
which the courts formulated over time the principles of English
land law.

Both remedies are discretionary. This means that they are not
available as of right. By contrast, common law remedies, notably
damages, are available as of right once the plaintiff has proved
his case (*e.g.* that a contract has been breached by the defendant). The only discretion or flexibility which the court pos-
sesses in an award of common law damages is in fixing the
amount or "quantum" of those damages. This discretionary
quality of equitable remedies means that in certain circumstances the plaintiff will be denied his equitable remedy even
though he has proved a wrong against him which is normally
remedied by equity.

There are four main circumstances where the equitable
remedy will be denied. First, where damages at law would
provide adequate compensation for the wrong suffered. Secondly, where the plaintiff's own conduct is reproachable ("He
who comes to Equity must come with clean hands"). Thirdly,
where, because of what has happened, it is impossible or
impracticable to award the equitable remedy. Sometimes, for
example, because third parties are involved, awarding specific
performance of a contract would only lead to further litigation.
In these circumstances, where the plaintiff would normally have

been given his decree of specific performance but for the complication of third parties, the courts have jurisdiction to award equitable damages in lieu of specific performance. Although the plaintiff will only receive financial compensation instead of the promised performance, an award of equitable damages can lead to the award of a significantly greater quantum of damages. This is because the *quantum* is assessed on the loss as it stands at the time of the trial of the action, rather than on the loss at the time of the breach of the contract (which is the basis for assessing contractual damages at common law). Finally, the remedy is normally denied where the person asking for the remedy of specific performance is a volunteer, that is, has not given consideration. An example is the recipient of a purely voluntary promise.

THE EQUITABLE JURISDICTION AND THE JUDICATURE ACTS

In the mature period of equity, when its courts had come to be integrated into the ordinary judicial apparatus of the English polity, its jurisdiction was described by lawyers as threefold: the exclusive, the concurrent and the auxiliary jurisdiction:

The exclusive jurisdiction involved the enforcement of equitable rights; the concurrent jurisdiction involved the enforcement of legal rights. This jurisdiction was exercised "either because the remedy in equity was a more perfect remedy than the remedy at law or because the remedy at law either never existed at all, or [had] become unavailable" (Snell, 1908, p.424). The auxiliary jurisdiction:

> "was applicable primarily to the better enforcement of legal rights,—and only (by a sort of analogy) was it applicable to the enforcement also of equitable rights . . . (in the case of legal rights) the decision of the common law court thereon was conclusive in equity; but . . . (in the case of equitable rights) the opinion of the common law court (where equity thought fit to take that opinion) was for guidance only,—and the verdict also of a common law jury (where equity thought fit to obtain such a verdict) was for guidance only" (*ibid.*, p.603).

All matters relating to trusts, mortgages, married women and lunatics were part of the exclusive jurisdiction; the remedies of specific performance and the injunction were at the core of the concurrent jurisdiction; orders for discovery and delivery of documents, were, for our purposes, a central element in the auxiliary jurisdiction.

In former times, litigants sought the assistance of equity where their rights derived from the common law partly because of the remedies which equity courts made available, and, in some cases at least, because of the absence of a jury (which was once common in civil actions). A case from 1735 provides a good example.[12] A Duke owned an antique altarpiece, which had been taken and sold to a goldsmith who knew of the Duke's claim. The Duke presented a bill in equity for delivery of the thing. The goldsmith said the court should leave the plaintiff to his remedies at law. Delivery of title-deeds ("writing savouring of the realty") and heirlooms, he conceded, might be appropriate things for equitable assistance, but if bills like this were allowed, he argued, the equity courts would be swamped with petitions concerning the wrongful taking or retention of things which had previously been tried in the courts of common law, a form of argument, of course, which is as old as the hills.

The Lord Chancellor helped the Duke out. With things of "curiosity or antiquity", he thought, it would be hard if plaintiffs could only recover their value; that would be like a forced sale. A later judge supplies a further clue. The Duke had brought his bill before the Lord High Chancellor of England; but pursuit of things of curiosity and antiquity through the common law courts might have proved to be quite a different affair. The common law required the thing to be found, and most moveables could be hidden. It was thus much more likely, going down that road, that a plaintiff would end up only with financial compensation, and the amount would fall to be determined by a jury.

"The Pusey horn, the patera of the Duke of Somerset, were things of that sort of value that a jury might not give twopence beyond the weight. It was not to be cast to the estimation of people who have not those feelings. In all cases where the object of the suit is not liable to a compensation by damages, it would be strange if the law of this country did not afford any remedy. It would be great injustice if an individual cannot have his property without being liable to the estimate of people who have not his feelings upon it."[13]

To invoke the assistance of a court of equity, it was insufficient to make good your claim at law. Unless you could assert an "equity" (*i.e.* something that warranted an appeal to equity, preferably, of course, grounded in the established practice of that court), you would be left to your remedies at law, such as they were.

In the 1870s, significant procedural and administrative changes were made which enabled the rules of equity and the rules of common law to be discussed in the same court before the same judge. These changes culminated in the abolition by the Judicature Acts of the existing common law courts and the Court of Chancery, and their replacement by a single unified High Court of Justice, divided up into three main divisions: Queen's Bench, Probate, Divorce and Admiralty (now Family), and Chancery.

Lawyers still debate the precise consequences of the Judicature Acts. What is clear is that they brought about a change in procedure, such that both equitable and common law remedies are now available in the same court. Before these Acts, many litigated issues to do with property and title belonged exclusively to the courts of common law. Equity was resorted to in order to supplement the jurisdiction of the common law, which was the foundation of the auxiliary jurisdiction.

This ceased to be necessary after these Acts came into effect, because this supplement of equity was now available in every court. But the conceptual foundations of the distinction between law and equity remained in place. So property lawyers continue to distinguish ownership "at law" from ownership "in equity", even though such distinctions are no longer reflected in differences between institutions or in divisions and sometimes conflicts between jurisdictions. In this respect, the Judicature Acts simplified the "administration of justice", and, to a limited extent, the substantive law itself. There were matters on which the rules of law and the rules of equity overlapped but were inconsistent. These principally occur in the area of contractual obligations; one example must suffice. A lease, the nature of which is explored further in Chapter 7, commonly today contains a rent review clause. If the lease provides a timetable for such a rent review to occur, and the timetable is not complied with, what is the position? As lawyers put it, is time, in such a context, of the essence of the contract? Law and equity diverged here in the past. The common law gave effect to the private law of the parties. If the arrangement provided a date, that was decisive. Equity's attitude, however, was different, so far as agreements which came within its purview were concerned. The practice of equity came to be that stipulations in a contract as to the time of performance would not be regarded as being of the essence unless the contract expressly said so. After the Judicature Acts, the equitable view always prevails, which means that, so far as questions of this order are concerned, the old common law rules are effectively obsolete, and the only operative rules are those which originate from the practice of the courts of equity.

So the maxim "Equity prevails over law" still applies. Whereas it originally resolved a jurisdictional problem between two different decision-making institutions, it means today that the equitable rules prevail if there is a conflict with the legal rules. For example, in the case of the trust, the legal rules indicate simply that the legal owner (the person with the legal estate) is entitled to the property, but the equitable rules indicate that he holds the legal estate as a trustee, that is for the benefit of someone else (whom we will call the beneficiary). Thus, the legal rules say the legal owner is entitled to the property, and the rules of equity say the benefit is with the beneficiary. In this conflict of interpretation, the equitable view prevails.

EQUITABLE INTERESTS: THE BASIC SCHEME

It is against this background of the availability of equitable remedies that we can speak of equitable interests, or equitable rights as property rights. Three examples will now be considered: the estate contract, the restrictive covenant and the beneficial interest behind a trust. This order of presentation is adopted for simplicity of exposition; it is not an historical sequence of the progressive recognition of different kinds of rights by the courts of equity.

The estate contract

This is a contract between a prospective seller and a prospective purchaser of land. If the seller, having entered into the contract, later refuses to transfer the title to that land—refuses to convey the title—as he has promised, the only remedy available to the buyer at common law is a remedy in damages, financial compensation based on what the buyer has lost. But for centuries equity has taken the view that, in relation to a contract for the sale of land, damages for breach are not adequate, even though they usually are sufficient for breach of contract to sell chattels. Because equity viewed contracts for the sale of land as special, it was prepared to decree specific performance of these contracts. It would not leave a would-be purchaser to his remedy in damages at law, but would help him to compel the seller to do what he had promised and convey the title to the land. Because the purchaser could normally (see p.102, above for the exceptions to this general rule) get specific performance of a contract to sell land, he came to be viewed as the owner of the land "in equity" as soon as the contract was made. The legal title, of course, remained with the seller until the conveyance (the act of transfer of title) but the purchaser, because he could get specific performance against the seller, was viewed as having an equitable interest in the land. This means that the effect of the contract is in some sense to transfer certain property rights from the seller to the purchaser.

Why is it important to say not simply that the purchaser has more remedies than parties to many other kinds of contracts (because he can get specific performance) but in addition that the purchaser has an equitable interest in the land—a property right? It is because third parties in certain situations will, as lawyers say, "take subject to" these equitable interests, that they have the character of property rights.

EXAMPLE

V contracts with P1 to convey the title to his land. V then conveys the title to P2. What is P1's position? At law, his only remedy is against V in damages for breach of contract. P1 cannot sue P2 at law on the contract because P2 is not a party to the contract and so is under no contractual duty towards P1. (This doctrine of English law, that only the parties to a contract have rights and duties under it, is known as privity of contract.) In limited circumstances, P1 may have a remedy in tort against P2, but this requires P1 to prove that P2 persuaded or induced V to break the contract, and even if P1 can prove this, the remedy is limited to common law damages. But in equity, P1 has an equitable interest because he could have obtained specific performance of his contract against V. In certain circumstances, P2 will be made by equity to take subject to P1's rights because P1 has an equitable interest. Under the old law, this would arise if P2 knew or ought to have known (lawyers say "had notice") of P1's rights.

What does it mean to say that P2 "takes subject to" P1's rights? The effect of the conveyance by V to P2 is to transfer the legal estate in the land from V to P2. But if P2 has notice of P1's rights, he takes subject to them. This means that P1 can pursue the same equitable (but not common law) remedies against P2 as he could have pursued against V. In short, P1 can invoke the assistance of equity against P2 and get a degree of specific performance against P2. In other words, P2 will be compelled to convey the land to P1. P2 will then be left to pursue a remedy at law against V.

The restrictive covenant

An owner (V1) of a large piece of land might sell off an outlying portion of that land to a purchaser (P1), extracting a promise known as a "covenant" from that purchaser at the time of the conveyance that the land being sold will be used for residential purposes only. So the purchaser is promising in the covenant to limit the uses to which he may put the land. If he later goes back on this promise, that would be a breach of contract by the purchaser, and the seller could sue for damages at law in respect of that breach. But his covenant, viewed simply as a contract (that is, through common law spectacles), could have legal effect only as between the parties to the covenant. In what circumstances, if any, could the covenant have an effect if V1 sold the land he had retained to V2, and P1 sold the land he had bought to P2? Could V2 enforce the covenant against P2, if P2 proposed to use the land for non-residential purposes? Neither is a party to the covenant as a contract, and so under common law principles the covenant would be of no legal effect as between the two. But in the nineteenth century, the Court of Chancery came to give effect to the covenant in equity, and would grant the equitable remedy of the injunction to restrain breach of the covenant by P2 when its assistance was invoked by V2. Because we have now stepped well outside the common law confines of privity of contract, and relationships between non-contracting parties are being regulated by means of the injunction, we can say that V2 in this situation has a property right or equitable interest against P2. The land in P2's hands is burdened with a third-party right (V2's right to enforce the covenant).

V2, although he has no legal rights in P2's land, and although he has no contract with P2, has equitable rights which affect or burden P2's land. But V2's rights are only equitable, and therefore if he sought to enforce them against P2, we would in the past have needed to ask if P2 knew or ought to have known (*i.e.* had "notice) of the covenant. If P2 had no knowledge of the covenant made between V1 and P1, and had no way of knowing about it, the covenant would have been unenforceable by V2 against P2 because, to revert to the origins of the equitable jurisdiction, without notice of the rights or claims of others, his conscience was not bound.

The interests of beneficiaries behind a trust

We have already seen that the trust was a creation of equity. Part of equity's jurisdiction over trustees centres around equity's jurisdiction to restrain a breach of trust. If trustees propose to do something which is a breach of trust (for example, something which is contrary to the purposes for which the trustee acquired the legal estate as legal owner, or something which, under the terms of the trust, the trustee has no power to do) then the beneficiaries can go to the court and get an injunction, by which the court will restrain the trustee from committing the breach of trust.

The jurisdiction over breaches of trust extends further. Trustees are not allowed to take a personal benefit from administering the trust. If they do, the beneficiaries can go to court to restrain the trustees from taking a personal benefit. If the beneficiaries suffer a loss as a result of the way the trust has been administered, they can go to court and get compensation from the trustees for the loss which they have suffered.

EXAMPLE

T1 and T2 have the legal title to a fund, but they hold the fund as trustees. A has a life interest in possession in equity in respect of this fund, and B has a remainder in fee simple. This means that for the duration of A's life, he is entitled to the income from the fund and on his death, when the equitable life interest terminates, B is beneficially entitled to the capital itself—the whole fund—because his equitable fee simple—the whole beneficial interest in the trust property—has now come into possession. But during this time, legal title to the fund, and thus managerial control over it, are in the hands of trustees. The trustees are in charge but are compelled by equity to deal with the fund for the benefit of the beneficiaries.

Here again, the jurisdiction may extend to people who are not themselves trustees. Although the legal estate in land might be vested in a purchaser P, who would have been regarded in the common law courts as entitled to the property, equity would, under some conditions, intervene to restrain the purchaser P from deriving any personal benefit from the land because of the circumstances in which he had acquired that legal estate. Equity viewed him as a legal owner who was a trustee, with obligations to a group of people who were not on the legal title, whom today we call beneficiaries.

EXAMPLE
A is the legal owner of Blackacre as trustee on behalf of B and C. He transfers the legal estate to P. Does P acquire that legal estate subject to the rights of B and C or not?

In practice, this problem is only likely to arise if A runs off with the money or becomes bankrupt. Normally, if there is a difficulty, B and C will pursue their remedies against A, the trustee. But what if A is penniless (what lawyers call a "man of straw")? Can they get at P? Again, under the old law, this depended on whether or not P knew or ought to have known (had notice) of the rights of B and C. If he did, then he took subject to them, and if he did not, he took free. This would mean that if B and C between them were entitled to the whole enjoyment of the property (that is, had between them the equitable fee simple in possession), then P would, if he had notice of their rights, have acquired a worthless legal estate. This would be because he would hold that legal estate he had acquired by conveyance from A as trustee for B and C, and, because they were absolutely entitled in equity to the beneficial ownership of the land, he could himself derive no benefit from the land. On the other hand, if P had no notice he took free, and would himself, as purchaser of the legal estate, be absolutely entitled to the enjoyment of the land.

Since whether a purchaser took subject to equitable interests affecting the legal estate depended on whether or not he had notice of these interests, equitable interests might seem to have operated as an exception to the basic principle of *nemo dat* (see p.66, above). A, as trustee of a legal estate, was not entitled to derive any benefit from the land; the beneficial interest, in our example, is in B and C, yet if P had no notice, the rights of beneficial ownership would not affect him. In other words, P, without notice, could be in a better position than A, the seller, had been. This anomaly or distinction in fact highlights the different ways in which legal rights (that is, rights recognised by the common law) and equitable rights worked in the past. In asking whether a particular legal owner was affected by equitable interests in the land, equity looked at the circumstances in which the person had acquired his legal title.

MIDDLE-CLASS FAMILY SETTLEMENTS IN THE NINETEENTH CENTURY

Trusts provided an important vehicle for middle-class wealth-holding until well into the twentieth century. Unlike the dynastic settlement associated with large landed estates, and their preservation over time by means of primogeniture and entail, these middle-class family settlements were more flexible devices typically used to settle on trust the ownership of funds and stocks and shares as well as land. They commonly involved partible inheritance, and a more significant role for the wife/widow than most dynastic settlements. Middle-class settlements had two core features. First, legal title to the settled property or capital was held by trustees (often solicitors) in order to secure an income for a married couple during their lives. The role of the trustees was to look after the settled property and to pay the income to the beneficiaries. Secondly, the final choice as to the descent of the settled property to the next generation was postponed until the children were grown up. On the death of the parents, the final task of the trustees was to distribute the settled property among the children in accordance with the original trust instrument or with decisions made subsequently under powers conferred by the trust instrument.

The marriage settlement thus involved the transfer of property, at the time of the marriage, to trustees. The income from the capital was normally to be paid to the husband during his life, to the wife if she survived him and, on the death of the spouses, the capital fund was to be distributed among the children equally, or in such shares as the father and mother jointly or the survivor by deed or will should appoint. As with the jointure, the wife had only a provision during widowhood, but, by contrast with the dynastic settlement, a wife who survived her husband had the opportunity to determine the descent of the property to the next generation, especially if the husband died before many of the children had attained their majority, thus reducing the likelihood of a joint appointment having been made prior to the husband's death.

In this form of settlement, it was common to insert a covenant by the wife to hand over to the trustees any property (over a certain value, conventionally over £200) which she acquired subsequently to the marriage. Such property would then be secured for transmission in due course to the next generation. The trustees conventionally itemised the husband's and wife's property separately, and in the event of no children of either sex, the husband's property reverted on his death to his heirs by will or on intestacy, and the wife's property to her next of kin (though she often had a power of selection among them). Sometimes in these settlements, property was settled upon the wife as the first beneficiary. This was done by inserting a formula requiring the trustees to pay the income to her "separate use". This would give the wife the income in her own right, independently of the husband, even during his own lifetime. This device was particularly suitable where the family of the wife considered the husband to be feckless or improvident, or where the husband engaged in "trade", with which the idea of bankruptcy, in the nineteenth century, was particularly associated. At the end of the eighteenth century, a new device had been invented and subsequently recognised by the courts called the "restraint against anticipation". Such a restraint meant that the married woman had no power to alienate or "anticipate" her life interest during the marriage. Technically, this device was valid if it was attached to a settlement of property to a married woman's separate use. In other words, in order to have the benefit of a restraint, it was necessary to use the formula of separate property. Under a settlement which did not use this device, the husband and wife could alienate or anticipate their lifetime income rights by assigning them to a money-lender in return for a capital sum. By contrast, if property was settled by means of the restraint device, future income entitlements could not be exchanged for a capital sum; the future, as it were, could not be mortgaged. Any such transaction would be treated as nugatory by the courts.

Against this general background, the courts of Equity formulated what was called the "equity to a settlement". This was a discretionary award made by the court on the application of a wife or widow who did not have a marriage settlement nor proof of an agreement to make one. If the wife had brought property into the marriage, the court would award her a settlement to her separate use. This would usually be on the husband's death or bankruptcy.

The practice of this type of settlement lasted well into this century, despite various legislative changes, notably the Married Women's Property Acts of 1870 and 1882, which reduced the need for some of the technical chicanery relating to the legal position of married women that had become common in nineteenth-century settlements. The Matrimonial Causes Act of

1857 enabled marriage, for the first time, to be formally dissolved by a secular court. This Act had to accommodate the fact of middle-class settlements, and make provision for what was to happen to the settlement in the event of a divorce. The courts were empowered to order maintenance of the wife, or to order a fund to be set aside and an income for life secured for the wife upon it. It was in a juridical sense a more final version of a separation agreement, which was itself merely the obverse of a marriage settlement, or a modification thereto. None of this legislation was, in any direct sense, a manifestation or a cause of the discontinuation of the practice of settlement, but part of a movement of formal equality, liberty and rationalisation of the law which co-existed with it. The disappearance of these settlements came about largely for a range of other reasons. For present purposes, one of the most important was the rise of owner-occupation and joint ownership of the family home as a substitute device for family wealth-holding. This is the central topic of the next chapter.

6

MODERN EQUITY AND THE RISE OF OWNER-OCCUPATION

We have already seen that before 1926 the legal fee simple absolute in possession could be split up into a number of lesser legal estates, and that the right to enjoyment of these different estates could be spread out through time (interests in possession, in remainder, reversions, etc.). The effect of the 1925 legislation was that the legal fee simple absolute in possession became the only pre-1925 freehold estate which could exist at law. The life estate and entail could thereafter only exist in equity (*i.e.* behind a trust), and all future interests (*i.e.* interests in remainder or reversion) must also take effect in equity. Equally, all interests of tenants in common could only exist behind a trust. More recently, as we shall see, the equitable entail has been abolished for the future, and the type of trust behind which tenancies in common can exist has been modified (Trusts of Land and Appointment of Trustees Act 1996).

These changes mean that what would once have been disputes about legal interests in land, with equitable remedies being sought simply to secure these legal interests, now tend to be disputes couched as claims to equitable entitlements as such, whether or not these claims explicitly involve trusts. Equity has thus come to provide in large measure the language and concepts in which most rights to enjoyment of land must be articulated. Conceptually, this can blur the distinction between interests behind trusts and other kinds of equitable rights, which here we call the "new equities". A famous nineteenth-century case provides a good illustration. In this case, a housekeeper who claimed that she had right to remain for the rest of her life in the house where she had lived and worked after her employer had died, and whom his heirs were trying to remove, resorted to the jurisdiction of equity merely in the old way for remedial assistance. What she sought was a legal life estate, arguing that she had an equity to get one through a decree of the court.[14] In the modern world, any such person must not just make a case for equitable intervention, through establishing an equity in the old sense of the word, but must also conceptualise in the language of equity the substantive nature of the right to which he or she is laying claim. As we shall see, many of the "new" equitable interests are not new in substance, but they are new, first, in that they operate "in equity" and not "at law" and, secondly, in that they arise informally and do not originate in formal documents nor can their continued existence be so proved. Although it is often repeated that equity looks not to form but to substance, it must be stressed that this informal character of the new equities is not connected with the fact that these rights are equitable. (As we shall see in the next chapter, the common law was long familiar with dealing with entirely informal tenancies, and much of the work of courts of equity, over a long period of time, centred around the construction of formal documents such as trust instruments and wills, and remains so today). Rather, informality derives from the circumstances which generate the disputes. We return to this in the final chapter, where the idea of form and substance in English land law is reappraised. In this chapter we look more closely at the first aspect of what is new, the fact that the framework of the 1925 code forces many disputes concerning land to be couched in the language of equity rather than the language of law.

The 1925 code transformed the conceptual scheme within which disputes about the ownership or occupation of land could be framed; quite different factors informed what such disputes, in substance, could be about. The principal focus of the discussion is housing. The first point is the rise of public housing in this century. So long as such housing remains in the public sector, it cannot generate disputes which impinge upon the lawyer's understanding of what property is. Transfers of council tenancies, and succession to tenancies on the death of the existing tenant, are all matters for specific, statutory schemes and local authority policies. The rise of this housing sector coincides with the decline in the relative significance of the private rented sector. Because this sector embraces some of the acutest manifestations of social deprivation in modern Britain, it has understandably been the focus of intensive study by progressive lawyers. But its significance for the development of the law of property since the enactment of the 1925 code has been negligible by comparison with the explosion of the owner-occupied housing sector, the sector whose contextual importance has been only enhanced by government policies promoting the sale of council houses to their tenants (see Murphy and Clark, 1983, pp.1–13; Swenarton and Taylor, 1985).

The owner-occupied housing sector has continued to grow exponentially in the past decade, both in fact and as a subject of public and governmental interest. The Land Registry now publishes house price figures from 1995 to the present on its website, and the growth of the private investment ("buy-to-let") market survives both the creation of private pensions and (recent) fears of a burst in the housing bubble. Prices and speculation continue to grow. Equity and trusts gain increasing importance in terms of the possibilities of legal disputes in this housing landscape.

Against the background of mortgage-financed owner-occupation, the range of probable disputes relating to housing is fairly limited. Principally they concern either the ownership or occupation of residential property, and for the most part arise in disputes between "homesharers" on marital or quasi-marital breakdown or on death, or on insolvency of one of the homesharers. Since 1925, the legal owner of the property must either have an estate in fee simple or a leasehold estate, the nature of which is elaborated in the next chapter. A dispute at law can only arise between legal joint tenants, where, for example a couple are joint owners of their home and are both on the title. In such circumstances, the principal kind of dispute which can find its way to a court is over sale of the house, in respect of which question the courts now have a broad discretion conferred by statute to make such order as they think fit (s.30 of the Law of Property Act 1925, now modified by s.14 of the TLAPA 1996, discussed below). In disputes between most homesharers, a legal analysis of the relationship in terms of landlord and tenant is more or less obsolete, for reasons outlined in the next chapter. All other attempts to assert rights of ownership or occupation are necessarily pushed either into the domain of equity or into the (legal) province of contract.

All these changes boil down to two things for the development of land law in recent years. First, the legal life estate has had, in effect, to be reinvented, through the conceptual resources available to modern lawyers. Because of the changes brought in by legislation in 1925, this reinvention has been forced to occur in equity. Secondly, lawyers have had to find a way of defining the basis upon which people other than those on the title can establish a claim to a share in the fruits of owner-occupation even where no formal trust has been created.

We now outline, in turn, each of these accommodations, beginning with the second. This came first because, until the 1970s, the courts had to apply the general principles of property law to marital breakdown. And because of the changes in the context of such disputes, since one of the relatively new matters which required resolution on marital breakdown was the ownership of the matrimonial home, there was pressure, at the level of equity, to specify the circumstances in which people acquired ownership rights in equity even if they had none at law, that is, were not on the legal title to the house or flat in question. Change in context, in brief, led to change in text. But the text was not that of the conveyancer but that of the judge. This is what was new. If the conveyancer's context had always been social relations, the judge's context had traditionally been the text prepared by the conveyancer. The 1925 legislation was assembled on the basis of just such a scheme of things. But now this changed: it was social relations themselves, unmediated by the conveyancer's text, which served as the object of judicial activity. Judges had to interpret the world of everyday life, without assistance from the specialists in the business of formalising inheritance and transfer by sale. That their own prejudices thus became more transparent, and that they were forced to resort to drawing upon their own understandings as to the meaning of action in the social world, was inevitable. Inevitably, too, such transformations led to confusion, because judges were called upon to deal with matters of which they had no deep experience and therefore no established legal framework within which to proceed. It would, however, have been scandalous to admit this directly, which is why, even given clear signs of unease which are manifest in the written record of decisions, the judges, as living oracles of the law, were constrained to present the decisions which they made as consistent with the tradition (when they were not), or as "adaptations" of principle, when they were, in fact, departures. This is another reason why land law is difficult for the student; judicial decisions continually rewrite legal history without admitting to it.

THE REFORMULATION OF OWNERSHIP RIGHTS IN EQUITY: THE ADAPTATION OF IMPLIED TRUSTS

Once trusts were recognised by the courts of equity, they came to be formalised and elaborated by conveyancers, although they rarely rivalled the strict settlement of land in complexity and intricacy of composition. But trusts of this type—which we call "express trusts" because they are deliberately created, with the help of lawyers, in the social world—could also serve as a model permitting the equity courts to extend the reach of their remedies. Equity came to impose trusts on legal estates, justifying such imposition with reference to the circumstances in which those who held these estates had acquired them. There were several instances of this, but only one concerns us here: this is what is called the "resulting trust". Where land was conveyed to a nominee and the purchase price paid by another who intended no gift to the nominee, equity would impose a resulting trust upon the nominal purchaser of the estate in favour of the real purchaser, looking to the "substance" of the purchase (the source of the money) rather than to the "form" of (the name on) the conveyance.

The resulting trust provided the most accessible device for modelling the analysis of modern disputes about ownership of the matrimonial home, when that was necessary. It is less important today, in property disputes between married couples, because the courts now have statutory powers to vary the property rights of spouses on divorce or judicial separation. But where the disputants, whatever the precise nature of their relationship, are not married, it remains the principal mechanism for framing a dispute about ownership. The difficulty which courts have experienced centres upon specifying the boundary conditions for its deployment; in deciding, that is, who is or is not to count as a real purchaser.

The difficulty in adapting the resulting trust to modern conditions is rooted in changes in practices of land purchase. It was not uncommon for people in the past, as we see in the next chapter, to finance the purchase of land by borrowing money secured upon a mortgage of the purchased land. What is different is the manner in which such loans are repaid. The legal framework within which judges of the past worked and around which the 1925 code was organised took the servicing of the loan out of rental income as its operational model. Indeed, as we shall see, repayment of the borrowed capital was in one sense not fundamental to the mortgage device, which was equally a way of securing the entitlement to interest upon the capital advanced by the lender. Now it is different. Building societies and banks, who lend money for the purchase of houses or flats, do so on the basis that the money lent will be repaid along with interest, within a period of time indicated in advance. In most cases, moreover, it is assumed that the repayments will be made from the earned income of the borrower. This in turn means that the mortgage repayments simply form part of the outgoings of a household, along with the bills for gas and electricity, telephone and food. Put simply, then, the problem is the difficulty, in life and therefore in a dispute about ownership, of separating contributions to the repayment of the mortgage loan from other household outgoings. And since the practice of lenders has tended in the direction of refusing, or being reluctant, to lend a sum equal to the whole purchase price, most purchaser-borrowers have had to find a deposit for the purchase price. Given that all this can take place over a number of years, it can often be difficult, in retrospect, when a relationship between homesharers ends in a dispute, to work out who has borne the acquisition costs of the home. However people arrange their affairs, there is always room for argument, along one of the lines suggested above, that someone who is not on the title is entitled in equity to a share of the value of the property. There are a number of reasons why people with a claim in equity to be recognised as owners might not have their names on the legal title. Once again, such reasons spring more from life than from law.

In the past, the majority of such ownership disputes would have been mediated by the paperwork of conveyancers in which, it could be assumed, the intentions of the relevant parties to disputes had been crystallised. Judicial dispute resolution was therefore primarily oriented to the task of construction of the meaning of the words in these documents. The circumstances of the parties at the time of disputes reaching court, and the informal interpersonal conduct of the parties over time preceding the arrival in court of disputes, were at best a supplement for the process of adjudication. In many modern disputes surrounding owner-occupation, however, the position is different for reasons we have highlighted. One judge has recently drawn attention to the problems for courts which result from these changes, stressing "the difficulties which these cases pose for the honest recollections of witnesses and the barrenness of the terrain in which judges and district judges who try them are required to search for the small evidential nuggets on which issues as to the existence—or the proportions—of beneficial interests are liable to depend".[15]

The courts have come to impose a resulting trust today where there is an "actual common intention" that the claimant should have a share of the property and where, secondly, the claimant has made direct or indirect contributions towards the costs of acquisition. What the first requirement means is not exactly clear. As formulated, it seems to conflate the traditional ground for imposing a trust of this kind—the generation of an equity through the payment of purchase money—with the quite different idea of agreement providing the basis for equitable intervention, a frame of reference, in other words, which is very close to the idea of a contract. But the main function of this requirement seems to be that it provides a way of excluding claims where, upon close analysis of the particular facts, the court concludes that no share was intended. Conversely, where the most plausible interpretation of the facts is that a share was intended, "actual common intention" provides a superficially attractive catchphrase to justify the imposition of a trust upon the legal owner.

The second requirement, which does seem to echo the traditional rationale of the resulting trust, is perhaps best understood as an attempt to draw a line somewhere and in that sense as a general guideline for the judicial processing of disputes. It is generally accepted today that monetary contributions will be recognised and result in the award of an interest in the event of a dispute. There are a few cases, all somewhat unusual, which suggest that exceptional work on a property can lead to a similar award. But ordinary domestic labour—maintenance and repair, and childrearing—has usually been excluded. Inevitably, such decisions can be seen as underpinned by a certain ideology, and inevitably too, the rhetoric of "direct or indirect contributions" can be interpreted as a means of rationalising a distinction between claims which the judiciary wish to uphold and those which they do not. But from the point of view of judicial administration, the central difficulty, in this relatively uncharted area, is how to achieve at least the appearance of consistency in decision-making. What makes consistency in decision-making difficult to ensure is the need in these disputes for careful judicial scrutiny of the particular facts of each case, and the inescapable need for an individualised judgment to be made by the court once the facts as disclosed to the court have been studied. Explicit agreement between the parties from the outset is the best way to circumvent this problem, and we return below to the general policy issues surrounding such agreements. But such agreements may in any event often be absent. As a result, what can look to the observer like differences in the law being applied to analyse these relationships often boil down to differences in the facts and in judicial perceptions of these facts—in the history and position of the parties, in what it is sensible in retrospect to have expected them to have said or done at the relevant time or times, and so on.

"When people, especially young people, agree to share their lives in joint homes they do so on a basis of mutual trust and in the expectation that their relationship will endure. Despite the efforts that have been made by many responsible bodies to counsel prospective cohabitants as to the risks of taking shared interests in property without legal advice [*i.e.* without formalisation of the relationship], it is unrealistic to expect that advice to be followed on a universal scale. For a couple embarking on a serious relationship, discussion of the terms to apply at parting is almost a contradiction of the shared hopes that have brought them together. There will inevitably be numerous couples, married or unmarried, who have no discussion about ownership and who, perhaps advisedly, make no agreement about it. It would be anomalous, against that background, to create a range of home-buyers who were beyond the pale of equity's assistance in formulating a fair presumed basis for the sharing of beneficial title, simply because they had been honest enough to admit that they never gave ownership a thought or reached any agreement about it."[16]

Apprehension of "real-life" context is crucial, at least according to this recent Court of Appeal judgment. Thus an earlier Court of Appeal decision,[17] where the beneficial shares were quantified on the strict basis of respective direct financial contributions, was distinguished on the basis that it involved "the part-pooling of resources by a middle-aged couple already established in life whose house-purchasing arrangements were clearly regarded by the court as having the same formality as if they had been the subject of a joint venture or commercial partnership".[18]

It follows from this that the modern rules about the acquisition of ownership interests are necessarily framed in a rather open-ended way. Once an equitable interest is successfully asserted through direct contributions, and where there is no evidence of an express intention as to the sizes of the respective shares of the beneficiaries,

"... the duty of the judge is to undertake a survey of the whole course of dealing between the parties relevant to their ownership and occupation of the property and their sharing of its burdens and advantages. Their scrutiny will not confine itself to the limited range of acts of direct contribution of the sort that are needed to found a beneficial interest in the first place. It will take into consideration all conduct which throws light on the question what shares were intended. Only if that search proves inconclusive does the court fall back on the maxim that 'equality is equity' ".[19]

Because the courts now have statutory powers to make property adjustments on divorce which override the principles of property law introduced here, the resulting trust is principally relevant, in a marital relationship, where there is a dispute between the couple and a third party, as in the case where a bank or building society seeks possession of the house because they have defaulted on the mortgage repayments.

In this section we have used the term "resulting trust". In some decisions the term "constructive trust" is also encountered. One can agonise about whether there is a difference between the two; but this is a largely futile exercise. The more a claimant's case relies upon financial contributions to the acquisition costs of a property, the easier it is to see the analogies in the facts with the factual basis of the old-style resulting trust. The more, by contrast, that a claim is assembled on the basis of shared understandings and a course of dealings built up over time between the parties, the more a court is called upon to make use of some model of "fair dealing" or "justice", and some judges prefer to speak of a constructive trust in this situation. Whatever labels are used and old precedents invoked, the basic question is simply this: when, in the absence of a formalised arrangement between the parties, will the courts impose a trust upon one of the parties or award a beneficial entitlement to the other?

When considering the acquisition of interests, the courts continue to waver between allegiance to the old model of formalisation and the new model of presumption and imputation which is based directly on social relationships and sociocultural norms rather than on the "usual terms" written into documents by lawyers (for more general discussion, see Chapter 11, below). In parallel with this, there are two possible main directions for legalisation of this area to take in the future: contractualisation or further legislative imposition of presumed appropriate distributions of property based on social status and social relationships. Contractualisation means people are required to spell out in advance the legal consequences, including the property consequences, of their relationship, and thus, even if the form and content (and underlying rationale) of such agreements may have changed, the relationship of law and society remains structurally rather similar to that in place in the nineteenth century. Alternatively, legislators determine appropriate regimes for solving disputes and awarding shares to disputants. As always, the choice between these two strategies can be posed in conflictual or complementary terms: legislative imposition can be mandatory or something out of which it is possible to opt contractually.

LIFETIME RIGHTS AND OCCUPATION RIGHTS

A certain ambivalence lies at the centre of the English lawyer's way of thinking about rights to land which are less than full, absolute, ownership. As stressed above, the "enjoyment" of land can take two forms: receipt of the rent which land generates or physical enjoyment of the land. If "land" means a house, you can rent it out and pocket the income or live in it yourself. This duality is not peculiar to land. Exactly the same could be said, for example, about a trust of an Old Master, under which someone had, for his or her life, the right to hang the picture at home but not the right to sell it and receive the proceeds of the sale. But the property disputes of recent years which have found their way to the courts, and thus called for a response, have not, for the most part, been about pictures but about houses, and, in particular, about specifying the conditions in which people who live in houses which belong to others can continue to live in them for the duration of their lives, or, at least, for as long as they wish.

In the nineteenth century, most people were tenants or lodgers in the houses they inhabited. Not so with owner-occupation. People who live in houses which belong to other people are more likely to be living there because of some social relationship with the owner which, in the event of a dispute about occupation, must be identified from a spectrum which spans relatives, lovers and people who are simply sharing a house without any sexual or emotional involvement with one another. There have been a large number of reported decisions in this area and a proliferation of conceptual tools for the analysis of such disputes. Thus we find counsel presenting arguments or judges analysing facts in terms of "contractual licence", "personal licence", "equitable licence", "equity", "proprietary estoppel" or just "estoppel". In one case, the owner tries to get a possession order against the occupant and is denied the order because the occupant has an equitable licence to remain. In another, the owner, the court says, is estopped from evicting the occupant because of "equities" which arise in the occupant's favour. This causes anxiety to a student, since, by any yardstick of legal relevance, it seems impossible to see what in the facts of the two cases justifies the deployment of different analytical tools. The answer is perhaps to distinguish between the superficial—and trivial—difference in labels and the underlying continuity in substantive approach. Labelling differences are merely symptomatic of the fact that these kinds of disputes are relatively new and different judges are trying to find a preferred way of talking them through.

Beneath these differences are straightforward differences in circumstances. On the one hand, there are occupants who claim the right to remain based on agreement, whether or not they pay rent to the owner. These can be called contractual licences, though they are not invariably. As we see in Chapter 10, such arrangements are now often regarded as equitable interests capable of binding third parties like purchasers and mortgagees. Imposition of a "contractual" tag upon the relationship requires, of course, something in the facts which can count as consideration to support the owner's promise that the occupant can remain. Sometimes this is impossible, though often it is not, because if the occupant does housework or keeps the garden in order, that can, if the court wishes, be treated as consideration. But more generally, a contractual label may "feel" inappropriate because the relationship between the parties has shifted and drifted over time; is too diffuse, in other words, to be called an "agreement". Here, estoppel or even constructive trust sometimes seem to provide more comfortable means of arriving at awarding lifetime occupation rights to the occupant, especially where the facts are amenable to the conclusion that the occupant has acted to his or her detriment on the understanding that occupation could continue indefinitely. What counts as "detriment" is also a matter for the judgment of the court. We have been told that payment of money is not necessary, and that "lost opportunities" will suffice. Yet it is inescapable that one judge presents as a matter of contract what another presents as a matter of equity or trust. Finally, we should note that this barrage of concepts is not confined to the formulation of lifetime rights but of rights of occupation generally. But it is chiefly in the context of relatively elderly defendants, seeking to remain in occupation of property belonging to someone else who is seeking to evict them, that the higher courts have had to resolve these disputes. This is why it has tended to be the case that successful defendants have been permitted to remain for the rest of their lives.

It is difficult to assess the importance of such indeterminacy in the present practice of the courts. There is nothing new about the judicial attempt to preserve leeway or room for manoeuvre. All that changes is where such flexibility needs to be sought at any point in time. But for the law student oppressed by the need to distill from the cases an analytical certainty usable in the examination room, the deeply engrained pragmatism of English law can be frustrating, even disturbing.

The judicial desire to keep things vague is not new, but where the leeway which vagueness permits is to be found is new. In matters concerning property, and especially title to land, leeway hovered in the margins of formal documents of title. That all these products of the new vagueness, these diffuse rights generated by contract or by equity, are capable of binding purchasers of land would probably not have surprised a nineteenth-century conveyancer, as we shall see. But that such rights could come into existence without any formality, and yet amount to a right to enjoy land for life, would have seemed bizarre and dangerous. Occupants whose rights rested solely on the fact of their occupation, and whose rights did not rest upon legal formulae inscribed on paper, were perfectly familiar to conveyancers. They were the tenants and lodgers mentioned above. But their rights were short-term and relatively fragile in strict legal terms. In the nineteenth-century conveyancer's frame of reference, lifetime rights of occupation were formalised into legal life estates or into leases for lives. That was how things were done. And as we shall see, the 1925 legislation was constructed on the basis that things were done as they should be.

We will need to discuss further below how these new equities potentially mess up the design of the 1925 scheme. As we shall see, what matters to lawyers investigating title as part of their role in managing land transfers is often hypothetical possibilities of the claims of people other than the owner. But it would be misleading to imply that in practice a large number of claims of the type discussed in this section are made through the courts each year. The extension of the basis on which beneficial entitlements to a share in the ownership of property can be established, considered in the previous section, is much more important, although it should also be recognised that at their edges the distinction between these beneficial entitlements and the new equities may become somewhat blurred. The new equities are in many ways solutions tailor-made for particular ensembles of facts which can be seen as giving rise to a demand for justice. As such, strictly irrelevant factors, from a legal point of view, like the relative ages of the parties, may propel a decision in a particular direction while at the same time making it perilous to generalise from it to applications in other cases. It also follows from this characteristic that this type of dispute is less amenable to a legislative solution in terms of the specification of generalised rights than may be the case with claims to beneficial entitlements.

TRUSTS AND OCCUPATION RIGHTS

The pressure on the courts to reformulate the equitable basis of the acquisition of ownership rights took place, for the most part, in the context of disputes about money and financial entitlements rather than occupation. Disputes about occupation as such tended, by contrast, to be routed through a different conceptual terrain, as we have seen. But these separate strands now need to be brought together analytically and as a matter of social policy, because in reality the differences between them are differences only of degree.

For reasons we examine more closely below, the question of the occupation rights of beneficiaries behind trusts has been difficult, because these interests were housed in a framework which, as the 1925 legislation came to be interpreted and applied, sat uncomfortably with the idea that such interests carried with them occupation rights. As we have emphasised repeatedly, this is less surprising once it is recalled that the basic meaning of land ownership in the past was the ownership of the right to receive rent and that occupants were usually, though not invariably, tenants or lodgers. Trusts of land, within this model, were therefore primarily trusts of rents, present and future, and the practical issue which mattered was the machinery for ensuring the beneficial entitlements in relation to receipt of these rents, rather than rights to occupy the physical property itself which was the source of these rents.

For this reason, as we shall see in more detail in Chapter 10, below, the 1925 scheme focused its conveyancing reforms on expanding the scope of equitable interests behind trusts of real property in order to simplify problems of transfer of legal title, but did so by largely ignoring the question of the occupation rights of such beneficiaries. The priority at that time was rather to keep the multiplicity of equitable claims away from the title and therefore away from the concern of third parties dealing with the land, so far as was possible. The result was, to simplify, that the interests of many beneficiaries behind trusts of which land was the initial subject-matter were conceived within this scheme to be interests in the proceeds of sale of the land rather than in the land itself, and pending such a sale, to be interests in the rents and profits accruing from the land. Within such a mode of thought, the linkage of equitable ownership rights and occupation rights was almost completely marginalised. As we shall also see, the strict settlement of land (see pp.84–90, above) received special treatment in 1925 (see pp.229–231, below), but this, too, proved to be of little relevance for the world which has since emerged.

With the rise of owner-occupation and the separate but linked shifts towards social norms of co-ownership underscored by mortgage-based financing of acquisition costs funded out of earned income, this model became increasingly obscure. Put simply, it came by the 1950s to seem entirely artificial to suggest that beneficiaries behind a trust which arose where a house was acquired for the purpose of occupation did not have a right to occupy the property unless they happened also to be trustees (*i.e.* on the legal title). The courts solved these problems pragmatically for the most part, modifying the operation of the 1925 framework by insisting on taking account of the purpose behind the trust, and this same notion of purpose also became the yardstick for guiding the exercise of the court's section 30 jurisdiction in a dispute between co-owners and/or third parties about whether or not the property should be sold.[20]

The Law Commission has now sought, in designing the Trusts of Land and Appointment of Trustees Act 1996, which came into force on January 1, 1997, to modify the statutory basis of the law in this area in order to bring it more closely into line with emerging judicial practice. We look more closely in chapter 10 at how this Act has remodelled the basic design of the 1925 scheme for land subjected to some kind of trust. The central point to grasp here is that the new Act moves into a pivotal position the concept of a "trust of land", in relation to which the beneficiaries' interests are no longer treated as interests in the rents or in the capital which the land might realise on a sale, but as interests in the land itself. This reconceptualisation clears the way for linking together explicitly beneficial rights to the property and occupation rights, and for developing mechanisms and procedures through which beneficiaries can claim or defend such occupation rights, whether or not they are on the title and therefore "double up" as trustees.

The 1996 Act both codifies some of the general equitable rules regarding the powers of trustees of land and expands on them. In particular, s.6(2) of the Act gives trustees the power to decide to transfer the title to land to beneficiaries of full age, expanding on the previous rule[21] that trust property should be transferred to adult beneficiaries where all the beneficiaries were adult and made a unanimous request for such a transfer of title. More generally, the Act brings adult beneficiaries, using two different formulae in different contexts—"of full age and absolutely entitled" or, in some cases, "beneficially entitled to an interest in possession"—more fully into the picture, by setting out a range of entitlements and possibilities for their involvement in decision-making relating to the administration of the trust. Trustees are to have wide powers to purchase land for investment, occupation by a beneficiary or any other reason (s.6(4)); but in exercising their powers they are to "have regard to the rights of the beneficiaries" (s.6(5)), whatever that means. However, all the statutory powers can be limited expressly in a "disposition" (*i.e.* an *inter vivos* trust or a will) (s.8), either by excluding the power entirely or making its exercise by the trustees subject to a consent. The Act also gives to trustees wide scope to delegate their powers to adult beneficiaries.

A duty to consult adult beneficiaries who are beneficially entitled to an interest in possession regarding the exercise of functions is retained (s.11(1)(a)) but this can be excluded by the settlor or testator expressly, and many solicitors are likely to take advantage of this opportunity in order to avoid giving what they may see as unnecessary ammunition to recalcitrant beneficiaries.

Some of the new Act is relatively technical reform. Apart from the elimination of the doctrine of conversion (the 1925 idea that the claims of beneficiaries were against the proceeds of sale rather than the land itself; see further pp.231–236, below), which had in any event become an archaism largely caught up with eighteenth- and nineteenth-century inheritance issues, little of substance has been changed at the practical level for settlors and testators who are using lawyers to create their own trusts of land expressly. This is because most of these statutory provisions operate as default provisions—they will take effect unless settlors or testators indicate otherwise. However, as before, the default provisions regarding powers and duties—or "functions" as they are described in the Act—will necessarily come into play where the trust of land is statutory rather than express. This will be significant in precisely those cases which were so awkward to accommodate within the 1925 scheme—the cases where the trust came into existence in the first place as an implied trust (a trust imposed "after the fact" by the court) rather than a purpose-built trust created in a lawyer's office with the usual formalities.

Occupation rights under the 1996 Act

Of more interest, perhaps, are the provisions relating to rights of occupation. These can be seen as a legislative response to the gulf which had emerged since the 1950s between the texts of the 1925 legislation and the judicial interpretation of these texts. Creative interpretation had been required in certain family disputes in order to squeeze the statutory words into something which approximated to what could be presumed to be the intention of the parties to the dispute. This is now tackled head on (in ss.12 and 13), although the prolixity of s.13 may have stored up some hostages to fortune.

The conceptual distinction between rights in possession (*i.e.* present rather than future interests) and rights to occupation is retained. A beneficiary who has an interest in possession is entitled to occupy the land at any time if at that time "the purposes of the trust include making the land available for his occupation" (section.12(1)(a)) or if "the land is held by the trustees so as to be so available" (paragraph (b))—a fairly disastrously drafted paragraph whose meaning is open to several different readings, subjective and objective. But this will not apply if the land "is either unavailable or unsuitable" for occupation by the beneficiary (s.12(2)), and all of this is subject to a long list of exclusions and restrictions of the right to occupy, which is set out in s.13.

The section is concerned with the basic problem of how to square the right to occupy with the situation where there may be more than one beneficiary with an interest in possession. In the traditional scheme, as we have seen, this problem was not in the foreground, in so far as many trusts and settlements had been essentially mechanisms for apportioning rents. But occupation-related issues have been foregrounded in the litigation of the last 40 years or so, and it is no doubt appropriate that this has been addressed in this legislation. The starting point is that the trustees must let in at least one of the beneficiaries with concurrent present interests (if, presumably, at least one so requests) (s.13(1)). In exercising this discretion, trustees must not unreasonably exclude an eligible beneficiary nor impose unreasonable restrictions on the entitlement to occupy (s.13(2)(a) and (b)). Trustees can impose conditions regarding a beneficiary's occupation, but they must be reasonable (s.13(3)). They include, specifically, requiring the occupying beneficiary to pay outgoings or expenses in relation to the occupation, and to take on any other obligation in relation to occupation of the land (s.13(5)(a) and (b)). Section 13(4) sets out "matters to which trustees are to have regard" in making these decisions (presumably these are intended to orient the notion of reasonableness introduced in this section). These are: the intention of the settlor or testator; the purposes for which the land is held; the "circumstances and wishes" of potentially eligible beneficiaries. Where occupation entitlements are excluded or restricted, conditions can be imposed on occupying beneficiaries involving payment of compensation to the excluded beneficiary (in effect an occupation rent) or involving foregoing a payment or benefit to which the occupying beneficiary would otherwise be entitled under the trust (s.13(6)).

Existing occupants of land cannot be involuntarily prevented from continued occupation through exercise of these powers without the consent of the court (s.13(7)).

The expansion of powers, discretions or "functions" is complemented by an expansion of the jurisdiction of the court from the existing s.30 of the LPA. Section 14 enables any trustee of land or any beneficiary to apply to the court, which is empowered to make orders regarding the exercise of any of the trustees' functions (which includes dispensing with any consent or consultation requirements), and to declare the nature or extent of a person's interests in the property.

A statutory framework is now provided to guide courts in the exercise of their discretion, though the list adds little to the existing case law and does little to resolve the tensions already visible in it. Courts are to have regard to: the intention of the settlor or testator; the purposes underlying the trust; the welfare of minors either in occupation or who have a reasonable expectation of occupying; the interests of secured creditors of beneficiaries. Where the application concerns the exercise of trustees' s.13 powers permitting a beneficiary to occupy, the court is also to take account of the "circumstances and wishes" of beneficiaries who have occupation entitlements. Regarding other applications (except the exercise of the trustees' power to transfer title to adult beneficiaries who are absolutely entitled), the court is also to have regard to the "circumstances and wishes" of adult beneficiaries entitled to an interest in possession or the majority by value of these interests where these circumstances and wishes diverge. A special regime is preserved for applications by trustees in bankruptcy (s.15(4) and Sch.3).

We return in Chapter 10 to those parts of the 1996 Act, and subsequently the Land Registration Act 2002, which substantially modify the design of the 1925 framework in relation to the conveyancing consequences of fragmentation of title. What needs to be emphasised at this point is that the 1996 Act did not set out to modify the modern methods for the acquisition of ownership and occupation rights. These difficult questions, which as we have seen are by no means simply technical, remain open to debate. Perhaps the most crucial is that of community property. The questions of implied trusts, estoppel interests and so on remain, and continue to give rise to difficult decisions in the event of disputes reaching the courts. In terms of legislative policy, the debate has recently shifted across or into entitlements to pension rights on the breakup of marriage and/or non-marital cohabitation relationships. Whether legislation is appropriate in this area remains debatable—the question of freedom of contract remains of some application here, as the rise of pre-nuptial agreements against the backdrop of community property legislation in the United States indicates.

SOCIAL JUSTICE AND PRIVATE ORDERING

The old law on settlements is, increasingly, ignored and regarded as irrelevant. But some of it contained important lessons about legal practice and about its relation to adjudication which may need to be recovered from the detritus of the past. Specifically, these concern the relationship between status and contract in relation to the property aspects of or implied by domestic relationships.

In the nineteenth century, Sir Henry Maine made famous the idea that the movement of all societies has been from status to contract:

> "All the forms of Status taken notice of in the Law of Persons were derived from, and to some extent are still coloured by, the powers and privileges anciently residing in the Family. If then we employ Status, agreeably with the usage of the best writers, to signify these personal conditions only, and avoid applying the term to such conditions as are the immediate or remote result of agreement, we may say that the movement of progressive societies has hitherto been a movement from Status to Contract" (Maine, 1917, p.100).

"Status" meant that social relationships were organised in terms of ascribed rather than achieved roles. A wife or child had the status or occupied the role of a wife or a child and should be dealt with by the law on that basis. In theory, the contract model, by contrast, meant that social relationships were organised by means of legally enforceable agreements between individuals—which meant that children tended to be excluded from the scope of this new framework, being below the age of capacity to form legally binding agreements. On this widely held view, traditional society was a society of status relationships, and access to or enjoyment of property was largely determined by birth. Nineteenth-century society, as Maine saw it, was characterised by a progressive contractualisation of social relationships and an erosion of status (ascription) as the basis of establishing interpersonal obligations. Some observers have argued that the social-welfare state of the post-War world has witnessed a counter-movement from contract to status. This is said to involve the displacement of the contract model by a new status model, recast, by comparison with its former version, in a more clearly emphasised social-welfare way in which the public interest is given more emphasis. This has the consequence that the traditional division between the public and the private is eroded and the state (whether by legislation and modern bureaucratic administration, or through the vehicle of adjudication) comes to interfere in or regulate with increasing frequency what had come, by the nineteenth century, to be regarded as the private domain free from outside interference. What then results is a kind of mutual antagonism between two models of social ordering: a liberal paradigm which stresses freedom of contract, the primacy of private property and "formal" equality before the law, and a social-welfare paradigm which stresses the "real" or "material" inequalities which underpin the liberal paradigm, and the importance of law and the state in redressing the balance through systems of social support in the interest of social justice.

In one sense, the issues to which these academic debates alert us remain central to the current policy agenda. To take some examples: what role should be played by pre-nuptial agreements relating to property matters? Should the courts be expected to enforce them, or to substitute their own decisions about the distribution of property as between divorcing couples, based on criteria other than those which the contracting parties had considered relevant? To what extent should the fate of children be regarded as a matter where the state should (at the beginning or in the end) decide (on matters of custody, property, etc.) or on the other hand should this too be left to parents to determine, either in advance of or on dissolution of the marriage? Are children to be regarded by the law as the property of their parents?

In the current regime for divorce, mediation is available to facilitate decision-making. Mediation, too, aims at (though does not always succeed in achieving) consensual outcomes— agreements which, as a form of "private ordering", bear some structural resemblance to contracts. Should these be allowed to be decisive or should the state, through its jurisdiction, review such outcomes in the public interest and, whether or not children are involved, insist on imposing its own view which might in some cases contradict what the adult parties to the dispute have decided either by themselves or through a mediation process? Critics of the contracting or private ordering model (within which it is in some ways sensible, as we have suggested, to include mediation) say that it leads to inconsistent results (because different individuals can agree to different outcomes); that it inhibits the development of general rules in the light of newly revealed social issues and problems emerging through the litigation process (because it channels interpersonal conflict into the private domain); and that it ignores the real problem in domestic conflicts, which is often (though not always) the inequality of bargaining power between the disputants (see Fiss, 1984).

While there are some issues of substance here, there is also a sense in which this is an arid dispute between models which are conceived in too abstract a way. Those who advocate the contract model—under which the agreements made by individuals should be allowed to determine their futures (which is close to the pattern of some of the underlying assumptions of the nineteenth century in relation to property)—have to recognise that what may be involved here is an unacceptable inequality of bargaining power leading to the formation of "unfair" contracts. In other words, there may well be scope for pre-nuptial and pre-partnership agreements, and perhaps the social-welfare emphasis of current discussions, notably those undertaken in academic circles, has obscured this, but there is still a need to consider how to balance status versus contract so far as innocent third parties (*e.g.* children) are concerned, and how to take account of what are widely known to be inequalities of bargaining power, which extend, of course, to relationships beyond the conventional marital relationship.

On the other side of the debate, where the contractual model is found objectionable, it needs to be recognised that any system of regulation by general classification or description will impose what is assumed to be the typical or model case on all cases, and that this will result in inappropriate results or outcomes. This is not exactly a new problem; the nineteenth-century world of private ordering as organised through lawyers was heavily governed by the accumulated weight of conveyancers' precedents and the practical "wisdom" based on experience which they supposedly contained—the wealth of clauses it was "advisable" or "appropriate" to insert into a settlement which themselves presupposed a society of status relationships. But the individual circumstances of the parties to such settlements, the particular social relationships between those involved, could often override the lawyers' habitual caution. General norms, in other words, did not prevent the creation of bespoke agreements. Modern legislative, administrative and adjudicative resolutions necessarily tend more towards consistency in rule-formulation and/or -application, and what is perceived as inconsistent adjudication is as often criticised for the arbitrariness or prejudice which, it is supposed, must underlie a lack of uniformity as it is commended for its sensitivity to the particularities of individual cases. And this is why the question which refuses to go away is the extent to which, whatever regime is adopted, it remains permissible to opt out of it; that is, to substitute by private ordering a particular regime for the individual parties which will prevail over general schemes, whether legislative or adjudicative in origin, which would apply in default of such arrangements.

Private ordering in the present context is primarily geared to spelling out entitlements and obligations in relation to property in advance of a possible breakdown of a relationship or joint venture. In this sense it shares many features of the old separation agreements, but, unlike these (which were agreements entered into as part of and at the point of winding up or redefining the relationship between a married couple), the current policy issue is whether parties (and not just married couples) should be encouraged to enter into such agreements when embarking on a homesharing arrangement, and whether the courts should be encouraged to hold the parties to the terms set out in such agreements.

The current regime dealing with unfair contracts, set out in the Unfair Contract Terms Act 1977, provides a model of limited if any use for these purposes. This regime is primarily geared to regulating the blanket use of clauses in consumer contracts designed to limit or exclude the liability of suppliers of products, in circumstances where competition and the market provide an insufficient guarantee of genuine freedom of contract for consumers, either because of the ignorance of consumers or because of *de facto* monopolies enjoyed by suppliers.

Private ordering in the sphere of owner-occupation, by contrast, is exposed to the risk that interpersonal inequalities, shored up by social and economic structural inequalities of class and gender, will be reproduced directly in private ordering arrangements.

Again, there are precedents for handling this kind of problem, notably the old law relating to unconscionable bargains—for example, the ability of courts to set aside bargains made by "expectant heirs". These were often rooted in perceptions of status, and provide limited assistance today if a regime of private ordering is to flourish. Moreover, empowering the courts to scrutinise private arrangements with reference to too broad a notion of unconscionability undermines the rationale of private ordering in the first place.

A more attractive approach in some respects is to move towards a procedural approach to potential unfairness. A substantial body of law has emerged in recent years in which the equitable notion of "undue influence" has been reinvigorated.[22] While this has so far been primarily concerned with the relationship between financial institutions and borrowers' wives, it is

capable of wider application. Following on from this is the need
for each party to a privately negotiated arrangement to have
independent legal advice. A role here could be conceived, too,
for government and/or the Law Commission, in developing
model or "off-the-shelf" agreements. If private ordering is
encouraged, practitioners will develop these in any case. Such
model agreements would themselves serve to foster a notion of
"good practice", against which particular agreements can be
assessed, and which can serve as a reference point for lawyers
where both parties have access to their own legal advice. The
advantage of this kind of approach is that it avoids some of the
rigidities which tend to accompany legislative schemes, thereby
permitting more customised arrangements. At the same time, it
has the potential to circumvent some of the arbitrariness which
inevitably accompanies adjudication in this area.

7

TENANCIES, LEASES AND MORTGAGES

So far we have outlined the principal ways in which, in the past, title to land could be fragmented in English law, and indicated the general strategy pursued in 1925 for overcoming the complexities which these practices of fragmentation generated for the transfer of title. The machinery adopted to implement this strategy, and the reasons why what was adopted was chosen, are examined in later chapters. First we must introduce a further range of property interests, which from one point of view can be regarded as "encumbrances" upon a title. That is, we are concerned with a range of "rights", which, in the English lawyer's scheme of things, are property rights and not mere contractual or personal rights, since they possess some of the attributes of durability and transmissibility singled out above, but which in some way or other amount to something less than the unqualified right of enjoyment which lawyers have associated with holding an unencumbered freehold estate in land.

In this chapter, we consider tenancies, leases, which are a particular form of tenancy, and mortgages, which can, in the modern law, take the form of a lease. In the following chapter, we consider a number of rights and liabilities which can be latched on to titles, to benefit them or to encumber them, all of which concern the manner in which landowners are entitled to use the land which they own.

Attention has already been drawn to the historical importance of the rent relation. As we have said, most of the varied legal forms which the relation assumed in the past have now been eclipsed. What remains is the tenancy. Rent is not an essential ingredient of what lawyers mean by a tenancy, although almost invariably the relation between landlord and tenant will involve the payment of rent by the tenant to the landlord. But what does the lawyer mean by "rent"? It is the "annual profit arising out of lands and tenements corporeal", a profit which can, and usually does, consist of money, "or of money's worth, as, for example, of arms, horses, corn, or of other things" (Bullen, 1899, p.20). Rent "must issue out of the land, and not be part of the land itself; so that the grass, herbage, or other vesture cannot properly constitute a rent". Rent is the reservation of a thing "not in being", "to be newly created or produced out of the land or tenement demised" (*ibid.*). These distinctions between being and non-being are perhaps the closest English lawyers, with their reluctance for speculation, came to articulating the metaphysical undercore of their thought.

TENANCIES AND LEASES

A tenancy could perhaps be called a temporary ownership right: "ownership" in the sense that, while it lasts, the tenant has exclusive use of the property; "temporary" in the sense that at some time in the future these rights will cease and the right to possess and enjoy the land will revert to the landlord. Secondly, as we shall see, a tenancy is a form of "conditional" ownership, in that the relationship between landlord and tenant usually involves obligations which impose duties on both parties relating to the manner in which the tenant may enjoy the property during the time that he has exclusive possession of it.

Of all the interests in land considered in this book, the tenancy is the most difficult to classify by means of the distinction between fragmentation of and encumbrance upon title. There are two reasons for this. First, it is a matter of perspective: it all depends on which way you look at it. A lawyer whose client wants to buy a landlord's title views a tenancy as an encumbrance on the title he has to investigate for his purchaser. It is an interest adverse to the title he wants to buy; it limits the enjoyment of the land by the person who has the title, and the lawyer's task is to investigate the extent of that limit. By contrast, a lawyer whose client wants to buy the tenancy approaches the tenancy as a title in its own right. His concern here will be primarily to ascertain the extent of the enjoyment afforded by the tenancy viewed as a title, and the conditions attached to that enjoyment. Secondly, the temporary nature of the relationship between landlord and tenant varies considerably, depending upon the nature of the arrangement upon which both have embarked. Some tenancies, in a practical sense, are much more like titles in their own right than others. If we cease to view the opposition between fragmentation of title and encumbrance on title as a rigid either/or, and dissolve the opposition into a spectrum of possibilities, we can say that tenancies range from being very close to absolute ownership, in a practical sense, to being very minor and temporary encumbrances upon title.

The extent of the involvement of lawyers in the creation of a relationship between landlord and tenant varied considerably in the past. In some cases, their stylised drafting skills were lavishly deployed in formalising the relationship. But in many other cases tenancies were completely informal, without lawyers being involved in their formation or their subsequent course. Such tenancies, from the practical point of view of the lawyer, were essentially encumbrances on the landlord's title, things to be checked out on a transfer of that title, and, it should be added, encumbrances of a type which were readily observable and which caused relatively little difficulty in practice. We will see later that it was the existence of formal tenancies as encumbrances on the landlord's title which presented more difficulty from the conveyancing point of view. In modern conditions, the growth of various regimes of regulation of landlord-tenant relationships has increased the involvement of lawyers—and the degree of formalisation—in most of these relationships.

The "lease" is a "formalised" tenancy. It is this device which lawyers have in mind when they describe a tenancy as a "term of years absolute". It is leases rather than tenancies in general which are often best grasped as an instance of fragmentation of title. In the past, indeed, the lease really was another way of carving "lesser" interests out of the largest interest, the fee simple. Such leases could be carved up in exactly the same way as fee simples, as where leases were granted for successive lives especially by the Church of England and by some of the great landowning colleges of Oxford and Cambridge. And this is why, in 1925, it was provided that the only legal estate in land which could exist in the future, alongside the fee simple absolute in possession, was the term of years absolute, *i.e.* the lease.

The legal concept of a lease involves two principal requirements. First, for a valid lease to be created, it must give to the lessee exclusive possession of the land or buildings which are the subject-matter of the lease. "Exclusive possession" means, principally, possession exclusive of the lessor, and is the yardstick for distinguishing a leasehold estate from a lesser right, from easements in particular, as we see in the next chapter. Secondly, it is said, the maximum duration of the lease—the term which it creates—must be known at the outset if a valid lease is to be created. So instruments purporting to grant leases of buildings in London "for the duration of the [Second World] War" were held not to create legal leases,[23] but mere tenancies terminable at short notice by the landlord. Finally, it is provided by statute that a "deed" is required to create a term valid at law of over three years.[24]

A lease is a conveyance of title. Therefore, much of what needs to be said about the law of leases is discussed below when the role of lawyers in the management of transfers of title to land is examined. Moreover, it is obvious that in practical terms, a very long lease—say for 999 years—is at first sight a conveyance of title not much different from that obtained by a conveyance of a fee simple. (We will see in due course, however, that there is a difference which will normally arise in practice, because, while a lease must have a maximum duration, it need not have a minimum duration. There is a range of ways in which leases can terminate ahead of time, which is rarely the case—though it is not impossible—in a conveyance of a fee simple.)

In this century, a substantial body of functionally differentiated statute law has grown up around the landlord-tenant relationship, such that today the nineteenth century rules have limited—though still very important—practical application. But to get the subject as a whole into perspective, it is necessary to look back to the past. In historical terms, the landlord-tenant relationship is, perhaps, from a social as well as legal point of view, the most important one examined in this book. While all lessees are tenants, not all tenants are lessees. The formal definitional rules stated above apply to all tenants, if a little artificially, but they are really formulated with lessees in mind. We can clarify this by examining the legal and social historical contexts of the relationship.

The principal contextual distinction is between the rural and urban sectors, or, slightly differently as we shall see, between agricultural land—farms—and housing. What follows is necessarily overgeneralised, because there were considerable regional differences in landholding forms, but it does delineate a framework which many people used to think did hold generally true, and on the basis of which assumption the regulatory framework of the twentieth century has been constructed.

The rural context: farms[25]

Our discussion of settlements of land, above, stressed that what was fundamentally being provided for in such settlements was the distribution of rents through time among family members. Some of these rents—in many cases, the bulk of them—took the form of agricultural or farm rents. The "broad acres" of a landed estate were in fact composed of a number of farms, each yielding a rent paid by the tenant farmer who worked the farm. Until changes which came in the wake of the First World War, in which the scions of landed families fell alongside the sons of tenant farmers in the trenches by the Somme, such tenancies, to judge from the evidence, commonly remained in one farming family over several generations. But such tenancies were very often extremely informal, something those devoted to the cause of improving the state of agriculture in England criticised with growing intensity from the middle of the nineteenth century. Why were they informal and why was this informality criticised by agricultural reformers?

People of the time called these farming tenancies "tenancies at will", as do today's historians. Strictly, lawyers call them "yearly periodic tenancies". But the same thing is meant by both, for a simple reason: the legal conceptualisation of the relationship was largely a matter of clothing fact with right. The landowner could terminate the tenancy at his pleasure, but, given the nature of farming, at pleasure would normally mean giving notice on certain days of the year, and allowing the tenant six months, principally in order to gather such crops as he may have planted. At one level this meant that the exiguous legal structure of this relationship afforded much social power to the landowner, whose ability to terminate the tenancy at pleasure might hang like a sword of Damocles over the heads of his tenant farmers. But the legal relationship was, for the most part, enveloped in a broader normative framework, as well as being underpinned by the brute fact of mutual dependency. The landowner, in many cases, was principally concerned with the long-term preservation of his rental income. In a time of severe agricultural depression, for example, the landlord might do better to allow his tenant farmers to go into arrears rather than exercise his legal rights, in the hope that, over time, things would balance out. Resident landlords, who had to coexist over time with their tenants, were likely to be particularly subject to these diffuse normative pressures. This, more than anything, was perhaps the problem underlying absentee landlords, most notably in Ireland. An English landowner's Irish estates were, all too often, merely a source of rental income and not in any larger, more normative sense the fulcrum of a set of face-to-face social relationships, in which legal rights, social norms and political power were all interwoven in a largely undifferentiated way.

The modern regulatory scheme for agricultural tenancies springs principally from the problems of Ireland. It is interesting to note that legislation was required, because, as noted above, mid-nineteenth-century reformers thought that most of what was needed could be achieved by formalising the relationship by means of a lease. Let us return to why they thought this to be so.

Informal tenancies were largely governed by traditional localised norms, so that lawyers were commonly faced with a *fait accompli*. But in the nature of things, these norms might be rather diffuse and vague. As between landowner and tenant farmer, rights and duties might not always be clearly spelt out. People interested in agricultural improvement in the nineteenth century—in improving farming methods, in increasing the potential yield of land and in methods of improving the manner of storage of its produce—saw the formal lease as a mechanism for spelling out in advance precisely who was responsible for what, and for enshrining in legal terms how the land was to be utilised. Those who advocated the adoption of leases hoped, by formalising all this, to focus the minds of the parties at the time of entering into the transaction. The traditional tenancy, because of its informal character, was seen as an obstacle to improvement in these respects. Moreover, its vagueness, it was said, enveloped the tenant farmer with a cluster of disincentives. Given that only a sense of fair play, and not the law, deterred the landowner from terminating the relationship at will, what incentive was there for the tenant farmer to engage in agricultural improvement? Why should he build barns, drain land, clear wasteland and so on, if his landlord could turn him out at any time and reap the benefit of the improvement himself? These questions, which were posed with most intensity in the Irish context, because, on the whole, absentee landlords behaved that much worse, shaped the form taken by legislative interventions. A regime providing some security of tenure was laid down (see now principally the Agricultural Holdings Act 1948, as amended); and provision was made for "tenant right", whereby the tenant farmer could be compensated on the termination of his tenancy for improvements made during his time.

Both could largely have been accommodated through the adoption of formal leases; that they were not was largely due to inertia. In the face of inertia, a general legislative framework was established.

The urban context: housing[26]

It is even harder to generalise with any accuracy about the legal forms through which the occupation of houses was arranged. The most that can be said at present is that the arrangements which we now examine were common in some towns, cities or regions, and that these forms, whether real or merely perceived to be so by legislators and reformers, have left their imprint upon the framework of the present law.

Whatever the position in remoter times, when most people lived in the country, the urbanisation of England in the nineteenth century meant, among other things, that farmland adjacent to what were once small towns became the target of urban development. People who owned such land at the time that pressure for development came upon it—whether industrial or residential (indeed, obviously, the two went together)—were faced with two choices. They could sell the land to a developer; but such a course of action would involve the problem of finding alternative safe places for the proceeds of sale. So the course which was widely adopted was not to sell up entirely but to grant leases of land wanted for development. Such leases would draw upon all the expertise of lawyers, and contain detailed plans for how the land let to the builder should be built upon. Lawyers called these leases "building leases", which were typically of 60 or 90 years' duration. Under such leases, the builder/developer would be responsible for erecting a building or a number of buildings upon a particular site, and detailed provision might be made for the manner of their construction and continuing maintenance, even down to the type of subsequent letting of the buildings which was to be permitted, for example, the social status of permitted occupants. The lease would reserve a "ground rent" for the landowner. Relative to the rental income which the building, once constructed, could yield to the builder, or the capital value of the lease if he sold it on (see below), this ground rent would constitute a small amount per annum. From the landowner's financial point of view, its significance lay simply in the fact that, by comparison with the yield which could be derived from agricultural land, urbanised exploitation was a much more intensive form of exploitation so far as revenue generation was concerned. The broad acres of rural England might be replaced by stretches of suburbia which seem to us to epitomise England, or, for that matter, by tenements which, in their way, also do: the ground rent for each parcel might be small, but such a process of development permitted many more such rents to be created. When many agricultural rents came under pressure in the 1880s, it was those landowners who owned many ground rents who best withstood the storm: a few families did. While landowners were unconcerned to encase their rental incomes from farmland in the guarantees of law, their urban rental incomes from ground rents were wrapped up in as much law as you could get at the time. But what happened to these buildings, once constructed?

The speculative, "capitalist" builder was faced with a choice of his own. He could sell on the term (as lawyers say, "assign" it), or he could rent out the property. If he sold on, the capital value would be assessed in relation to the potential future rental yield, in the light of the outstanding term of the lease. As we shall see, it is all different today.

So in the urban context we encounter two rental incomes generated from the same physical entity: the ground rent and the house or occupancy rent, whether actual—because the house is let out—or notional—that is, a rent which serves simply as a measure for calculating the capital value of the lease.

In a practical sense, then, there were two different things which could be "owned" over a long period of time: the ground rent on the one hand, the building on the other, which is why you find lawyers at the time talking about house owners when the interest is in fact leasehold and subject to the payment of ground rent.

When we come to the nature of the position of those using such houses or buildings as residences, it is necessary to draw distinctions, however roughly, in terms of social class, as people did at the time. Broadly, middle-class families considered it sensible to embark on formal leases, though often of fairly short duration, in much the same way, no doubt, as it is thought sensible today for anyone with a job to buy a house or flat. In many industrialised parts of the country, working-class housing, by contrast, was primarily arranged through informal weekly tenancies, in principle determinable on the giving of one week's notice by either side. Rent books recording payment (or non-payment) of rent came to be used by rent collectors, which served as evidence of the tenancy and, more importantly, could serve as a testimonial for a good tenant seeking a tenancy from a new landlord (Dennis, 1984, p.170). In the twentieth century, legislation has made such rent books mandatory.

The shape of the present regulatory framework, mainly derived from statute, arises, as we have said, largely from these practices of the past. In 1915, the War Cabinet sought to keep down the wages of its munitions workers through a mandatory regime controlling the rents which landlords could charge their tenants, and the interest rates which mortgagees (*i.e.* lenders on mortgage) could charge their borrowers (that is, in terms of the assumptions of the time, landlords of working-class houses who had borrowed money on mortgages secured on the houses that they owned). This statutory scheme protecting tenants survived the war more or less permanently, though some governments have sought, prospectively, to "decontrol" rents, and their successors to reimpose controls (see Daunton, 1987, pp.26–32).

Statutory control has had two principal elements: public control of the level of rent and security of tenure for the tenant. Public officials have been empowered to set rent levels for a particular property if so requested by either landlord or tenant (though the precise criteria such officials are to use have varied over time) and statutes have imposed a range of limits upon the landlords' ability to regain possession of the rented property, at the end of the contracted term, through the judicial process.

The details of this history are beyond our present scope; with one exception, this can be regarded as a quite separate body of statute law, throwing up the usual problems of statutory interpretation for the courts, but with minimal impact, despite its practical significance, for the general fabric of English land law. This is signalled in the terminology which lawyers use today in describing tenancies which come within one or other of these statutory regimes: the "contractual" tenancy is contrasted with the "statutory" tenancy, which indicates the contrast between the relationship actually bargained for—say a one-year tenancy taken by a group of students—and the relationship imposed upon the parties by the statutory scheme, which comes into effect when the "contractual" tenancy expires.

There has been much debate over whether the imposition of such statutory controls is directly responsible for the overall decline in the private rented housing sector, though this decline is in any case unevenly distributed across the country. Rent control is a disincentive only if, first, the officials controlling rents set them at uneconomic levels. What is uneconomic depends, secondly, upon what alternative opportunities are available for investment in urban land, and a comparison of the returns from such investments with the returns from alternative sources of investment, such as shares. To the extent that the substance of litigation can serve as an indicator to what is the major disincentive (and here, as anywhere else in the law, that is very problematic), it is security of tenure which has most troubled private landlords, and which has led to attempts to find ways of circumventing statutory control. This is not surprising. From the landlord's point of view, rent control affects the level of income that land will yield; any established system of official decision-making on rent levels within a particular town or region will, over time, enable permissible rent levels to become relatively predictable and therefore calculable in advance. But security of tenure is not so calculable, it involves a level of contingency analogous to that involving certain kinds of leases in the past.

Suppose in the past someone bought a freehold estate which was subject to a lease for two successive lives. The price would take account of the rent reserved under the lease, and the contingency that "full" enjoyment of the land by the purchaser would depend on the duration of the lives in question. The purchaser took a gamble: if the lives were long-lived, his freehold would remain in reversion for a long period; if both died soon after the purchase, the lease would quickly be at an end and the purchaser would then be free to sell unencumbered. The effect of security of tenure imposed by statute is broadly the same, with the added contingency, operating in the landlord's favour, that the tenant might decide to move out and thereby terminate the statutory protection of the tenancy.

In their nature, the old leases for lives were voluntarily created by an owner of the estate at some point in time. By contrast, their modern equivalents are imposed by statute, and where statute imposes, owners of property often endeavour, with the help of their lawyers, to find a way around the imposition. So the attempt was made to find ways through which residential property could be exploited commercially to yield an income without the label of "landlord and tenant" being attached by the courts to the relationship between owner and resident. This led, in other words, to pressure upon the definition of the concept of "tenancy" in English law.

Initially, the question was presented in terms of the distinction between commercial and non-commercial, especially family, arrangements. If someone allowed his brother to live in a house which he owned, in return for the payment of a weekly sum of money, the courts described the arrangement as a contractual licence not a tenancy, with the result that statutory control did not apply. This approach, however, suggested that any commercial arrangement would fall within the statutory scheme, at least where, under the arrangement, the resident obtained, in fact or by express agreement, exclusive possession of the premises in question. This led in turn to a greater formalisation of commercial residential lettings, where the principal technical aim was to construct an agreement under which the resident would not be permitted exclusive possession of the property. These were, and are, known as "non-exclusive occupation" agreements, under which the landlord purports to reserve the right to confer the right to possession of the premises upon someone other than the contracting residents. The effect of these agreements has been much litigated. The House of Lords has held that the crucial question for the courts to ask in interpreting them is whether, taking all the elements of the actual relationship into account, the resident is in practice a lodger, being supplied with services by the landlord, or a tenant with exclusive occupation.[27] If the latter, then the relationship is within the scheme of statutory control. Put in other terms, the lower courts have been urged to view with suspicion these blatant attempts at avoiding statutory control, and to concentrate upon the substance rather than the form of the transaction between owner and resident. This can involve completely disregarding "unreal" or "sham" clauses in written agreements which the courts do not consider represent the true character of the transaction between the owner and the resident.

LEASES AND LAWYERS

Three principal sets of questions have exercised lawyers regarding the contents of a lease and their legal consequences. The first set concerns what provisions should be put in a lease and the manner in which these should be formalised. The second involves the question how a lease can be terminated, which in turn divides into two different scenarios: the mechanisms available for consensual termination by landlord and tenant on the one hand, termination "ahead of time" as an additional remedial device for landlords on the other. The third concerns the legal effect of the contents of a lease once either landlord or tenant transfers his interest to another.

It must first be stressed that the contents of a lease constitute a kind of private law, where lawyers create the regime to which landlord and tenant are to be subject. Here, as more generally with the preparation of all land transfer documentation, the expertise of the lawyer is essentially formulaic. The courts have had very little to do with setting the terms of the relationship, although legislative intervention has now made a difference in certain areas. No general rights and duties can usefully be said to be imposed by common law upon the landlord-tenant relationship as such, beyond a very small number imposed in specific, rather narrowly drawn contexts. The common law tradition must be understood as essentially abstentionist in this area. It is for the parties to create their private law.

From this point of view, the repairing covenant is perhaps the most important item in a lease. Buildings in the English climate are prone to all kinds of dilapidation. Wherever there is a lease, good legal sense suggests that attention should be given to the allocation of responsibility for repairs and maintenance of the fabric of the building. If you look at the pages of the specialist books on landlord and tenant, acres of words are devoted to the subject of repair. Nearly all of this learning is concerned, at bottom, with the question of formulae. What forms of words will make the lessor or the lessee responsible for renewing the roof or the windows and so on? It is not a matter of law versus policy, rather a matter of style.

In a lease of any significant duration, the repair obligations are commonly placed upon the lessee, whether the lease be of commercial premises or of residential property. The precise form these repair obligations take varies, as does the extent. Specifying the parts of the building to which they extend is essentially a matter of the formulae, and that is why so much learning on the subject is described in the lawbooks. Once, however, the answer to that is ascertained—and often there will be no room for argument because the lessor's lawyer has done his job properly (or, to put it the other way round, if there is, he has not)—the role of the court is simply to enforce the covenant where the lessee allows the buildings to fall into disrepair. Directly, the court hears an action for, and then awards, damages. But such covenants can also be enforced indirectly. The lawyer who drafted the lease may have attached to the covenants in the lease a clause stating that failure to perform the covenants entitles the landlord to re-enter. That is, what is called a forfeiture clause has been put in the lease. If the tenant fails to perform, the landlord can go to court and seek to repossess the premises. This process of repossession or forfeiture has been regulated by statute in two ways since 1925. So far as repair covenants are concerned, this gives the lessee two opportunities to repent.[28] First, s.146 of the Law of Property Act 1925 requires the lessor to serve a forfeiture notice on the lessee and to require the breach of covenant—here, in our example, the failure to repair—to be remedied if it is capable of remedy. The courts have now interpreted this to mean that the lessor must require remedy of the breach if in a practical sense the landlord can be put back into the position he would have been in had the tenant not defaulted on his obligations. If the landlord serves such a notice and the tenant does the repairs, then the breach is in effect cured and the tenant can remain. But if he does not remedy the breach, the landlord can repossess unless the court grants the tenant relief against forfeiture.

The basis of this jurisdiction to grant relief matters little at present. What matters is rather to explore what lawyers suppose to be the proper function of the court when the jurisdiction is invoked. The courts do not wave sabres of justice at this point. The lessor, via his lawyer, has laid down in the lease a private law and this private law is the basis on which the lessee has entered into the relationship and taken on the property. The courts tend to approach this private law with circumspection; that is, they are there to facilitate its implementation, not to rewrite it. This is what is expected from them by practitioners. Such expectations form the basis for what practitioners do when they draw up leases, as well as when they advise on the likely outcome of a lawsuit. A lessee who had deliberately broken the terms of his lease, or refused to remedy his breach, is extremely unlikely to succeed if he appeals to a court to relieve him from the consequences.

The first opportunity for a lessee to save himself is by remedying the breach and this opportunity, we have just seen, the statute requires him to be given. But it only arises where the breach is capable of being remedied. Some breaches are not, it has been decided (notably breaches of covenant which forbid assignments or sub-lettings of the lease without permission from the lessor). In such circumstances, tenants involved in forfeiture proceedings can never save themselves from the landlord except by availing themselves of the relief jurisdiction, by throwing themselves upon the mercy of the court. And here, precisely because remediability is ruled out of court, there is scope for seeking relief. If the breach cannot be remedied, but is innocent or innocuous, relief may be granted. The tenant then gets relief because at worst he has broken the private law unintentionally, and at best he had done nothing wrong.[29]

Forfeiture is the main mechanism by which a landlord can terminate a fixed-term lease ahead of time. Most of the other mechanisms for terminating a lease are quite straightforward and unsurprising once the very limited role which the courts have assumed in relation to these matters has been grasped. A fixed-term lease may contain a provision empowering either side to give notice to quit, and the common law would give effect to this, although a tenant may now have some security of tenure in this situation under one of the statutory regimes mentioned above. A lease will also end if a landlord accepts a surrender of the lease from his tenant; and if the tenant buys the reversion on his lease, his leasehold interests and the reversion he buys "merge" and the independent leasehold interest thereby ends. The difficult, if usually academic, question is whether a lease can also determine through the application of the doctrine of frustration.

The doctrine of frustration is concerned with specifying a set of circumstances in which people can be released from contractual obligations which would otherwise have to be performed. While there is no canonical formula for stating what these circumstances are, the basic idea, which suffices for present purposes, is that where the whole basis upon which the parties made the contract has been destroyed, the doctrine will apply. So people who hired window seats to watch Edward VII's planned coronation procession did not have to pay up when it was postponed because the King was confined to bed. The application of such a doctrine by judges is thus more a matter of delicacy than difficulty. The question is what, if any, scope does this have for leases?

Any properly drafted lease for any significant duration is likely to provide in advance for the consequences of foreseeable risks. Thus leases commonly contain provisions relating to building insurance, to deal in advance with the problem of fire. Since the allocation of such risks is part of the bargain itself, there is, so far as they are concerned, no scope for the doctrine of frustration, which rests, in another formulation, on the idea that "this is not the bargain into which I came". What, however, about the unforeseeable? If you rent a warehouse for storage purpose, and then the public authorities seal off all access to and from the building so that it is unusable, does rent remain payable? This brings to the fore the underlying conceptual nature of a leasehold interest and thus warrants closer scrutiny. The obligation, contained in a lease, to pay rent is a contractual obligation of sorts, although failure to pay rent by the tenant gives rise to the additional common law remedy of distress, which enables a landlord to enter and seize a tenant's moveables and sell them in order to recoup rent arrears. Distress is quite independent of the contractual nature of the relationship and is, rather, rooted in the property relationship between landlord and tenant. The lease is in some sense a mixture of contract and conveyance, because the bulk of its contents comprises obligations working out the responsibilities of landlord and tenant respectively, concerning the use and maintenance of the premises let over time, as well as the rent due. But how should this mix be conceptualised?

Property lawyers used to put it in this way. The lease is a conveyance of title, the transfer of a fixed term to the tenant. The covenants contained in this conveyance comprise a set of independent rights and duties made, by the parties, incidental to the term of years. The lease is not one bargain which can be taken as a whole, but creates an estate in land to which unrelated obligations are attached. This means that a tenant cannot refuse to pay the rent if the landlord defaults on his repair obligations, nor could the landlord set off rent he is owed if the tenant sues him for his default. Each obligation is treated entirely independently. On this view, the only way in which the relationship could end through something analogous to frustration is if the land in which the tenancy exists itself ceases to exist, as where a house on a cliff falls into the sea through erosion. In such an event, all the covenants in the lease would lose their force because there is no longer anything in which either landlord or tenant can have an estate, and therefore no possibility any longer for a landlord-tenant relationship to subsist, no estates to which obligations can be annexed. However, this view has lost its attraction, mainly because it seems artificial, and the latest decision on the question[30] holds that a lease is capable of ending through frustration, though this ruling was qualified by saying that in considering whether the doctrine can be invoked in a particular case, all the factors must be weighed up, not least the relationship between the frustrating circumstances and the length of the outstanding term. In place of the traditional position that the doctrine "never" applied to leases was substituted the position that it would "hardly ever" apply. This formulation has the advantage of flexibility, giving scope to judges to apply the doctrine in a strong case which warrants intervention. It also provides an interesting example of the rather commonplace contemporary judicial reluctance to be bound by what has come to be seen as the shackles of the traditional conceptual repertoire of land law. The practical difficulties which this approach involves are experienced by law students and their teachers brought up to expect something different from the judges.

Applying the doctrine of frustration to a lease is to treat the lease as a contract. But the lease is a conveyance as well as a contract. It is a title to land, to which obligations can be attached. They commonly originate as promises, but their subsequent enforceability is based on their attachment to a title rather than on the fact that they have been promised. This becomes clear when we consider the third concern of lawyers. What is the legal effect of the contents of a lease if either landlord or tenant pass on their respective interests?

When a transfer of title takes place, the transferor may seek, if he is retaining adjacent land, to make some express stipulation with a view to binding the purchaser as to the use in the future to which he may put the land he is buying. To this extent, the courts have been pressured into recognising certain enduring rights and duties between adjacent landowners, and to the extent that this recognition of durability is afforded, these rights are, for lawyers, property rights, and are further explored below in the next chapter. But in the case of the lease, the problem is both slightly different and at the same time more pressing. A lease throws up a problem of adjacency which is not necessarily one of physical proximity. What is adjacent to, indeed is at the core of, the landlord-tenant relationship, is the conjunction of two estates in land, of the tenant's term of years and the landlord's reversion. This is what lawyers call "privity of estate". And since both may intrinsically endure concurrently over a vast stretch of time, the common law had to formulate a response to the question of the enforceability of leasehold covenants, once either the term or the reversion or both had passed on into new hands, as, in the case of a long lease, was more or less inevitable.

The covenants attached to the term, so far as both sides are concerned, are integral to the relationship which is created. A tenant's covenants endure throughout the term. The tenant who acquires a lease for 90 years remains liable on his covenants for that term. But since he has acquired what is recognised by force of statute as an estate in land, he has something of (often considerable) value which can be sold on in the marketplace. If he sells on the term ("assigns it"), will his purchaser (the "assignee" of the lease) be liable on the covenants the original tenant undertook? By the late sixteenth century an affirmative answer was reached by the courts to this question, provided that the covenants in question could be judged to "touch and concern" the land which was the subject-matter of the lease. The position of new landlords who acquired the reversion of the original lessor had been earlier dealt with by statute in broadly similar terms.

This is nothing to do with contract. Rather, the rights and duties enshrined in the covenants "run" with the land—or more precisely with the respective estates of landlord and tenant— such that anyone who acquires one of these estates takes it subject to and with the benefit of all covenants which relate to the land. The original tenant remains liable on his covenants throughout the term because they are his covenants. Statute make most burdens placed on landlords pass on to their assignees, in this respect overriding the law of contract. Assignees of the reversion thus acquire rights to sue the original tenant on his covenants, even if the new landlord acquired his rights after the original tenant had passed on his interest. By contrast, assignees of the lease are only liable for those breaches of covenant which occur during their time. The position of landlords and tenants over time in respect of leasehold cove-nants is thus asymmetrical, but the lack of symmetry flows from a combination of the logic of the situation and the intervention of particularistic legislation long ago.

To return briefly to the question of the doctrine of frustration: since at its core the doctrine is based on the destruction of the basis or "substratum" of the bargain, it is difficult to see how it is applicable after a lease has been passed on by assignment. One can see how, conceptually, the doctrine could apply to the tenant's liability on his covenants because his enduring liability, after he has assigned his lease, is based on the fact that they are his covenants and is, in other words, a contractual liability. But the assignee is bound by the covenants which touch and concern the land simply because they are incidental to the estate, the term of years, he acquires in the assignment. The only bargain such an assignee enters into is with his assignor before taking the assignment (unless, as may happen in some commercial contexts, the assignee is required to enter into a new set of direct covenants with the landlord).

THE NEW STATUTORY SCHEME FOR ASSIGNMENT

The mix of long-established common law and statutory rules relating to the consequences of the assignment of the interests of landlords and tenants have perhaps always been both logical and anomalous. It is logical to distinguish between the original parties to a lease and their successors in title because the lease which constitutes the foundation of the two proprietary interests—the landlord's reversion and the tenancy itself—will typically contain covenants given by the original landlord and tenant on behalf of themselves, and their successors in title. Therefore each undertakes obligations which, as a matter of simple contract, bind them for the duration of the term of the lease. This means that they are exposed to liability even if they have parted with their interest in the property in question. Successors in title, by contrast, as we have seen, are liable only for acts or events which occur while they enjoy an interest in the property. This distinction has come to seem anomalous or inconvenient or even unfair. Take two examples. First, as is commonplace in many cities, the conversion of a large dwelling house into flats which are then sold off on long-term, typically 99-year, leases. Why should the liability of the first flat-owner differ from that of the later ones (for payment of ground rent, insurance, etc.)? Similarly, why should the liability of the first tenant of a shop in a shopping development differ from that of the later tenants? A gap appears here between legal form—the fact that the covenants in the lease are in the name of the original parties—and economic realities.

New legislation—the Landlord and Tenant (Covenants) Act 1995—has sought to tackle these perceived anomalies. In its essentials, the Act does two things. First, it provides for the automatic release of tenants from their obligations under the lease when they assign their interests, and for the release of the landlord from his liability with the consent of the tenant or the court. In other words, privity of contract in this area is abolished. Secondly, the Act now puts on a statutory basis all the rules relating to the transmission of the benefit and burden of covenants in leases. We will look briefly at each in turn. But the main provisions of the Act are not retrospective. They will not apply to pre-1996 leases. This means that the existing rules sketched above, and the distinction between privity of contract and privity of estate, will remain applicable for many years to come, given the long-term nature of many leasehold interests. The paradoxical price of reform is added legal complexity.

Release of the original parties from liability on their covenants

The Act provides a framework for the release of both landlords and tenants from liability on their covenants for acts or events occurring after they have parted with their respective interests. The scheme of the Act treats landlords and tenants differently. In general terms, the release of tenants is automatic whereas the release of landlords is not. The rationale behind this differential treatment is that in most leases the landlord can assign his reversion without the consent of the tenant, whereas the assignment of the tenancy commonly requires the landlord's consent. So most landlords can block what they consider to be an unsuitable assignment of the lease, whereas most tenants are not able to stop unsuitable assignment of the reversion. In each case, the classic example of unsuitability would be an assignment to someone who is not in a financial position to meet the obligations contained in the covenants. But because the terms of most leases enable landlords but not tenants to stop this occurring, automatic release is "safe" for a tenant's liability on the covenants but not for that of a landlord's.

So if a landlord wishes to assign the reversion on the lease, a procedure of reciprocal serving of notices is established by s.8 of the Act to enable him to be released. The landlord must serve a notice of the assignment on the tenant, who then has four weeks to object in writing. If the tenant does not object within this period, the landlord is released from future liabilities. If the tenant does object, the landlord can apply to the court for a declaration that a release is reasonable.

Some types of assignment are excluded from these provisions. If the assignment is in breach of a covenant governing assignment (typically, for example, a lease contains a covenant stipulating that an assignment by the tenant requires the landlord's approval, so that an assignment of the lease without such approval would constitute a breach of the covenant), liability is not released but deferred until the next assignment which takes place in conformity with the terms of the lease. Secondly, what are in a sense "technical" assignments are excluded from these provisions. These are assignments which take place "by operation of law", *i.e.* automatically, for example on the bankruptcy or death of the holder of the interest, which passes automatically to the trustee in bankruptcy or executor. The liabilities of landlord or tenant are kept alive in such instances of transfer of title and again are deferred until the next transfer.

The automatic release of the original tenant from liability is modified, however, in an important respect. The Act contains (in s.16) provisions whereby an outgoing tenant can be required to give a guarantee for the performance of his immediate assignee. The guarantee, in other words, can cover his own assignment but not beyond that into the next assignment, as was and is the case under the old rules. The landlord will only be able to extract a guarantee of this sort if the lease contains a covenant requiring his or some other person's consent to the assignment on terms which are lawful. The Act also modifies or rationalises the rules relating to the granting or withholding of consent by landlords to tenants' assignments, which connect up directly with these provisions regarding guarantees. Previous legislation had enabled a tenant to challenge the withholding of consent to a proposed assignment on the grounds that it was unreasonable. But this left, in the end, the test of reasonableness to the courts and required the parties to litigate in the event of a dispute. Under s.22 of the new regime, the original parties can make explicit provision in the lease as to the grounds on which the landlord can reasonably withhold consent to an assignment of the lease. This means that it can be anticipated that new leases will contain a covenant requiring the tenant to enter into an authorised guarantee agreement as sketched above as a condition of the landlord giving consent to an assignment.

The new statutory code

For the rights and obligations contained in the covenants of leases created after 1995, the LPA 1925 provisions as interpreted since by the courts will no longer apply, and a new, modified, regime is substituted. Perhaps most important from a conceptual point of view, the long-established requirement that after the first assignment only covenants which touch and concern the land are binding is abolished. In its place for the future is a contrary emphasis: all covenants will bind successors in title to the lease or the reversion unless they are undertaken as the personal covenants of the originating parties. Secondly, the enforceability of covenants which restrict the use to which leasehold property can be put is extended (by s.3(5) of the Act) to any "owner or occupier" of the premises covered by the lease. The first change dispenses with the distinction between privity of contract and privity of estate or dispenses with part of the traditional rationale for imposing obligations beyond privity of contract (that certain—in practice, most—obligations in leases benefited "land" and not just persons). The second change dispenses with the notion of privity or proximity itself. Paradoxically, perhaps, this change means that obligations are now to be firmly anchored to land, whether or not, in legal terms, they "in fact" benefit it.

The Act also reformulates the rules regarding the passing of benefit and burden in respect of breaches occurring prior to an assignment. Neither benefit nor burden of past breaches passes on an assignment of the lease, but where the lease contains a forfeiture clause, as is normal, the assignee of the reversion can forfeit the lease on the basis of a pre-assignment breach. Assignment will no longer affect the ability of the assignor to sue for pre-assignment breaches.

PRACTICAL PROBLEMS OF MODERN LEASES

The landlord-tenant relationship, as stated above, has encompassed a wide range of functionally distinct social contexts. This is one reason why special statutory regimes have seemed necessary to cater for the deficiencies left by a largely abstentionist and formalist common law. It is beyond the scope of the present work to discuss these regimes or their deficiencies, which would, in any case, require close examination of the divergent social contexts in which these problems emerge. These regimes, as indicated above, have their own special procedures, officials and tribunals to administer them, and in large measure the role of the ordinary courts in respect of them is now confined to questions of statutory interpretation which arise from time to time as to the precise scope of any particular regime.

What can be questioned here is whether it is satisfactory that those social relations whose legal character still rests upon "general principle", if that it can be called, are adequately dealt with by the present law. We can concentrate on the remaining high ground of common law abstentionism, on that area where some questions remain about whether or not there is a need for either statutory regulation or modification of the common law. This is the area of the long-term lease of residential houses and flats, usually of 99 or sometimes 999 years in duration. It is difficult to say in statistical terms how important this area is today, but, if anything, in large conurbations it is of growing significance. We have outlined (above) areas where in some respects the legal framework of property law seems to be more complicated than is required to meet the needs of ordinary people. This is particularly true of the lease.

(1) If you buy a freehold property, you assume that its care and maintenance are up to you. There may be rights and duties that arise in respect of neighbouring property, which we discuss in the next chapter, but for the most part people's expectations as to the nature of what they are buying, and the legal character of the rights they acquire, coincide. This may not be the case at all with leasehold property, especially leases of parts of buildings under multiple leasehold occupancy. Restrictions on use, allocation of repair obligations between tenants, even the identity of the present ground rent holder, may all be unknown to a prospective purchaser. All are treated by the estate agents and lawyers involved in the transfer process as technical matters rather than being part and parcel of what is or is not for sale. When the prospective purchaser first puts in his offer for the property, he is commonly forced to do so in ignorance of the precise regime of private law into which he is proposing to buy, *i.e.* the terms of the lease which strictly represents and encapsulates the estate in land he is, in reality, acquiring.

(2) The more serious question centres around why it is necessary or preferable for buildings enjoyed in multiple occupancy to be parcelled out as leaseholds rather than freeholds. We shall elaborate below on why; for the moment we simply note that it is extremely difficult as the law stands at present for obligations relating to maintenance or repair of buildings to be directly enforced between freeholders. The general practice of building societies, as a result, is to refuse to lend money to buy "flying freeholds". So if a building contains 10 flats, the most convenient way from a technical point of view to ensure that each flat owner is obliged, in legal terms, to contribute to the cost of maintaining the building as a whole is by means of leasehold covenants owed to a landlord or freeholder. In this

situation, the freeholder is best seen as a purely technical intermediary, inserted for remedial purposes, between the respective tenants. The old function of ground rents has not been lost for a landlord with a sufficient quantity of them, but in many cases the leasehold form is adopted purely because, from the point of view of the enforceability of obligations between tenants, and the ability of prospective purchasers to obtain mortgage finance, it has advantages of a technical kind which lack any substantial foundation in the realities of social life. No simple or cast-iron mechanism for embedding such obligations between the tenants themselves is available in English law. And so the combination of an inactive freeholder and a recalcitrant tenant may pose severe obstacles to the maintenance of a building.

The simplest solution to these problems would be to make obligations to do things—such as contribute towards the cost of repair—attachable to land so that they were enforceable between freeholders. A less radical solution, though one which cannot solve all the difficulties, is to confer upon tenants the right to buy out the freeholder, as has been the case for some time for leasehold owners of houses.[31] Ideally, what is needed is to implement some form of "commonhold" tenure (proposals for which have existed for some time) tailored to the specific requirements of multiple-occupancy dwellings such as blocks of flats.

EQUITABLE LEASES

A lease was, and is, a conveyance of title. So it was, and remains, common for the execution of a lease to be preceded by an agreement, by a contract which sets out the terms of what is to be formalised. If the contract was concluded and then the landowner refused to execute the lease, the best course of action, for someone who could afford it, was to go to the Court of Chancery, because of the availability of its decree of specific performance. What if the "lessee" took possession under the contract and before execution of the formal lease? Let us confine the question for the moment to the situation where the contract for the lease was in writing or evidenced by writing. As we shall see (pp.200–202, below), there were particular problems where such a transfer of possession took place on the basis of a purely oral agreement. For the present purposes, all that needs to be said is that this problem was short-circuited by the Judicature

Acts of the 1870s. If a "tenant" had taken possession under a contract for a lease, but without the execution under seal of the formal lease for which he had contracted, it ceased to be necessary to await, through the issue of a decree from equity of specific performance of the contract, the physical coming into existence of the lease which had been promised in the contract. In the event of a dispute between any relevant parties, it became possible to ask what the position would be if the contract for a lease had been carried into effect, and to determine the dispute, whatever its nature, as if the lease had been brought into existence along the lines provided for in the contract. In its essentials, an "equitable lease" is no more than this: a short-circuiting of the adjudicative process effected by the organisational changes of the 1870s in the system of adjudication in England.[32] It does not follow from this that an agreement for a lease is equivalent to (or "as good as") a lease; in particular, there are important differences regarding the liability of assignees on the covenants in a formal lease, on the one hand, and of obligations in a mere agreement, on the other, though in the future these will need to be read subject to the provisions of the 1995 Act (pp.156–157, above).

MORTGAGES

The changing character of the mortgage

Lawyers—and bank managers—talk about personal loans and secured loans, and distinguish unsecured from secured creditors. A personal loan is just a contract. The terms of the contract will provide for the terms and time of repayment. If the borrower does not honour these but, say, falls behind with his repayments or fails to repay the lump sum on the due day, the lender's remedies are purely contractual: principally, an action in debt for the sum in question, as happens, for example, today with people who fall seriously into arrears with their credit card repayments.

Where the loan is secured on property, the position is quite different. The lender can still sue for the sum owed, as with a personal loan; but, in addition, he has the ability to seek a court order which will enable him to take over the property which serves as security, sell it and take from the proceeds whatever amount is needed to wipe out the debt. A mortgage is the principal device used for this purpose, in which estates or interests in land serve as the security for loans. The mortgage, generally, is an essential component of the development of a credit economy in land. Most people today have a mortgage during part of their lives. They borrow some or all of the money they need to buy a house or flat from a bank or building society and repay the loan over a number of years. The repayment structures have become increasingly complex in recent years, as the principal loan providers—banks and building societies—have encouraged borrowers to purchase other financial products in combination with the loan secured on the property, notably savings or insurance policies and pension schemes. We are not concerned with the detail of these arrangements, since for present purposes what continues to underpin these schemes is that the capital advanced by the lender is secured via the mortgage device. However, it should be noted that many of these alternative schemes do not involve direct repayment of the loan to the lender. Rather, the borrower's payments are channelled towards the insurance or pension scheme, in the expectation that sufficient capital will accrue at some date in the future to repay the whole of the initial loan.

The lender secures his loan by means of a mortgage on the property. In the normal case, the owner (the "mortgagor") grants a legal mortgage to the lender (the "mortgagee"). In the modern law, this arrangement can either take the form of a long lease, or of a "charge by way of legal mortgage", introduced by the LPA 1925, s.86. This can be described as a simpler and more realistic way of creating a mortgage; it does not involve leases, but the mortgagee has all the same protection, powers and remedies as he would have under the lease-type mortgage. The advantages of this system are that it is short and easy to understand, it can be used to mortgage freehold and leasehold land together and, in the case of a mortgage of a leasehold, it will not constitute breach of a leasehold covenant against subletting. Many lenders choose to use this form, but in any event, any legal mortgage of registered land will now take effect as a charge by way of legal mortgage (s.51 LRA 2002, s.51).

This last device, introduced in 1925, is the first time that English law has recognised a conveyancing device which in formal terms is constitutive of the mortgage as a distinctive kind of interest in land. As we will see, this is the main reason why the involvement of the law in mortgages has been so complicated. For most of its history, the form of the mortgage has been "borrowed" from other legal forms. This meant that, for centuries, lawyers devoted much energy, especially in the litigation process, to working out criteria for distinguishing what was really a mortgage from what was really something else. Traditionally, the mortgage took the form of a purchase of some sort by the lender of the borrower's land. In formal terms, the mortgagee was, and is, a purchaser, and some of the rules and procedures governing purchasers applied and apply with equal force to lenders on mortgage. Indeed, Cyprian Williams suggested that the investigation of a title by a prospective mortgagee's solicitor should be even more meticulous than in the case of a straightforward conveyance on sale. There were two reasons for this, both of which are still relevant today in certain respects. First, although the mortgage is a type of "purchase" for English lawyers, it is not usual for a mortgagee to take possession of the mortgaged land from the borrower at the time the loan is made. And so, before 1925, this meant, almost invariably, that since:

"... a mortgagee ... gets only a parchment security, and does not, like a [purchaser], enter into possession of the land, there is the more reason for seeing that the evidence of the mortgagor's title is in every respect complete. The title deeds especially should be examined with most particular care; for frauds and forgeries have been far more frequently effected in connection with the mortgage of land, where there is no transfer of actual possession, than upon sale" (Williams, 1922, p.478).

As we shall briefly note, there were exceptions to this, notably what were called "Welch" mortgages, under which the mortgagee did take possession of the land. But in the standard mortgage—and this remains true today—the mortgagor kept possession of the mortgaged land. In the past, this meant that the borrower continued for the duration of the mortgage to receive the rental income from the land, and in the normal case, pending repayment of the capital advanced by the lender, paid interest on the loan as agreed in the arrangement.

Secondly, in former times:

"purchasers generally buy land with the view of occupying or enjoying it [*i.e.* taking its rental yield]; they seldom buy it for immediate resale. But the object of a mortgagee is simply to obtain good security for the repayment of his money, whenever he may desire to call it in . . . While purchasers, therefore, so long as they can obtain a good holding title, are often willing to waive defects of title which will be cured by lapse of time or may be covered by special conditions on a resale, a mortgagee will always desire to get a good marketable title; for he contemplates the possibility of having recourse to a forced sale, when special conditions, in spite of the avidity with which they are usually swallowed at the auction mart, may be depreciatory" (Williams, 1922, p.477).

Modern mortgages of residential property are somewhat different, in that immediate resale is not envisaged, but only the ability to resell without difficulty should the borrower default. However, as we shall see, lenders on mortgage in the past by no means had their eyes fixed always on resale, and many were content to leave their capital outstanding on mortgage, drawing interest upon it, for very long periods of time. What remains true, in very different conditions, is that those who lend on mortgage are likely, because of the legal advice which they receive, to worry more about possible defects of title, or inconvenient incumbrances upon title, than the purchasers to whom, in the modern world, they advance loans.

The modern mortgage with which most people are familiar is different in a number of ways from the more traditional form of mortgage. This legal form has been adapted, from a technical if not a social policy point of view, fairly adequately to meet modern needs, but the form itself, and the rules which give it expression, were all geared to transactions of a quite different character.

Mortgage transactions, viewed as a whole, are best regarded as a form of investment, the mortgage device being the mechanism whereby that investment is made secure. This remains true today, although mortgages are also used for a range of different purposes. (For example, and subject to shifting fashions in competition law, brewery and petroleum companies lend money to retail traders largely as a means of securing an outlet for their products). Where investment is at the heart of the transaction, the investment or the profit which the lender makes is the interest payable on the capital sum lent. What is different about modern home loans is that their structure is geared fundamentally to repayment of the capital as well as interest on the capital (subject to the complexities noted above, which result from the association of mortgages with the sale of other financial products). This distinguishes it from the traditional use of the mortgage. So long as the paradigm of what land ownership meant was essentially a rental income, the traditional mortgage can be seen as another means of parcelling out the total annual rents, or as a mechanism through which people other than owners of land could participate in its financial fruits. Today, however, most mortgage debt is covered by the earned income of the borrower, out of which, within a finite period of time, both capital and interest is to be repaid. Servicing the debt owed under a traditional mortgage diverted a portion of the rental income from land or houses away from those with interests in possession and towards the mortgagee. The repayments on the modern residential mortgage, by contrast, effectively operate as a rent paid by the borrower to the lender in return for enjoyment by the borrower of occupation of the land.

The other side of this comparison between the present and the past is that today we think of the lender as more powerful than the borrower—the ordinary person versus the institutional lender with huge assets and considerable capacity for loss spreading. In the past, by contrast, it was often, although not always, the other way around: the borrower was the person with social and economic power in many transactions; it was the lender, a small person seeking a safe place for his or her capital, who sought through the mortgage device a safe way in which the capital could generate an income over time. The pervasive Victorian literary theme of the beleaguered family mortgaged to the brink of ruin was a part, but not the most important part, of the former social and economic reality of mortgaging (*cf.* Cannadine, 1977; Beckett, 1986; Beckett, 1994).

For lawyers in the past, there was generally a mutuality in the relationship between mortgagee and mortgagor. In the nature of things, the mortgagor represented land and the mortgagee represented money. Money was, for centuries, regarded as morally suspect. This was reflected in usury laws which sought to regulate the charging of interest on loans, but more fundamentally in a view which saw something dangerous in the shifting, moveable nature of money, in its liquid form and ephemeral mode of functioning. Land, by contrast, was immovable and constant. The preservation of the status quo, of the established order of society, not surprisingly, seemed to be connected, in an intimate way, with the preservation of the relation between lineage and land, and, less grandly but not less importantly, the maintenance of the security of titles, which, in the present context, could include protecting them from the depredations of "money". Here, the courts of equity came to play a crucial role.

A mortgage transaction would commonly identify a particular day upon which the borrower was to repay the capital advanced. Around this date the mutuality of the relationship centred. On the one hand, once this date had passed, the lender was entitled to call for repayment. If at this time the borrower could not repay, the lender could take possession, if the court permitted, of the mortgaged land as absolute owner. This process was known as "foreclosure". But the other side of the coin, as the equity courts came to view the matter, was that where the borrower wished to remove the mortgage from his land by repaying the sum advanced, he would be permitted to do so. This was because the equity courts would always compel (except where foreclosure had occurred) the mortgagee to accept payment in these circumstances as an effective discharge of the mortgage. As a result of this policy of the court, this right became known as the equity of redemption, that is, the right, enforceable in the courts of equity, for a borrower to "redeem" or buy back his mortgaged land from the lender, even after the contractual time for repayment had passed.

But this in turn meant that it was necessary to develop criteria to distinguish a mortgage from a conveyance on sale. In formal terms, mortgagees were purchasers, as we have indicated. Unusually, then, the equity courts, in their desire to protect landowners, were here compelled to address a fundamental distinction between the form and substance of a transaction prepared by lawyers.

Form and substance of the mortgage

What you find in law books about mortgages in English law is very complicated and more than a little tedious. There are two main reasons for this. The first derives from the traditional nature of the mortgage as such. As a form of carving up rental income, it always made possible, once recognised as a device, the pledging of land as security to more than one mortgagee, up to the total capital value of the land proffered as security, not least because, in the traditional mortgage, the capital advanced on mortgage was commonly much less than the capitalised value of the rental income yielded by the land. (This is one further manifestation of the fact that in the past borrowers were the big men while lenders were the little people.) In other words, it has long been the case that English lawyers needed to develop principles of *priority* as between several mortgagees in the event of disputes arising between them when the debtor/ mortgagor defaulted. In analytical terms a similar question of priorities as between mortgagees arises today against the backdrop of home ownership. But the underlying practical realities of this situation are radically different: these mortgages are almost always a profit-making device dependent for repayment on the earned income or business profits of the borrowers, where the possibility of plural mortgaging depends in the end upon anticipated permanent inflation in real-estate book values.

The second reason for the complexity of the law concerning mortgages, and from a conceptual point of view the more conspicuous, is best grasped in terms of the distinction drawn between form and substance. This is an expression much used by lawyers in the common law world, as much in property law as elsewhere. And, commonly though not exclusively, this distinction, when applied to a legal transaction, can be mapped on to the institutional and jurisdictional distinction between law and equity: common law is "form", equity is—or regards— "substance". But much of the time the drift of this proposition is, at least to modern eyes, not especially profound. It means, for example, that in considering whether an obligation imposed upon someone is genuinely "negative" or not—as we shall see in the next chapter when restrictive covenants are elaborated— equity asked, whatever form of words was used in the covenant, whether the obligation so created was really negative in nature. So a covenant requiring a building to be used for residential purposes only could be treated as in substance imposing a negative obligation even if it seemed on its surface—in terms of the form of words—to be positive: really, such an obligation meant that the covenantee undertook not to use the building for any other purposes. What made the application of the form and substance distinction to mortgages somewhat unusual was that it went well beyond this question (to us rather minor, even if it was not to people of the past) of the meaning of words. In the area of mortgages, it was the meaning of *transactions* rather than *words* which was at stake in the development of the law by the equity courts, and what is striking about this is the manner in which the courts departed from their conventional stance *vis-à-vis* the formulaic tradition of the conveyancers and the abstentionism they adopted in relation to leases. It is difficult to believe that this was not related to the higher social or cultural value placed upon land ownership over the mere possession of money, the superiority of "property" over "wealth" (*cf.* Sugarman and Warrington 1996).

The legal mortgage of a legal estate took the form of a conveyance of title—whether freehold or leasehold—coupled with a covenant given by the mortgagee to reconvey the title upon repayment ("redemption") of the capital advanced. Against this backdrop, under the banner of looking to the substance of the transaction so created, equity courts asserted a jurisdiction to intervene in favour of the borrower which became known as the "equity of redemption".

The basic idea here was that the borrower should always be allowed to redeem if he could repay the loan with interest. In more modern times, it has further been stressed that the borrower's equity here extends to the ability to redeem free of any "collateral advantages" taken by the mortgagee at the time of the loan. There must be, it is sometimes said, no "clogs or fetters" on the equity of redemption. This is a rather convoluted way, to modern eyes, of directly posing the question of in what circumstances the courts will give relief against what they consider to be unfair or oppressive transactions.

Why should it follow that where, in substance, a transaction is a mortgage, the borrower must always be able to redeem his land once the legal period for redemption has passed? It is circular to explain this simply in terms of "equity" or "justice": equity developed this set of principles because of the way the common law was constrained by the terms of the conveyance and covenant to reconvey, which it simply had to construe and then uphold. The answer might be that English law lacked a separate clearly defined concept of a mortgage along the lines of the civilian "hypothec" until the specialised concept of a "charge by way of legal mortgage" was introduced by statute in 1925. Until then, the legal forms or mechanisms used to create mortgages were parasitic upon the standard forms designed for the transfer of title. Such forms, when used to create mortgages, usually contained special covenants which made it clear that they were really mortgages but in form they were more than that—they were outright transfers of title. This parasitic use of a legal form thus helps to explain the pressure upon courts to distinguish transactions which were, both in form and substance, outright transfers of title from transactions which were similarly transfers in form but in substance designed as mortgages. This does in part explain the equity of redemption, since without it the mortgagee in possession of the title deeds could sell on the title, and the mortgagor would be left, at law, with no more than his remedy in damages on the covenant to reconvey. (The equity to redeem is necessary today because the legal redemption period is so short: but this is a conveyancing convention; setting a redemption date at law, as part of the bargain, has been allowed to atrophy because of the equity to redeem. Home purchase mortgages, which are pivotally geared to the direct or indirect repayment of capital, have built-in redemption dates, though the date may fluctuate during the life of the mortgage.)

This discussion illustrates very sharply a pervasive feature of English property law, and one which accounts for why it often seems difficult or inaccessible to its students. Instead of simply developing a set of principles, either by statutory regulation or by the casuistry of the common law method, to give assistance in the face of oppressive transactions, lawyers must talk in a complex and convoluted code when addressing quite simple (which is not to say easy-to-answer) questions. Not only do you not need sledgehammers to crack nuts; if you use one, the results can be messy.

Foreclosure and power of sale

As we have indicated, the converse of redemption was, traditionally, foreclosure, through which the lender would gain possession of the mortgaged land. The alternative remedy for a mortgagee was to sell the land under a court order and recoup what was owed from the proceeds of sale, and this is in the normal case the remedy used by modern institutional mortgagees like building societies. When people fall behind on their mortgage repayments, the bank or building society can go to court and in due course repossess the house or flat, put it on the market and recoup its losses from the purchase price. (One might note that, in these circumstances, an institutional lender may well provide the finance for the new purchaser, so that in economic terms a repossession followed by a sale is, for the lender, a book transfer of the mortgage liability from the defaulting purchaser to the new purchaser. Legally, however, this would normally involve the discharge of the old mortgage and a fresh advance of a loan under a new mortgage.)

There is nothing new about the spectre of foreclosure or repossession haunting a landowner; the burden of debt on the landed estates of the past sometimes became so immense that little if anything from the rent rolls remained after the annual charges had been met, though most great landowners of the past managed to pull back from total ruin (Beckett, 1986, pp.302–315). Only a few suffered the fate of the second Duke of Buckingham, who ended his days in Paddington in the Great Western Hotel (Thompson, 1955; Beckett, 1994).

But because, as we have already seen, mortgage-financed owner-occupation has become the dominant form of tenure in modern England, and because these mortgages are largely financed from earned income, not from rents as in the past, the high levels of unemployment which have been experienced since the late 1980s coupled with a slump in house prices during the first half of the 1990s have led in turn to a significant increase in the volume of mortgage defaults, and have thus hooked up to the more general problem of homelessness. Whether or not the present procedures which regulate the processing of repossession claims by mortgagees through the courts are adequate cannot be elaborated upon here; but the "right to buy" policies of Mrs Thatcher's administrations have meant that what for lawyers is a relatively prosaic element of the judicial process has already assumed a sharpened significance for a widening section of the population in the wake of the long recession at the end of the 1980s.

As with leases, mortgages involve the creation of a private law of the parties to govern their relationships, including the possibility that parties on one side of the relationship—tenants, mortgagors—will lose their interests in land to parties on the other side—landlords, mortgagees. We have suggested that the law traditionally gave more protection to mortgagors than to tenants, but in general terms the problem is the same in each case: when, and on what grounds, should the courts intervene to prevent one side asserting his contractual and proprietary rights against the other?

In the case of modern residential mortgages, the practical issue is to determine when the courts are entitled to prevent a bank or building society from evicting a home owner who has defaulted on his mortgage so as to sell the property with vacant possession. Such possession actions are commonplace, though their scale is clearly linked to the economic cycle: 116,181 in 1993; 79,941 in 1996; rather fewer in the first half of 1997.

Section 36 of the Administration of Justice Act 1970 confers a broad discretion on the courts in this situation. Under this Act, where a court considers that the borrower will be able within a reasonable period to repay the sums due or remedy any default, the court can either adjourn the possession action or give a "suspended order" for possession. Suspension means that the court can set terms for the repayment of the outstanding debt—usually payment of current mortgage instalments and some of the arrears plus interest on them—and, provided that the borrower complies with them, the eviction will not take place.

8

LAND USE AND LAND OBLIGATIONS

Lawyers have been required to invent devices for the exploitation and restriction of the use value of land. Not surprisingly, given the well-planned character of Roman, and especially Graeco-Roman, cities, precedents for such conceptualisation already existed in Roman law. Predictably, what most interested medieval lawyers—and what had been most elaborated by Roman jurists—were what we would call "private" mechanisms for controlling land use. Medieval lawyers had two principal ways at their disposal of doing this: grants of use rights and promises as to use, which became easements and profits on the one hand, and covenants on the other.

On the one hand, lawyers came to recognise, by analogy with the process of granting estates in land, the grant of ancillary rights of use known as "easements", to benefit the enjoyment and exploitation of land (both agricultural and urban), such that these benefits (and their correlative burdens) could be attached to the land and so run with it, *i.e.* benefit and bind successors in title. The content of such rights of use of land belonging to another was principally bounded by the limit that such rights should not involve the expenditure of money. By contrast with mortgages, the courts stopped at permitting heirs to be burdened for the future with expensive charges so far as land obligations were concerned. "Covenants", solemn promises to do things or not to do things, were a different matter. If the performance of a promise cost money, it cost the money of the person making the promise. The benefit of such promises could be allowed to run with land—to enure to the benefit of successors in title to the original person taking the promise—but the obligation was not so permitted to run. We have already seen that the position was for a long time different with leasehold covenants. Here the courts were willing to enforce

covenants contained in leases beyond the original parties provided that it benefited the land which was the subject-matter of
the lease. In the nineteenth century, equity came to afford
similar recognition negative covenants restricting land use
between freeholders.

To summarise: in practical terms, these rights take two main
forms. Some enable one landowner to enter the land of another
and do things on that land—such as walk across it, hang a sign
on it or store goods on it—even though that land does not, by
definition, belong to him. The other main type of right takes the
form of enabling the person with the right to require the landowner subject to the right either to do things on the subjected
land or to refrain from doing things on that land, either of
which will benefit the holder of the right in his enjoyment of his
own land. Examples include the obligation to maintain hedges
and ditches, or to refrain from using agricultural or residential
land for commercial or industrial purposes.

Broadly, the first type of rights come within the category of
easements, while the second take the legal form of covenants.
Both types of rights can, with less ambivalence than was the
case with the lease or the mortgage, be regarded as ancillary to
ownership   rights,   or,   for   land   transfer   purposes,   as
incumbrances upon title rather than as fragments of title. In so
far as this distinction can be given a clear meaning, we might
say that these "subsidiary" rights which we now examine are
for the most part—again there are exceptions—rights which
possess the quality of durability through time but lack the
quality of independent transmissibility. These are rights, in
other words, which are transmissible in a limited way, but are
only recognised if attached or annexed to a freely transmissible
interest such as a lease or a fee simple. They are rights which
cannot be detached from the title to which they are ancillary and
the enjoyment of which they benefit or enhance (though they
may be exercisable too by those with derivative titles). They are
rights which cannot be transferred in their own right but only in
the course of the transfer of something else, which, in principle,
can.

EASEMENTS

As we noted in a previous chapter (p.59), distinctions which are
meaningful for lawyers are not always observable in the brute
facts (if they can be so described) of everyday life. If one farmer

lets his neighbour drive his cattle across one of his fields, lawyers can conceptualise the arrangement or transaction as involving the grant of an easement, or as a mere licence. An outside observer, however, may have no idea at all whether the relationship in legal terms between such farmers is one involving property rights or not, since whatever the nature of the legal relationship, the mode of use may be the same, equally intensive or equally sporadic.

Lawyers distinguish easements from ownership rights on the one hand and from personal rights on the other. Easements differ from ownership rights both in their scope and in the extent to which they are transmissible. Ownership rights involve the right to possession of the land (though as we have seen, there are many ways in which the right to physical possession can be postponed, as in the reversion on a lease). It is usually said of easements that they must not be so comprehensive: an easement cannot amount to conferring exclusive possession of the land over which the easement is claimed. An easement enables one landowner to tap the resources of an adjacent owner, to make limited use of land belonging to another. Sometimes this distinction between easement and ownership is clear-cut. If one farmer has a right of way over the land of a neighbour, he may from time to time drive his cattle across the neighbour's land, but otherwise the neighbour's freedom to use his land fully is unimpaired. But in the case of easements of storage, the limitations upon the owner's freedom may be more extensive. If one farmer has the right to store sacks of corn in a neighbour's barn, the owner of the barn can hardly be said to "enjoy" it while it contains the other farmer's sacks. In a case of this kind, it is not obvious where ownership ends and easement begins.

Easements are also transmissible in a sense much more limited than ownership rights are. They are ancillary to, or annexed to, title; they run with the land. This means that the owner of a field may sell it or give it away to anyone he chooses. Easements are transferrable only to the person to whom ownership is transferred. Easements are property rights because of their (limited) transmissibility and because they can endure against successive owners of the land over which they are held. In both respects they differ from licences. Licences are "personal" in two senses: the rights they confer may be enjoyed only by those to whom they are granted, and they bind only those who grant them.

Easements are sometimes called "servitudes", after Roman law, indicating that the core idea is the subjection of one land ownership to another. The land on which the obligation is imposed is called the "servient tenement" and the land which derives the benefit is the "dominant tenement". The more ponderous term used by English lawyers to describe such interests is "incorporeal hereditament". This emphasises the nature of the right rather than the obligation. Whatever we call it, we are here dealing with property rights which take the form of attaching rights in the one case and obligations in the other to titles to land. For lawyers, these are property rights precisely because they are attached to titles and possess, for the most part, the same durability as the titles to which they are attached.

As we have noted, most easements involve a right to do something on land belonging to another without taking any of the produce of that land, while covenants impose obligations upon the owner of land subjected to the covenant to do or refrain from doing something on his own land. But this neat distinction itself disintegrates when we examine certain rights which have been recognised as easements. Certain rights which lawyers have long treated as easements function more like covenants in so far as they involve restraining action by the servient owner on his land rather than conferring active benefits upon the owner of the land to which the easement is attached. Examples of this are easements which prevent the disruption of the flow of light or air to premises, which confer a right of support for buildings on one piece of land from soil or buildings on adjacent land, and rights which restrain a landowner from interfering with an established flow of water through his land to the land of another.

The difficulty which we here encounter of drawing clear—or tidy—conceptual boundaries once again results from the imprint of the past upon the present. Many rights that are still recognised today as easements—for example, rights of way, light and water—have been recognised since medieval times for the simple reason that the functional pressures for their continued recognition—pressures which flow from some very elementary and long-lasting aspects of the spatial organisation of settled social life—have operated for centuries and not ceased to exist. In this respect, negative easements, which restrict the activities or scope of the servient owner rather than enabling or enhancing the capacities of dominant owners, are best seen as an early response to basic problems which arise in situations where the enjoyment of one plot of land or building is intrinsically affected by the activity of the owner of the adjacent land. And the antiquity of easements is reflected in the way lawyers talk about their creation even today. They are said to be created by "grant" or "reservation", and one means of asserting a prescriptive right (*i.e.* a right generated from proof of long-term factual use) is by "lost modern grant". The kind of right which is capable of being an easement, it is said, must "lie in grant".

All this, while no doubt analytically sound, can make the study of easements rather obscure. In practical terms, in the modern and not so modern world, easements come into existence in two essentially different ways. First, where part of a block of land is sold off, vendor and purchaser may expressly direct their minds (or their lawyers may direct them) to the question whether, after the sale, either side should obtain any easements—say, rights of way—over the land retained or acquired by the other. Secondly, even where the parties' minds are not expressly directed to the question, so that nothing is written down in formal language in the transfer of title to the plot being sold, a dispute may subsequently come before the courts, and the court will have to decide whether an easement should be implied into the transfer of title, as part of the bargain, in favour of the former vendor or purchaser. Both of these matters are best regarded, for the most part, as pertaining to the business of the management of land transfer and the adjudication of disputes consequent upon the management of land transfer by lawyers.

The second complex of problems which have presented themselves to lawyers spring from life—or the social organisation of land use—rather than law. This is the acquisition of easements by prescription, which essentially means that a landowner should be entitled to continue to do something on a neighbour's land just because he has in fact done it for a very long time. This is another case of clothing fact—what actually happens—with right. No legal system can ignore the problem of prescriptive rights and their acquisition, but the extraordinary complexity of English law in this area suggests considerable discomfort with the whole idea.

One final point should be noted. We have stressed that for the benefit of an easement to be enjoyed as a property right, it is necessary for that benefit to be annexed to land. In English law, though not in some other common law jurisdictions, this requirement is taken to exclude the possibility of the creation and enjoyment of easements "in gross", that is, easements the benefit of which is not attached to land. Modern examples would include the right to lay cables or conduit pipes across private land, or even rights to hang signs and posters. Many utility companies have acquired such rights through special legislation, and in many other practical cases a contractual arrangement with a landowner will no doubt suffice. But it is not entirely obvious, in the modern world, that it is necessary or desirable to continue to limit what rights can be created as easements by means of the requirement of a dominant tenement.

PROFITS

Most of the law books discuss, alongside easements, a category of "use rights" called "profits". A profit gives its holder the right to take something from land belonging to another: to dig clay or cut turf, to pasture animals, to catch fish, to shoot game, to mine for coal or extract oil. These are commonly treated as servitudes, and share, with easements, the characteristic that whatever the content of the individual's right, it involves— subject to some exceptions regarding easements introduced above—the individual entering upon land belonging to another in order to perform some operation there. Here, however, the common characteristics stop, since the profit can better be regarded as another legal mechanism for carving up the fruits of the land.

This distinctive feature of the profit has long been recognised by lawyers in so far as they allowed the profit, but not the easement, to exist "in gross", that is, to operate as a property right even though its holder had no land of his own to which the right was attached. Obviously, profits could be annexed to land and through so doing make that land more valuable; but there has long been no requirement that recognition of a profit as a property right should depend upon such annexation to a title taking place. The fact that such rights could be annexed may be one reason why profits have tended to be classified alongside easements—or subsidiary rights—rather than being incorporated into the analysis of how title to land can be fragmented. But perhaps there is another reason for the classificatory difficulty. Easements and profits are both ways of fashioning rights relating to the physical use of land. When we talk about "the use and enjoyment" of land, two different things may be meant: its monetary yield (that is, the rental income it is capable of generating); or its enjoyment in physical terms, whether this means walking across it or picking the fruit or cutting the timber growing on it. English lawyers drew a fairly sharp division between the two, the first underpinning their analysis of title, the second their analysis of servitudes. To refer again to the metaphysics of the common law, a profit was a right to the substance of the land, as in a right to take minerals; as we have seen, a rent was a right to what the substance could be made to yield. Of course, as always, there were exceptions. Thus Bullen observes: "In the case of mines . . . it seems that a rent may consist of a portion of the ore, which is the substance of the land itself" (1899, p.20n.).

COVENANTS

Covenants restricting the way in which a landowner can use his land are more recent in origin. That they have emerged as a separate type of property right or servitude can be explained in fairly simple terms. The way lawyers conceptualised easements reflects a social context in which the capacity to confer ancillary benefits annexed to titles to land could increase the value of a particular estate, but, for the most part, except so far as securing flows of light and water were concerned, it did not seem necessary to enshrine in the form of a property right what a landowner could do with his land. The courts might, and did, come under pressure to provide remedial assistance where a landowner's use of his land was particularly noxious or unpleasant to his neighbours; hence that branch of the law of tort called "nuisance". But in the past, standards of tolerance were perhaps higher and the technological capacity to cause disturbance more limited. The layout of most medieval towns suggests no great concern with prospect or amenity. "Merrie England" was a country of filth, fire and stench.

Nonetheless, for reasons which cannot be expounded here, by the eighteenth century social values seem to have changed, and new urban developments came to be more carefully laid out and planned. Lawyers first gave expression to this in terms of the kinds of covenants they inserted in, for example, building leases. In due course, however, they endeavoured to insert similar covenants in conveyances of freehold, where no continuing landlord-tenant relationship could support the obligation created by covenant once the title had passed out of the hands of the original covenantor.

Covenants are property rights to the extent that, although they originate in agreement between individual landowners, and as such are enforceable as contracts by the original parties, they are treated as attached, by analogy with easements, to the dominant and servient tenements concerned. Again by analogy with easements, they are not recognised as capable of being so attached unless this proximate relationship of benefit and burden can be shown. A further requirement is that the content of the covenant undertaken by a landowner is negative in character, where, in other words, no positive action is required of him. Covenants which impose positive obligations—to maintain a fence or wall or to dig a ditch—have always been treated differently.[33] The benefit of such covenants, it has long been recognised, can attach to the land so that the right to enforce them will run automatically with the land. (Whether it does or not is for the parties to decide when the covenant is made.) But the obligation so created cannot be attached to the land of the covenantor; it remains personal to him and will become unenforceable when his title passes on or he becomes unobtainable.

This has an important practical consequence today, particularly concerning whether the obligation to maintain or repair buildings can be made to run with land. The lease was and, at the time of writing, remains the only secure way in which positive obligations can be attached to titles to land.[34] Such obligations are important, for instance, where neighbours share common structural elements of a building—the foundations, the roof—as is the case in flats and tenements. A flat developer today gets his basic return by selling leases of the flats he has developed. He must sell them as leases because the purchasers will not be able to raise mortgage finance if he sells the flats as freeholds. And the purchasers will not get such finance because as things stand at the time of writing positive covenants relating, for example, to repair, cannot be enforced between freeholders, and therefore freehold flats are considered to provide poor security by institutional lenders. In other words, today, the "lease" is used as a form which has been disengaged from the substance of the transaction. Leases of this sort have become the vehicle of a new kind of practice: the service charge of the freeholder of a building converted into flats by way of leases containing positive covenants relating to repair and maintenance. The brute fact is that the lessees—the owners of the flats—must pay the costs of maintenance and repair. But if a lease places the responsibility for carrying out the work upon the lessor (whether it does or not is largely up to the initial developer), there is a risk that the lessor may charge almost regardless of the service he provides. Statute now gives lessees of flats the right to go to court if these charges are unreasonable (Landlord and Tenant Act 1985). An alternative approach would be to change the old rules and enable positive obligations to be attached to freeholds. This would have the added advantage of making it possible to simplify the esoteric form in which the ownership of units in multiple dwellings is organised today. The statutory introduction of a "commonhold" system making this possible is still awaited.

Because restrictive covenants were enforced by the courts of equity, their enforceability against a landowner depended upon the doctrine of notice (see p.108, above and 213–216, below), and a purchaser without notice of a covenant binding his land took free from it. Various procedures for the registration of such covenants were introduced in 1925, and are outlined in a later chapter. It can be noted at this stage, though, that the books rightly insist that, in deciding whether a particular covenant is enforceable as a land obligation, you must, once beyond privity of contract, ask whether the benefit has passed to the plaintiff and the burden to the defendant as two independent questions. This might suggest that there is a symmetrical relation between the two sides. But this is not exactly the case. There is one question relating to both benefit and burden: whether, in each case, it "passes", which is part of the body of learning concerning land transfer and the appropriate conveyancing procedures. A second question arises with the benefit alone: "Does this claimed right 'in fact' benefit the plaintiff's land or title?" This is a question which operates at a quite different level.

In previous chapters we have considered how the past grips the present in the way English land law is put together and how this makes many matters more convoluted or oblique than seems necessary. Questions which could be put directly are put indirectly, or have to be considered in a curious, obscure code. The same is true with land obligations. But perhaps because the questions here are not just questions for conveyancers, that is, questions of form or of mechanics, but also questions of substance, some of the fundamental distinctions in this area have been discredited. In particular, the Law Commission has now proposed that positive and negative covenants should be assimilated. The old metaphysics of the common law has lost its appeal for the modern mind.

PUBLIC CONTROL OF LAND USE

The use of covenants in building leases and in schemes of development marked a further extension of the private regulation of land use. To the extent that these devices were upheld and enforced by the courts, they constituted a private law which governed and governs the use of land by its owners. Limited inroads have been made upon this practice. In particular, legislation now empowers the Lands Tribunal to set aside restrictive covenants which have become obsolete.

More generally, the whole system of private control of land use now exists in parallel with a public system of control. For centuries, public control of the use of land took the form of prohibition: the issue of regulations forbidding anyone to erect a building more than such and such a height and so on. In the twentieth century, public control has assumed a more positive role.

Here it is necessary to distinguish two processes: public control of land development, and forward planning of land development by public authorities. Public control of land use aims at maximising the sum total of land values by minimising the costs and negative side-effects of the intensification of land use. In essence, this is done by requiring individual landowners who wish to carry out certain operations on their land, or change its use, even if the land is subject to no privately imposed restrictions, to seek planning permission from the local authority for such change of use.

Since the Second World War in particular, following the mass destruction of many urban areas through bombing, a range of attempts have been made to plan how land is used. Local authorities have been required to produce plans for the general nature of development in their areas, which, in turn, have been supervised or overseen by the central departments of state.

Control of land use by public authorities does not require plans, though the existence of plans may make the decision-making process on particular applications seem less arbitrary. If plans for cities, counties or regions exist, then decision-making on particular proposed changes of use can be made with reference to such plans and, equally, the formulation of proposals for development by private individuals or companies can use the plan as a point of reference for predicting the likely success of their proposal (since the formulation of proposals costs time and money). It is largely with reference to this broad objective of planning that local authorities have been empowered to compel private owners to sell to them land required for development.

The history of the planning system is largely caught up in the history of the land development industry on the one hand and the history of central and local government relations on the other, and lies beyond our scope here. Given the nature of modern life, and the very considerable side-effects which uncontrolled development can generate—especially in the area of transportation—it is generally accepted that public control is inevitable and necessary (see the reforms to Part II of the Town and Country Planning Act 1990, introduced by the Planning and Compensation Act 1991). These types of planning control were primarily concerned with the regulation of the construction of new buildings and with the type or manner of use of property. Alongside that system, and in part as a reaction to some of the products of that system, has grown up a concern with preservation of the old for aesthetic or social reasons (for some of the general issues which arise here, see Chapter 1, above). The institutionalisation of this concern with the remains of the past has, at its core, various procedures for the listing of buildings, which impose various obligations on private owners as to maintenance and repair, and restrict their freedom to alter the physical appearance of these buildings. A parallel regime has been established to protect undeveloped land which is of scientific interest or outstanding natural beauty. Even trees or birds' nests may be protected. Some notion of the public interest again provides the underlying justification for the inroads which these controls involve upon the freedom of property owners.

It follows from this brief discussion that an owner of land or an interest in land in modern society is potentially subject to a plurality of restrictions and controls on his freedom to enjoy the property as he wishes. If the property in question is a leasehold flat, for example, the owner's freedom of action may be limited by covenants in the lease, by restrictive covenants affecting the building as a whole, by planning controls (which may limit the ability to add an extension to the property, for example), and by "heritage" controls (which may limit, for example, the type of renovation work which can be undertaken, such as the replacement of windows). At the other extreme, the owner of an undeveloped rural field may be subject not only to private limitations of his freedom to enjoy contained in leasehold or freehold covenants, but also be prevented by public controls from building on the land, or from cutting down trees. The enforcement of these controls and restrictions differs, of course, depending on whether the restriction is private or public: in the former case it is for the holder of the right to enforce it; in the latter case it is primarily the responsibility of local authorities to ensure that public controls are complied with by owners of property.

9

TRANSFER AND THE CIRCULATION OF THINGS

THE MEANINGS OF CIRCULATION

In most Western societies today, the transfer of things is conceived primarily in terms of markets, secondarily in terms of gift, and a strong cultural distinction is emphasised between sale and gift. This framework, which lawyers have helped to consolidate, neglects a number of other aspects of what occurs in and through the transfer and circulation of things, and these opening paragraphs seek to focus attention on those questions.

After the sharing of food, the transfer of the possessions of someone who has died, few though they might be, to those who still remain has, in most societies, to be resolved. The Pharaonic solution (in which your possessions go with your body to the tomb), and the destruction of your possessions along with your body on a funeral pyre, are both relatively rare in human experience. Death is, however, only one moment in the developmental cycle, and the circulation of possessions is as widely associated with other decisive moments in this cycle in many societies, especially birth and marriage.

A number of things may be going on here, and different ways of making sense of them are not necessarily incompatible. First, the circulation of things, often linked, as with marriage, to the circulation of people (*e.g.* bridewealth and dowry), can be understood as an integrative mechanism, as social cement, although norms which concentrate the exchange of things at key points in the developmental cycle are as generative of conflict as of social peace. A semiological approach, on the other hand, sees exchanges signifying, as marking an event. People communicate with each other through the exchange of things. The circulation of things can symbolise or represent changes of status or the movement of honour within a social group. Mauss says that men could pledge their honour before they could sign their names (1925; tr. 1966, 1969, p.36), and quickly adds that they often used things as "pledges".

Moreover, in any society, many acts of exchange, through which things circulate between people, take place quite independently of the developmental cycle, as immediate responses to the needs of the moment. But the inner logic of exchange— what it means to the members of the group—is not necessarily economic, if by this we mean that "an economy comprises a separate sphere of instrumental or practical action" such that economic analysis "can be used to analyse patterns of livelihood everywhere" (Gudeman, 1986, p.vii). From such an economic perspective, exchange is understood as an instrumental or practical act. "Barter" is treated as an early form of sale, in which exchange involves the reciprocal transfer of a material capability, enabling each party to the transaction to satisfy, directly or indirectly, his material needs. So it is the satisfaction of these needs which serves to motivate the exchange.

Economists would no doubt readily admit that other, extraneous, elements may be visible in the transactions of real life: there may be elements which motivate exchange—as in the choice of trading partner—which are not readily attributable to the purely practical objective of the satisfaction of material needs. The main function or objective (obviously the two are not the same) of trading with particular partners may be to cement an alliance with them. This may be the indigenous explanation for the object of the exercise, or the interpretation placed upon the exchange by an anthropologist who observes it. In either case, this points to ways of seeing the exchange which diverge sharply from the model of economic rationality which we largely take for granted in the West.

These non-rational elements are more readily discerned in the way in which we think about "gift", which, as we shall see, lawyers, in contrast to many social scientists, do not treat as a form of exchange at all but as its opposite. The transmission of material capability—of the capacity to satisfy materials needs through the consumption of things—is clearly a feature of many gift exchanges, as with many practices of inheritance (for which see Chapter 1, above). But in our understanding of gift, other, additional, meanings are often at work. Wedding presents transfer material capability, but also cement relations between groups and mark important changes of status for the partners to the marriage. The functional and semiological aspects of the transaction are relatively visible. Sometimes, indeed, it is mainly the semiological element which renders the gift intelligible, as where the largest share in the family property passes to the eldest son by virtue of his position in the family but where such transmission confers no substantial material capability (the ancestral watch or one more goat than the younger brothers and/or sisters receive). Here, the principal role of the gift is to mark who he is.

In general terms, the economic understanding of the circulation of things provides limited, and often parochial, purchase on this central facet of human experience. As Mauss suggested many years ago, people communicate with each other in a complex variety of ways when they handle, exchange or destroy things. Honour and shame, political superiority and subordination, alliance and separation, maintenance and change of status: one or more of these can be at stake when things circulate between people as well as or in place of the transfer of the ability to satisfy material needs in which the economist would ground the logic of exchange (see generally Parry and Bloch, 1989).

Trade without rulers remains a common enough feature of social experience (see, for example, Northrup, 1978); nor does exchange, even today, require lawyers or courts. But the coming of literacy, more than anything, enables lawyers to get their hands on the business of exchange (Clanchy, 1979). This comes about in two ways. First, and most important, lawyers come upon the scene as writers, recording in writing the fact of transfer, and, in the process, developing a special language for the act of recording, until a point is reached where the writing ceases to be a mere record of an act and becomes constitutive of the act itself. Secondly, presupposing such developments, lawyers become readers of such writing, when the writing is scrutinised for proof of title, or by a judge in a dispute which is taken to court. We see in this chapter that the use of writing developed with particular intensity in relation to the circulation of titles to land. This has had the result that English land law is very largely the product of a dialectic between the work of lawyers as writers and lawyers as readers. The complexity of land law is largely attributable to the fact that lawyers have long been so good with words.

Alongside these dimensions to exchange we must set the development of markets. This is especially important in relation to land because, as we will shortly see, the idea that it is important to achieve the marketability of land has been especially influential in legal literature (mainly as a diagnosis of what is or was wrong with the laws which we have or had). Here we must stress that the creation of stable or reliable markets is an achievement, not a natural datum, and that the contribution of law to the achievement of such stability was and is always problematic. For medieval and early modern rulers, for example, the regulation of markets was an important concern—the timing and location of markets; what could be sold and its quality, however that was and could be assessed. For moveables, these considerations posed one kind of organisational problem: in essence that of bringing buyers and sellers together in the same physical location—paradigmatically, the street market. Today, this has been abstracted, first, into the supermarket and, secondly, into internet shopping. The activity of shopping signals the consolidation of markets and their establishment in particular places or locations; the internet holds out the possibility of unravelling some or much of this, as, earlier in the century, did mail-order shopping, which was first developed in a significant way in the geographically dispersed United States.

Land and housing markets have perhaps always been different in that the specific location of the land is an inextricable element of what is being bought and sold. The problem with land is the physical and temporal separation between the market and what is traded. A similar separation occurs in mail-order shopping, but this type of market presupposes the mass production of commodities, so that the general character and desirability of the commodity can be known by buyers even though they do not have the precise object in front of them at the time of the purchase. The specific character of a land market may help to explain why, in England, which had one of the earliest thriving market economies in both land and commodities, quite separate legal regimes came into being for the transfer of land on the one hand and of commodities on the other. As will be discussed below (Chapter 10), some aspects of these different markets may be merging to some extent. They will never be coterminous with each other, but some of the philosophies and techniques of electronic transfer may have a substantive effect on the position of land as a commodity.

LAWYERS AND TRANSFER MANAGEMENT

"The manner in which the alienation of personal chattels is effected, is in many respects essentially different from the modes of conveying real estate. In ancient times, indeed, there was more similarity than there is at present. The conveyance of land was then usually made by feoffment, with livery of seisin, which was nothing more than a simple gift of an estate in the land, accompanied by delivery of possession. This gift might then have been made by mere word of mouth; but the Statute of Frauds made writing necessary; and now every conveyance of landed property is required to be by deed. Personal chattels, on the contrary, are still alienable by mere gift and delivery; though they may be disposed of by 'deed'; and they are also assignable by sale, in a manner totally different from the conveyance requisite on the transfer of real estate. Each of these three modes of conveyance deserves a separate notice" (Williams, 1856, p.33, emphasis in original).

Moveables

Most moveables by definition are easy to transfer and circulate within a society with only minimal direct involvement on the part of lawyers. As already indicated, this is one reason why English conceptions of personal property are relatively undeveloped, and geared primarily to a system of remedies for the recovery of chattels or their value through the legal process. But, as we have seen, English lawyers distinguish property from the thing itself. This opens up the possibility that transfer of title will occur at a different time from transfer of the thing to which the title relates. In examining transfer in English law, we are looking at: (i) lawyers' recognition of the facts of life (clothing fact with right again: delivery of a thing as effecting a transfer of title); (ii) lawyers' development of artificial mechanisms for transferring title (notably deeds); and (iii) lawyers' specification of rules designed to determine in any particular case the moment in time when title passes. This third aspect is of particular importance in the context of buying and selling, and can conveniently be treated first.

Sale

Selling is a social process which can be privately arranged between two individuals, and this is what is meant, today, by the phrase "sale by private treaty". In the modern world, we often take this process of buying and selling for granted, since there are so many means of communication through which selling can occur. But in many societies, this is precisely the difficulty: establishing contact in the first place between buyer and seller. In this context the phenomenon of the traditional market, whether permanent (as in the bazaar or souk) or periodic (as in the market in the English country town), was the commonest form of organising exchange through sale. Transacting by private treaty still provides the model for the management by lawyers of the sale of land. The market, where exchange is rapid and many matters have to be taken on trust, provides the model for how lawyers think about the sale of most other things.

In English law, transfer of title by sale has two main ingredients. First, an agreement between buyer and seller. Secondly, a quid pro quo—you get the car and I get the money. This is what lawyers call "consideration". This second element is conventionally taken to distinguish sale from gift; we return below to this distinction. Unlike land, agreements for the sale of moveables need no formality to be effective in law. Indeed, nothing need even be said: you pay your money and take the thing away. The agreement is inferred from the conduct of the parties. Witnesses are not required. Written agreements or written evidence (*e.g.* a receipt) of the transaction will be of decisive importance if there is later a dispute, but legally they are "optional extras".

There is a significant contrast between this and the legal consequences of a contract for the sale of land:

"It is in this last and most usual method of alienation that the contrast presents itself between the means to be employed for the alienation of real property and chattels personal. When a contract has been entered into for the sale of lands, the legal estate in such lands still remains vested in the vendor; and it is not transferred to the vendee until the vendor shall have executed and delivered to him a proper deed of conveyance. In equity, it is true that the lands belong to the purchaser from the moment of the signature of the contract; and from the same moment,the purchase-money belongs, in equity, to the vendor. But at law the only result of the signature of a contract for the sale of land is that each party acquires a right to sue the other for pecuniary damages, in case such contract be not performed. Not so, however, the case of a contract for the sale of chattels personal. Such a contract immediately transfers the legal property in the goods sold from the vendor to the vendee, without the necessity of anything further" (Williams, 1856, pp.35–36).

So much for "agreement". Williams moves on to consider a second question: when does title pass? If you decide to sell your car, when does your title to the car pass to the buyer? Perhaps the most obvious answer is that title passes when he takes the keys and registration book from you and drives away. But what if the buyer puts down a deposit and you hold onto the car pending full payment? Are you still free to sell it to someone else? Who bears the loss if the car is stolen or destroyed pending "completion" of the sale? Even in the everyday world, people might be unsure about the question of title at that point. In fact, there are several possibilities. Title might pass as soon as you reach agreement and shake hands on the deal. It might pass when the full price is paid. It might pass at a time which the two of you agree it should.

Behind the question of time is the question of risk. Cars are dangerous and vulnerable things, easy to steal and easy to destroy. Cars are risky; insurance provides a mechanism for anticipating risk. Buyer and seller need to know about when title passes so that they know when the risk passes from one to the other, and thus who must insure what, and when.

Some civil law jurisdictions have a simple rule about the passing of title. It passes when the thing is delivered by the seller into the hands of the buyer. No doubt this seems sensible to many people. If you buy a guard dog, you would probably assume that it becomes yours from the time when you take it away, because from that time you have to feed it, make sure it does not maul innocent people, in short, become responsible for it. But English law treats the intention of the parties as decisive. The Sale of Goods Act 1979 provides that title under a contract of sale passes "when the contracting parties intend it to pass". If there is no discernible intention, title passes at the time the contract is made. The Act restates the common law position, explained here by a distinguished commercial lawyer, writing before the original legislation of 1893:

> "When the parties are agreed as to the goods on which the agreement is to attach, the presumption is, that the parties intend the right of property to be transferred at once, unless there be something to indicate a contrary intention. An agreement, therefore, concerning the sale of specific or ascertained goods, is *prima facie* a bargain and sale of those goods. But this arises merely from the presumed intention of the parties, and if it appears that the parties have agreed, not that

there shall be a mutual credit by which the property is to pass
from the vendor to the purchaser, and the purchaser is to be
bound to the vendor for the price, but that the exchange of the
money for the goods shall be made on the spot; no property is
transferred, for it is not the intention of the parties to transfer
any. In other words, a contract for the sale of specific chattels,
is *prima facie* a contract to transfer the property, in consideration of the purchaser becoming bound to pay the price; but if
the parties choose so to agree, it may be a contract to transfer
the property, in consideration of the purchaser actually paying the price, and not merely of his engagement so to do"
(Blackburn, 1845, p.147).

The essential elements of a transfer of title by sale, are, then,
agreement and consideration. But what else, if anything, should
concern a buyer who seeks to obtain a good title to moveable
things? How far is he concerned with titles "earlier" than that of
the seller? We have already seen that the general rule here is
that the seller cannot pass on a better title than he himself has
(*nemo dat quod non habet*). From this it follows that the buyer is at
risk if titles superior to that of the seller lurk in the background.
In this context, there are some exceptions to *nemo dat* which can
now be introduced.

These enable an innocent purchaser of moveable objects to
defend himself in defined circumstances against a claimant with
"good" earlier title.

(1) If you hand something over to an agent so that he can sell
it for you, the agent can pass a good title to a purchaser even
though title remains with you, provided he was given the thing
as an agent to sell it. So if a dealer sells your car while it is in his
hands to be repaired, title does not pass to the buyer under this
exception.

(2) If the seller lets the buyer take possession of the thing
before title has passed, the buyer can pass a good title to an
innocent purchaser even though he himself does not yet have
title.

(3) Conversely, if the seller remains in possession after title
has passed to the buyer under the contract of sale, a third party
can acquire good title from the seller.

The rationale of these exceptions to *nemo dat* is fairly obvious.
The innocent purchaser in whose favour these exceptions are
made is less able to protect himself than the person who would
succeed if nemo dat was strictly applied. If you sell through an

agent, you should choose an honest one. If you are selling, you should hold on to the thing until you have been paid. If you are buying you should take control of the thing once you have paid the price. The law assumes that such practical rules govern transactions in the marketplace.

Underpinning these exceptions is the more basic fact that titles in commercial transactions are commonly lacking in documentary support, and it is this, as we shall shortly see, which sharply distinguishes transfers of title to land in the English system. Put differently, there has always been pressure in the direction of enabling buyers to assume that those who have moveable things in their possession own them, at least if there is nothing clandestine about it. This is manifested clearly in the oldest exception to *nemo dat* which can be traced back to the Middle Ages (and which has no contemporary rationale).

(4) Until 1995, anyone who bought in "market overt" acquired secure title to the thing he bought. "Market overt" meant those open-air and street markets which were legally constituted by local laws or long established custom at familiar sites and times.

"With regard to ordinary choses in possession, a valid title to them is generally obtained by a purchase in an open market, or market overt, although no property may have been possessed by the vendor. And every shop in the city of London, where goods are openly sold, is considered as a *market overt* within this rule, for such things as by the trade of the owner are put there for sale. But the shops at the west end of the town do not appear to possess this privilege. If the sale is not made in *market overt*, the purchaser, though he purchase *bona fide*, acquires no further property in the article sold than was possessed by the vendor" (Williams, 1856, p.320).

This exception has now been removed by the Sale of Goods (Amendment) Act 1994. This abolition of the market overt rules was partly motivated by the increasing arbitrariness involved in determining what counted as a legally recognised open market under these rules. More generally, it can be suggested that the obsolescence of such rules derived from the fact that they were no longer needed to support or sustain markets in goods, since the existence and health of such markets had now come to depend not on the purposive actions of governments but on commercial imperatives driving the largely corporate retailing sector of the economy and the rise of modern consumer markets. Modern equivalents of traditional markets like the car-boot sale thus take place under the full rigour of *caveat emptor*.

Gift

As we have said, lawyers distinguish sharply between sale and gift. Lawyers see them as quite different transactions and attach different legal consequences to each. More precisely: lawyers classify promises into two distinct categories, using the presence or absence of consideration as the yardstick. Gratuitous promises, one-sided "unilateral" promises where I give you my promise—my word—but receive nothing in return, are unenforceable in law. But where promises are exchanged—where I give you my promise in return for your promise—the law will enforce each side of the bargain. If the promise relates to a transfer of title to a thing, the gratuitous promise as such has no legal consequences, whereas, as seen above, the mere exchange of promises is capable of passing title in law.

Lawyers look upon gift as at core a unilateral transaction, by contrast with the bilateral character of sale. Gift is not treated as a mode of exchange. In this respect, the legal definition of gift differs sometimes quite sharply from the social meaning of gift in many cultures, including, perhaps, our own.

In many societies, giving buys you prestige. As Mauss put it:

"Between vassals and chiefs, between vassals and their henchmen, the hierarchy is established by means of . . . gifts. To give is to show one's superiority, to show that one is something more and higher, that one is magister. To accept without returning or repaying more is to face subordination, to become a client and subservient, to become minister" (1925; tr. 1966, 1969, p.72).

Moreover, as Bourdieu has observed, in many societies gifts generate the obligation to give back. But such obligations are scripted in a complex way:

"In every society it may be observed that, if it is not to constitute an insult, the counter-gift must be deferred and different, because the immediate return of an exactly identical object clearly amounts to a refusal (*i.e.* the return of the same object). Thus gift exchange is opposed on the one hand to swapping, which . . . telescopes gift and counter-gift into the same instant, and on the other hand, to lending, in which the return of the loan is explicitly guaranteed by a juridical act and is thus already accomplished at the very moment of the drawing up of a contract capable of ensuring that the acts it prescribes are predictable and calculable" (1972; tr. 1977, p.5, italics removed).

Lawyers' involvement in giving arises in three contexts. First, the devising of mechanisms for giving which will be enforceable in courts. Secondly, the development of categories to conceptualise in legal terms what people do with their things in the course of ordinary life. Thirdly, the formulation of rules (beyond our present scope) to limit the effects of the general rules if people, in giving, harm others, notably their creditors.

Legal artifice

The courts will only enforce a gratuitous promise to transfer a thing if the promise is formally written down in a deed of gift. A deed is a written instrument (a stylised mechanism for achieving a result) signed and traditionally sealed (though the seal is no longer necessary) by the person making the gift and then delivered. "Delivery" is a ceremonial act which is accomplished when the donor places his hand on the seal and says: "I deliver this as my act and deed". In practical terms, such a deed functions to provide evidentiary support for the fact that a gift took place by actual delivery. However, its legal effect is the same whether or not the thing or the deed is handed over after the solemn declaration of delivery. And the desire to provide enduring evidentiary support for gratuitous transfers seems to be how this piece of legal artifice arose in the first place (Clanchy, 1979).

The deed itself is, then, the instrument which effects transfer of title by way of gift. But it stylises a more primordial—and still more common—mode of giving, namely the simple physical act whereby one person hands a thing over to another. The deed, one might say, has a representational character; it "stands for", substitutes for, but equally is premised upon, the act of giving itself.

"Every deed imports a consideration; but it was anciently supposed, that no person would do so solemn an act as the sealing and delivery of a deed without some sufficient ground. The presence of this implied consideration renders a deed sufficient of itself to pass the property in goods. It supplies on the one hand the act of delivery, and on the other the want of that actual consideration which always exists in the third and most usual mode of alienation of chattels personal, which is . . . by sale" (Williams, 1856, p.35).

Delivery

The transfer of title by actual, physical, delivery of the thing is not in its essentials a piece of legal artifice. Rather, it is something which happens in the social world, of which lawyers have to make sense. That is, it is a mode of social behaviour which lawyers had to draw in to their own conceptual scheme. Here, then, the rule is drawn from the social world: "Title passes with delivery". Lawyers conceptualised delivery, the physical act, as the instrument for passing title and, equally, treated the act of delivery as proving or establishing, in evidential terms, that a transfer of title had taken place.

". . . personal chattels are alienable by a mere gift of them, accompanied by delivery of possession. For this purpose no deed or writing is required, nor is it essential that there should be a consideration for the gift. Thus, if I give a horse to A.B., and at the same time deliver it into his possession, this gift is complete and irrevocable, and the property in the horse is thenceforward vested in A.B. But if I purport to assign the horse, and yet retain the possession, the gift, though made by writing (so that it be not a deed), is absolutely void at law" (Williams, 1856, p.33).

Given that transfer by deed is a piece of legal artifice, it posed only mechanical problems for lawyers, principally to do with verbal formulae, with the precise form of words which would achieve, in legal terms, the desired effect. But since delivery represents a legal conceptualisation of what people simply did and do, it inevitably throws up a range of problems concerning exactly what the legal concept of delivery means.

Actual physical transfer of a thing is simple enough. But some things may be so big or heavy that they cannot simply be picked up by me and handed to you. Further, if I want to give you a set or collection of things, do I have to hand over each individual item of the set for the law to recognise the transfer as valid? Yet again, I may not have the thing I wish to give you immediately to hand; it may be out on loan or buried among my mess. Must

I get it back or find it before I can give it to you? You might even have the thing I want to give you already in your possession, because you hired it or borrowed it, or are taking care of it for me. Must you return it to me before I can give it to you? Such routine questions required lawyers to stylise their conception of delivery itself. First, large heavy things could be transferred by "symbolical delivery". Delivery will be taken to have occurred by lawyers if, for example, the donor places his hand upon the thing and declares that he gives it to the donee, or if he hands over his receipt (from when he bought it) or some other document relating to the thing.

"In some cases it is not possible to make an immediate and complete delivery of the subject of gift; and in these cases, as near an approach as possible must be made to actual delivery; and if this be done, the gift will be effectual. Thus if goods be in a warehouse, the delivery of the key will be sufficient; timber may be delivered by marking it with the initials of the assignee, and an actual removal is not essential to the delivery of a haystack. But the delivery of a part of goods capable of actual delivery, is not a sufficient delivery of the whole" (Williams, 1856, p.34).

If someone else has the thing at the moment, say on loan or hire, the donor can pass title to you by telling that person of the gift and getting him to acknowledge that it now belongs to you. If the donor cannot find the thing but tells you where he thinks it might be, it will be yours if and when you find it. And words of gift suffice if the donee already has the thing at the time the donor wants to make the gift. In the case of sets or collections of things, however, each item must be handed over. I cannot give you my entire dinner service by handing over the sauceboat to you. If that is all I do, then that is all you get in law.

A gift cannot be forced upon someone. To this limited extent, although the law regards gift as a non-reciprocal relationship, it involves an element of consent. The donee can refuse the gift, as some universities and political parties have done recently for ethical reasons. It follows that where the donee is ignorant of the gift at the time that it is made—most obviously, in such a situation, where it is made by deed—he can, on discovery of the gift, repudiate it. In such perhaps rather unlikely circumstances, the legal position is not clear. Does title pass provisionally to the donee at the time of the gift and then revert to the donor on repudiation? Or does title remain with the donor until the gift is accepted by the donee? Or does a repudiated gift mean that title to the thing becomes vacant following the repudiation? We do not know the answers to these questions. As so often in English law, this may be because no practical pressures lead to them being asked in the first place.

Declaration of trust
Although, as Williams insists, a gift fails where the prospective donor remains in possession, the matter is different if in holding onto the thing he declares himself as a trustee:

> "It may, however, be observed, that if the donor should not attempt to part with the subject of gift, but should declare that he keeps possession of it in trust for the donee, equity will seize on and enforce this trust, although voluntarily created" (Williams, 1856, p.34).

Assignment of choses in action

Intangible things present problems of transfer which are absent in the case of tangible things. First, and most obviously, there is no physical thing to circulate, nothing to be delivered or received. Intangible things, as creatures of the law in the first place, require legal artifice for their transfer. Secondly, the transfer of title to some intangibles involve third parties in a way that is often not the case with moveables or land. Debt provides an example. Its transfer essentially involves ensuring that the debtor will pay the assignee of the debt. By their very nature, transfers of rights of this kind affect third parties as well as transferor and transferee.

Section 136 of the Law of Property Act 1925 provides a general set of formalities for transferring title to debts, which applies to both sales and gifts. It requires that the assignment be made in writing, and that written notice of the transfer be given to the debtor. The rules of equity are less stringent but apply only to assignments for value. Equity regards an assignment as effective between assignor and assignee as soon as the assignor has done all he can to divest himself of his interest. But the assignee's security against the debtor depends on notice being given to the debtor before a further assignment. So if the owner of the debt assigns it to two people successively, the first will have no claim against the debtor if the second assignee gives notice first.

The transfer of many types of intangibles is governed by special statutory regimes. To illustrate: the Companies Acts require shares to be transferred by writing and the transfer to be registered in the books of the company, unless the company's articles of association provide otherwise. The Patents Act provides that patents be transferred by deed and that the transfer be registered in the Patent Office. The Policies of Assurance Act requires a prescribed form of words to be used to assign an insurance policy, and further requires written notice to be given to the insurance company.

Land

In previous chapters, we have outlined the rather complex way in which lawyers have conceptualised rights in land by comparison with their approach to rights in other things. It is not surprising then that the business of land transfer is also complex. This complexity arises at three levels. The first concerns the nature of title in English law and the plurality of ways in which it can be fragmented. The second is the existence of a number of devices through which incumbrances can be imposed upon a title, which, as we saw above, are sometimes indistinguishable from the rights which result from the process of fragmentation of title. The third is the existence of property rights correlative to these incumbrances on title, such as the benefit of easements and restrictive covenants. All these facts of legal life must be provided for, and how this is done forms the subject-matter of the rest of this chapter.

Before we begin, though, let us repeat the fundamental point: the way English lawyers conceptualise property grows out of the nature of their involvement with it. With land, they have long been managers of its transfer. And so the complexities discussed in previous chapters and recapitulated above are largely the product, rather than the cause, of what lawyers have tried to do in the course of their management of land transfer.

Most people who buy a flat on a long lease realise that they are acquiring less than full ownership of the premises, even though they may remain vague about the precise nature of their rights, and the extent to which their purchase bestows less than full ownership. But even the purchaser of a freehold house is in fact buying a fee simple in the house, or, more precisely, in the land on which the house stands. Strictly speaking, he is buying a title—a property right—to land, not the land itself.

The physical nature of land means that its ownership is likely to have passed through more hands over time than in the case of most moveables. Moreover, purchasers are potentially more vulnerable to adverse claims both because the stakes are often high and because you cannot hide land away, as you can many chattels. So, when a purchaser proposes to buy land (strictly, title to the land) he needs to ask the seller for proof that he has title. How can the seller prove it? By showing how he himself acquired his title. How can he show this? Much of English land law has grown up around the range of problems embedded in this question and the search for ways of dealing with it.

In general terms, a seller of land traditionally established his title by producing the documents by means of which he acquired title from the previous owner. But this only pushed the question back one stage further. The purchaser would want to know whether that title, through which the seller derived his title, was itself a good title. How could that be proved? In exactly the same way. The seller had to produce the document through which the person from whom he had bought the land had himself derived title. Traditionally, there were two principal formalised ways through which such documentary support for the quality of a title could be marshalled: the will or last testament, and the conveyance. Although, as we shall see below, the 1925 legislation has made much of the traditional conveyancing learning less important in contemporary conditions, its nature and mode of functioning—and the problems it threw up—must all be understood if the fabric of this legislation is to be intelligible to its student today.

MECHANISMS OF LAND TRANSFER

Contract and conveyance

The traditional method of transfer of title to land was by a conveyance—a formal legal deed which stated that by means of the deed the seller conveyed or granted his fee simple to the purchaser. The execution of the deed—the affixing of seals, etc.—itself transferred the title. It was not necessary for legal purposes that there should be a physical transfer of possession and the widespread presence of tenants in both the urban and the rural context complicated the picture in any case. All that was required was the execution of the conveyance.

"The draft of the conveyance is prepared . . . by the purchaser's solicitors. It is then sent to the vendor's solicitors for approval on his behalf . . . Here it may be mentioned that when an instrument of assurance drawn by one conveyancer, whether counsel or solicitor, is sent to another to be settled on behalf of some party, whom the framer of the draft did not represent, the other should of course make all such alterations as he considers necessary to safeguard the interests of his client: but he should not alter the draft further or otherwise than is necessary to effect this end. In short, his alterations should be directed to matters of substance only and not of form; and it is a grave breach of conveyancing etiquette for one practitioner to amend another's draft in any point, on which his client's interest would not really be affected if the instrument were to stand as originally drawn" (Williams, 1922, p.652).

It was common, as this comment on "protocol" suggests, for lengthy negotiation to precede a transfer of title. In modern sales of residential property, the most important question, once the price has been agreed, is to decide when the transfer will occur and when the purchase price is to be paid, so that buyer and seller can arrange their affairs accordingly. All of these things are usually sorted out, prior to conveyance, by a contract. In the contract, the seller promises to sell and the buyer promises to buy and usually pays a deposit. This is the process which lawyers call "exchange of contracts", whereas the stage of the conveyance, when title passes at law, is called "completion". The contract is subject to all the normal rules of contract, and the common law remedy of damages is available for breach of it. But as we saw in Chapter 5, certain additional equitable remedies are available to enforce this kind of contract, which are not normally available where a contract is for the sale of chattels.

In the past, however, the complexity of title made the preparation of the contract an arduous and sometimes hazardous affair, since it was often necessary to include a mass of special stipulations and covenants in the contract, in order to circumvent any possible dispute which might rise between the parties in the future, whether before or after completion. And the more common such "special" contracts were, the more any general theory of good title was displaced by a contractual regime which invoked the idea of good title only to supersede it. The importance of this contract stage gave rise to another set of problems related to the formalisation of transactions, which it is convenient to consider now before returning to the question of transmission of title.

Contracts, writing and equity

The Statute of Frauds of 1677 provided, among other things, that contracts for the sale of land required written evidence if they were to be enforceable in the courts. This generated a new problem for the equity courts. Would the absence of written evidence of an agreement for sale always defeat a purchaser who went into possession under an oral agreement and later sought, through the courts, to acquire the title deeds and a conveyance of title from a reluctant seller? Over time, the courts came to afford remedial assistance in such circumstances. The difficulty was the question of defining with precision the circumstances in which the courts would intervene if asked. The grounds for affording this assistance came to be called "the equitable doctrine of part performance".

Social and economic life, in its very nature, commonly escapes the reach of the law, which only comes upon the scene after the fact. The oral agreement, which, after the statute, required written evidence to be enforceable in court, might have been acted upon without any writing being produced. Two different problems were posed for the courts, and which problem was the more important has never been adequately resolved. On the one hand is the problem that lies at the heart of much intervention by the equity courts: is there something in the dealings between the parties to the litigation which can be said to warrant the intervention of the court? This is what was meant when it was asked whether the petitioner had established an "equity", or where, as between the disputants, the "balance" of the equities lay. So the further the purchaser had proceeded on the basis of an oral arrangement and acted, as we would say today, to his detriment, the more the equities moved in his favour, in the sense that to put the clock back involved undoing what had been done on the basis of the bargain, in circumstances where it would be simpler, given what had happened, to compel the vendor to complete what he had promised to do, namely execute a conveyance of title in return for the payment of the purchase price.

On the other hand, the statute—which the courts could not simply ignore—was concerned with the need for evidence of a contract to sell land. The things done since the making of the oral agreement—the "acts of part performance"—could equally be viewed as making good the evidentiary deficiency caused by the absence of written evidence of the bargain. The canonical formula in which the doctrine of part performance came to be articulated at the end of the nineteenth century expressed precisely the tension between these two perspectives. It was held that the acts of part performance which would warrant court intervention must refer unequivocally to a contract concerning land.

More recently it has been said that this requirement was too stringent, and that a "balance of probabilities" test would suffice. That is, what was done following the oral agreement did not need to persuade a court that the only explanation was that there was a contract concerning land; it was sufficient to warrant intervention if it was more likely than not that what had been done was explicable because there was a prior agreement. What remained unresolved was whether the court must be persuaded that the acts of part performance occurred as a result of an agreement in general, or of an agreement concerning land. It might seem plausible to a judge, for example, that one of three daughters who gave up her job and returned home to look after her ailing parents for a considerable period of time did so as the result of some arrangement between them; but was the likelihood of such an agreement sufficient for the court to invoke the doctrine, or did the court have to be persuaded that the arrangement was more likely than not to have concerned the family home where the parents lived, which they owned, and which the dutiful daughter claimed after their death?

The Statute of Frauds requirement of written evidence was reproduced, with some modifications, in s.40 of the Law of Property Act 1925. That same section indirectly conferred statutory recognition on the doctrine of part performance by exempting from its scope transactions governed by the doctrine. As part of a package of reforms of the formal requirements relating to land transactions, sponsored by the Law Commission, s.2 of the Law of Property (Miscellaneous Provisions) Act 1989 now provides that s.40 shall "cease to have effect" and that all contracts for the sale of land must be *made* in writing (as opposed to the less stringent requirement of written evidence). The supersession of s.40 means the passing of the doctrine of part performance as a distinct category of equitable intervention. However, the new statute provides that this change does not affect "the creation or operation of resulting, implied or constructive trusts", a formula (not without its own problems) which has been appropriated from s.53(2) of the Law of Property Act 1925.

Both s.2 of the LP(MP)A 1989 and s.53(2) of the LPA 1925 will be affected by the new emphasis on electronic conveyancing in the Land Registration Act 2002 (discussed in Chapter 10). "Writing" in the sense of words on paper, which then make up physical documents, is undergoing a change in the new regime. The requirement is being erased, or otherwise diminished. For commentators and practicing lawyers, demonstrating the requisite evidence in electronic media—turning electronic documents into "deeds" by legislative *fiat*—raises the spectre of the same problems of permanence and security that had been addressed by the Statute of Frauds. In any event, this change does nothing to solve the basic problem faced by courts, which is to decide when it is right to grant equitable assistance in the absence of writing. It is doubtful whether the change of terminology ("trusts" in place of "part performance") will be sufficient to clarify the acceptable basis of equitable intervention in this area, and indeed some courts continue to refer to "part performance" in cases decided since the 1989 Act came into force. Old habits die hard.

Inheritance and title

Conveyance on sale was, of course, only one of several ways in which title to land could change hands. The seller's title might have been acquired not by purchase but through post-mortem inheritance. For example, his father might have bought the title, and died without selling it, but having left a will, which gave the land to his son. On his father's death, the title would vest in the executors of the will, whose job was to collect together all the property of the deceased, to pay off his debts and taxes, and then to distribute the property that was left in accordance with the directions contained in the will.

Alternatively, the father might have died leaving no will. Lawyers call this situation "intestacy". Here, relatives may apply to the court for letters of administration, so that they can wind up the affairs of the deceased, and then distribute the property to the next-of-kin. (The relatives who count as next-of-kin and the order of priority between them are set out in the Administration of Estates Act 1925.) If the son who is the seller in our example had acquired the title either through the will or through intestacy, a formal document known as an "assent", which vests this title in him, would be included in the title deeds. This document proved that he had acquired title not by purchase but by succession from a purchaser.

Finally, as we have already seen, a seller's title may derive from a settlement or from the combined effect of several settlements. Such titles frequently proved to be particularly difficult to investigate.

This collection of documents of transfer, showing a chain of title being transferred from one person to another, made up what lawyers call the "title deeds" to the property. A purchaser, in order to ensure that he got a good title, needed to check through all of these to be certain of an unbroken chain of transfers. In order to do this, he first obtained from the vendor's solicitor an "abstract" of the vendor's title.

Abstracts of title

"Evidence of title on sales being for the most part documentary, and such as can be weighed only by skilled legal advisers, it became usual to facilitate the task of judging of the effect of the title-deeds by making an abstract of their contents for the perusal of the purchaser's counsel. It appears that formerly the deeds were handed over to the purchaser for examination, and any abstract of them which he might require was made at his expense. But afterwards it became established that the vendor was bound to make at his own expense and to deliver to the purchaser an abstract of the title to the property sold . . ." (Williams, 1922, p.97).

The abstract was to begin with identifying a good root of title, that is, with "an instrument of disposition dealing with or proving on the face of it (without the aid of extrinsic evidence) the ownership of the whole legal and equitable estate in the property sold, containing a description by which the property can be identified, and showing nothing to cast any doubt on the title of the disposing parties" (Williams, 1922, p.98).

The basic idea, under this system, was that, in Sugden's words, "wherever he begins the root of title [the solicitor] ought to abstract every subsequent deed" (quoted in Williams, 1922, p.102). However, certain differences arose at this point, depending on whether it was legal or equitable rights which affected the state of the title.

"With regard to documents affecting the equitable but not the legal estate in the property sold, if they be documents on which the purchaser's title will necessarily depend, they certainly ought to be placed on the abstract. But as a purchaser for value, who takes a conveyance of the legal estate in any property, is not bound by any equitable interests therein, of which he has no notice, it is obvious that there may be many documents creating equitable interests only which are not necessary to the purchaser's title, so long as he obtains the legal estate without notice of them. For instance, the vendor may be possessed of documents showing that some former owner who appeared on the face of a conveyance to be entitled for his own benefit, was in fact a trustee, or that persons who had advanced money on mortgage were trustees of the mortgage money. In such cases it would be unusual to allow notice of the trust to appear in the abstract" (Williams, 1922, p.101).

And, as this illustrates, what came first was practical convenience. "This . . . is no doubt a departure from the general principle", commented Williams, "that it is for the purchaser's solicitor, and not the vendor's, to judge of the materiality of the muniments of title; but it is sanctioned by convenience and universal practice" (*ibid.*).

CONSEQUENCES OF THE TITLE-DEED SYSTEM

The process we have so far described was cumbersome and time-consuming. The fulcrum of the system was the conveyancing bar, the elite of the conveyancing side of the profession in the nineteenth century. It was their opinion that solicitors "in the field" would seek—or were supposed to seek—if difficulties presented themselves in the course of a transaction. And it was to their opinion that judges were encouraged to defer in litigation concerning matters of establishing and transferring title. Such a system inevitably had critics. A writer in the Edinburgh Review of 1821 observed a paradox here:

"There exists . . . an universal disinclinaton to the discussion of any subject purely legal; and whilst . . . all are willing to inquire and decide whether forgery shall or shall not be punished with death, few will attend to the merits of a question on a general registry of title-deeds, or the alteration in the modes of transferring property: and yet, there is scarcely any person who has not experienced, in his own case, or in that of some of his connexions, considerable inconvenience from the present state of the law on these subjects. In fact, the uncertainty, the intricacy, and the variety of technical expressions, the formalities to be pursued, and the long chain of evidence to be procured, render the disposal of real property a matter of so much difficulty, that many are deterred from bringing it to market" (1821, pp.190–191).

In short, the system was so cumbersome that transfer of title was often unnecessarily difficult, or even impossible.

It is perfectly clear that transfer management took a long time and cost a lot of money. Its complexity also meant that there was a relatively high risk that transactions would fall through in the course of negotiation, or, at any rate, that people thought there was such a risk, which is just as important. But it is probably an exaggeration to suggest that the system rendered land inalienable; more accurately, the system threw up a range of problems of a purely technical character which need not have arisen if a different system had been adopted. The ingenuity of conveyancing counsel largely overcame these problems; but it was not obviously desirable or necessary to deploy the ingenuity of counsel in this way. The 1925 code stands at the end of a century of "reform" through legislative intervention in the conveyancing process. But most of this legislation is best characterised as a vehicle for making available to all solicitors, directly, by force of statutory law, the best practice counselled by conveyancing experts in hard cases.

Beyond all the particular difficulties generated by the fragmentation of titles through the practices of settlement, and the encumbering of titles through mortgaging and leasing, was the more elementary problem generated by the fact of establishing title through a sequence of paper and parchment. On a transfer of title, the general rule was that all documents relating to the land should pass to the purchaser.

"The vendor is bound, in the absence of special stipulation, to deliver over to the purchaser on completion all documents of title, which are or should rightly be in his own possession and relate solely to the property purchased, whatever be their date and whether abstracted or not. The documents, which must be so handed over, include not only the title deeds and such other muniments of title as will pass without express mention by a conveyance of the land itself, but also all documents produced for the purpose of verifying the abstract in proof of any fact stated therein; such as certificates of baptism, marriage or burial, statutory declarations as to matters of pedigree or as to the identity of the property sold, or certificates of the result of an official search for judgements or other matters. But of course documents, such as a marriage settlement, merely produced to show that they do not affect the land sold, cannot be required to be given up to the purchaser . . ." (Williams, 1922, pp.639 *et seq.*).

So first, what about trust documents which contained information relating both to the property held on trust (the "subject-matter" of the trust) and to the beneficial interests in the property (the "objects" of the trust)?

"Suppose that land and personalty were vested in trustees by one deed of settlement, the land being settled on trust for sale, would the trustees be obliged on a sale of the land to hand over the deed of settlement to the purchaser? It is thought not . . . [However] the fact that the trustees have duties to perform under the deed, is [not] of itself sufficient to justify their retaining it. For where land alone is settled on trust for sale and the trusts of the purchase-money are declared by the same deed, it is considered that the trustees are not entitled to retain the deed of settlement on a sale of all the land; and for this reason it is the practice to declare the trusts of [*i.e.* the beneficial interests in] the purchase-money by a deed separate from the conveyance on trust for sale" (*ibid.*, pp.639–641).

(We return below to this concept of the "trust for sale" and the idea of separating documents vesting title in trustees from documents declaring beneficial interests "behind a trust".) More seriously, what about a transfer involving physical fragmentation of land itself, where there was an attempt to divide up one fee simple into several, whether by auctioning off a whole estate in lots, or simply where a landowner sought to sell off an outlying portion of his estate? In each case, the problem was the same: the purchaser's title would derive from the vendor's title, but what arrangement needed to be made concerning the vendor's documents of title through which, subsequently, the purchaser would have to prove his own?

First, the Vendor and Purchaser Act 1874 provided that, in the absence of stipulation to the contrary, a vendor who retained any part of an estate to which any documents of title related was entitled to retain such documents. But this still left the problem of how the purchaser was to prove his title in the future. Secondly, what if documents of common title retained by the vendor contained information relating to ancillary rights burdening or benefiting the purchaser's land? We now give some examples of how lawyers in the past coped with such problems, which illustrate both the difficulties of the paper title system and the pragmatism with which lawyers tried to solve these difficulties.

"By the Conveyancing Act 1911, where land having a common title with other land is disposed of to a purchaser (other than a lessee or a mortgagee) who does not hold or obtain possession of the documents forming the common title, such purchaser, notwithstanding any stipulation to the contrary, may require that a memorandum giving notice of any provision contained in the disposition to him restrictive of user of, or giving rights over, any other land comprised in the common title, shall, where practicable, be endorsed on, or where impracticable, be permanently annexed to some one document selected by the purchaser but retained in the possession or power of the person who makes the disposition, and being or forming part of the common title. But the title of any person omitting to require an indorsement to be made or a memorandum to be annexed is not, by reason only of this enactment, to be prejudiced or affected by the omission" (Williams, 1922, p.603).

"Where lands held under one title are put up for sale in lots, without any special stipulation as to the custody of the title deeds, it is considered that, if all the lots be sold, the title deeds should be delivered to the purchaser of the largest part in value of the lands (whether that part be contained in one or several lots), and that he should give statutory acknowledgements and undertakings to the other purchasers . . . [More generally] the vendor is, as a rule, bound to furnish the purchaser with proper statutory acknowledgements and undertakings for the production and safe custody of any title deeds or other muniments of title which may lawfully be withheld from the purchaser on completion, and are necessary to make a good title according to the contract" (*ibid.*, pp.642–643).

"... where the ownership of any land held under one title is divided, whether by sale, settlement or otherwise, and the title deeds remain in the possession of the owners of a part, the owners of the rest of the land have an equitable right, independently of any covenant, to enforce production of the title deeds in order to defend their title or effect any sale or like disposition of their lands ... if, while the lawful custody of the deeds is outstanding (as in the case of their being in the possession of a mortgagee or a tenant for life), the title to the land devolves upon joint tenants, tenants in common ... or upon persons entitled in severalty to different parts of the lands, then, on the termination of the right to custody of the deeds (as by the mortgage being paid off, or the death of the tenant for life), none of them has a better right than the others to the custody of the deeds; and if they cannot agree who shall have the custody of them, the deeds will have to be deposited in Court, and each of them will be entitled to inspect and take copies of them" (*ibid*., pp.645–646).

These examples illustrate the kinds of problems which the traditional system generated. The physical location of original paper documents was important; manual copying of such documents was inevitably exposed to problems of error creeping in during the copying process; and emergent global corporations such as Rank Xerox had not yet developed and marketed the technology of photocopying. As we see in the next chapter, registration of title deeds was put forward as the solution to many of the difficulties associated with establishing title through chains of private paper kept in private hands. As we will also see, practical devices such as the separation of trust instruments from conveyances of title, which were originally invented to accommodate the difficulties we have outlined above, could then serve as a model or inspiration for achieving rather different objectives.

PROOF AND INVESTIGATION OF TITLE

One of the most important historical peculiarities of the development of English land law lies in the complex relationship between, and the relative importance of, the common law courts on the one hand and the courts of equity on the other. This peculiarity is once again grounded in practical considerations, and therefore, since it is a matter of the involvement of courts in the process of transfer management by lawyers, it is a question of the remedial assistance afforded by the courts. Most of these matters, in practical terms, are today largely forgotten, but to grasp the framework of land law it is essential to understand the remedial structure of the past, because the shapes of the present are grounded upon the experience of lawyers in working within that structure.

At the heart of the tradition is the remedy of specific performance of contracts for the sale of land, which has been introduced above. For this reason, equity played a decisive role in the development of the ground-rules which contoured the land-transfer activities of lawyers. These rules were reworked in 1925, as we see in the next chapter, in a comprehensive way: but the agenda of reform was set by the practices of the past, and, as is inevitable in such circumstances, reworking works with as well as against the way things used to be. Rather than viewing 1925 as a sudden break with the past, it must be seen as carrying forward, as well as transforming, the traditional practices of lawyers.

Specific performance was, and is, a remedy available to both parties to a contract for the sale of land. To get such contract litigation into perspective, we should note that it is not fundamentally a matter of people refusing to perform contracts *tout court*; rather, it is often the more technical questions of: (a) purchasers whose advisors are unwilling to proceed to completion because they do not think the vendor has shown or can give good title, once the abstract has been investigated; and (b) purchasers who are unwilling to proceed because some defect—such as an underground water course—has been discovered in the land itself which in the purchaser's view materially alters the bargain to the extent that he wishes to rescind—to get out of—the contract. Thus the courts found themselves required to formulate rules regarding the investigation of title, not in some general or theoretical sense, but in a context always heavily mediated by the existing conveyancing practices of lawyers. In doing so, two main issues had to be addressed. The first was the question of what conditions a court should impose upon a vendor before ordering specific performance of a contract of sale in his favour. Secondly, what kinds of inquiries before conveyance would a court of equity require a purchaser to make?

"Good title": what vendors had to prove

We must always remember that a vendor does not contract to sell, and a purchaser does not contract to buy, land but a title to land. Titles to land can be more or less good or more or less bad. In the end, the question of what constitutes a good title is for the law (including equity) to determine.

"... every vendor of land is bound to show a good title to the property sold by him. This rule would appear to be of equitable origin. The courts of equity, in granting to a vendor the extraordinary relief of enforcing specific performance of the contract, considered that it was only fair to impose the condition, that he on his side should prove that he could actually convey what he professed to sell. [The law came to follow equity here.] What the vendor has to prove, in order to fulfil this obligation, is that he can convey that which he contracted to sell ... But the nature and extent of proof required was defined by a general rule of equity and law, adopted from the practice of conveyancers, whereby proof of title for not less than sixty years before the contract was held to be proof of a good title, if nothing appeared to the contrary ..." (Williams, 1922, pp.88–90).

Williams called this 60–year rule a merely "subordinate rule" which limited the amount of evidence a purchaser could require.

"It simply bound the purchaser to accept, as proof of a good title, evidence of sixty years' ownership ending in the vendor ... provided, however, that nothing appeared to show that the ownership so proved was not full or complete. But it was of no avail to show sixty years' title, if the result of the evidence produced were not to discharge the vendor's main obligation, that is, that he could actually convey what he sold" (*ibid.*, pp.88–89).

Williams insisted upon "this apparently simple distinction between the main rule imposing the duty of showing a good title, that is, a title to convey what was sold, and the subordinate rule defining the manner of proof" (1922, p.89):

"... omission to remember this distinction has been a fruitful source of error, especially in cases where the time for which title can be required to be shown has been limited by special stipulation [in the contract for sale]. In some such cases, the vendors, or their advisers, would appear to have forgotten that such a stipulation merely limits the evidence of title that can be asked of them in the first instance, and does not exempt them from the general duty of proving that they have the right to convey what they have sold" (*ibid.*, pp.89–90).

If the contract contains a special stipulation for a shorter period of proof than that specified by the general law, the stipulation ". . . must be fair and explicit, or the vendor, in seeking specific performance, will not be allowed to insist on it" (*ibid.*, p.100), another reminder of the discretionary basis of equitable remedies.

"If . . . a stipulation be made that the title shall commence with a particular deed less than forty years old, the purchaser is entitled to assume that the deed was made on an occasion on which the title would be investigated; and should this not be the case, as if the deed were voluntary, the vendor cannot force him, in an action for specific performance, to accept the title as limited by the condition. Such conditions, to be effectual as regards the specific performance of the contract, must clearly state the nature of the instrument, with which the title is to commence (ibid., pp.100–101).

Subject to these distinctions and this general practical logic, a 40–year period was substituted by statute in 1874, which was reduced to 30 years in 1925, and in 1969 was further shortened to 15 years. In broad terms these reductions indicate the regularisation and standardisation of the paper title system which have occurred in the last hundred years. We can clarify the mechanics, whatever the minimum period in force at any one time, with an example.

EXAMPLE

(1) 30 years ago, A conveys to B;

(2) 20 years ago, B conveys to C;

(3) 13 years ago, C conveys to D;

(4) Today, D is planning to sell to P.

Today, the question is how far back must P check the title? Using the current minimum period, he must look at the series of conveyances going back for at least 15 years. So he must look at

(3). But he must also look at (2) because he must go back to that conveyance, through which D derives his title, made at least 15 years ago. Conversely, D will normally be taken to be offering a good title if the chain of title is in order back to (2).

If P does not look at (2) this does not mean that the transfer from D is bad. It means that this title is at risk because he has not looked at the title deeds going back to transfer (2). Therefore, he is liable to attack from people in whose favour adverse interests were created by B. The other side of the rule—that he takes a good title if he goes back to (2)—means that the purchaser is not concerned with interests adverse to the title which could only be discovered by going back to (1). The rule, therefore, does not require him to go back to (2), nor to (1), but the consequence of failing to check (1) or (2) are different. Because of the rule, failure to check (2) may expose him to attack from third parties, but failure to go back to (1) will not. However, as we see in the next chapter, the introduction of registration of land charges in 1925 has both simplified and complicated the position.

Good title and the limitation of actions

How did this system take account of the rules of limitation of actions, which we saw above have a fundamental role in English property law?

Williams again:

> ". . . the Court will compel a purchaser to take a title depending . . . on the extinguishment under [the Limitation Acts] of the right and title of some person . . . who [is] shown to have been rightfully entitled. But it must not be supposed that this doctrine enables a vendor, who has been in possession for twelve or even thirty years, to escape the common obligation for showing forty years' title as proof of a good title. Possession for these periods does not give a good title under the [Limitation Acts] as against all the world; it does not bar the rights of remaindermen or reversioners not entitled to possession until the determination of some particular estate. It does not appear therefore that a vendor's obligation of showing a good title can be discharged by proof of thirty or even forty years' possession by himself alone, without showing, if the Statute of Limitations be relied on, who were rightfully entitled and that the vendor's possession has effectually barred their claims" (Williams, 1922, pp.96–97).

Although the minimum period for establishing good title (15 years) is now closer to the limitation period (12 years), the distinction drawn by Williams still applies in relation to the paper title system.

WHAT PURCHASERS HAD TO DO: INVESTIGATING TITLE AND CONSTRUCTIVE NOTICE

It must always be remembered that the courts of equity were principally geared to the resolution of disputes, rather than, as we too easily suppose today (precisely because of the routinisation of practice facilitated by improved communication networks within the legal system), the making of legal rules. Just as the rules concerning what vendors should do were parasitic upon—or grew out of litigation about—attempts by vendors to get specific performance of contracts for the sale of land, so the rules which emerged concerning purchasers were generated by disputes concerning either purchasers' attempts to tear up ("rescind") such contracts (where there was dispute at a more basic level as to whether this was a matter for law or for equity (Williams, 1922, p.154n.(d)) or by disputes between those who claimed as encumbrancers upon the vendor's title and the purchaser. The reach of equitable remedial assistance tended to stop, though not in every case, where the defendant could satisfy the court that he was a "bona fide purchaser of a legal estate without notice" of the claim asserted in the court. "Notice", in other words, was formulated in the context of land purchase, and came to involve positing a standard of enquiry into the state of a (legal) title to land. For this reason, the opinion of conveyancing experts was so important for the development of this equitable doctrine.

An example will again help to focus the key issues. Let us assume that A has the legal estate in Blackacre, and B has some equitable interest affecting the land (say an estate contract with A, or the benefit of a restrictive covenant to which Blackacre is subject). A conveys the legal estate to P. The contest in the courtroom is between B and P, A for whatever reasons having dropped out of the picture. The basic question, in these circumstances, was whether P "knew or ought to have known" of B's claim, and by asking and answering this question, in the light of what conveyancers regarded as "good practice", the courts came to formulate the "doctrine of notice".

What did it mean to say that P "knew or ought to have known" of B's equitable interest? Obviously, the "equitable interest" is not a physical, tangible, observable thing. Rather it is a right which arose originally because equity was prepared to grant B certain kinds of remedies against A because A's conscience was bound by what had happened between A and B.

First, B might argue that P actually knew of the prior relationship between A and B—that they had made, for example, a restrictive covenant or an estate contract. If B can produce evidence to the court to this effect, P's conscience will be bound in the same way as A's conscience was—in modern language, P will therefore take subject to B's rights. This is called "actual notice".

Secondly, the evidence may not extend so far as to prove actual knowledge on the part of P, but B may be able to argue that P would have found out about his equitable interest if he made the proper inquiries before taking the conveyance from A.

B is thus positing a standard of reasonable inquiry, and it is for the court to decide what this standard should be. This is called "constructive notice"—B is not arguing that P actually knew (actual notice) but that P ought to have known about his equitable interest because if P had come up to the standard of the reasonable purchaser, P would, in the course of his pre-conveyance investigations, have discovered B's equitable interest.

So what is this standard of reasonable inquiry which equity imposed upon a purchaser before he could take free of equitable interests which might affect the land?

Essentially, purchasers were required to make two different kinds of inquiry—first, to inspect the land and, secondly, to investigate the title deeds.

Investigative procedures

Inspection of the land[35]

"As a general rule if a person purchases and takes a conveyance of an estate which he knows to be in the occupation of another than the vendor, he is bound by all the equities which the person in such occupation may have in the land; for possession is *prima facie* seisin, and the purchaser has, therefore, actual notice of a fact by which the property is affected, and he is bound to ascertain the truth. Thus, if a person purchases property in the occupation of one whom he supposes to be only a tenant from year to year, he will be held to have notice of a lease under which he holds, and of the contents of it" (Hewitt and Richardson, 1928, p.195).

When a purchaser inspects the land which he is proposing to buy, he may discover that people other than the legal owner are in occupation or doing certain things on that land. This will "put him on inquiry", which means that he should find out what, if any, their rights in relation to the land are. If he does not inquire, and it subsequently turns out that these people have equitable interests affecting the land, the purchaser will take subject to those equitable interests.

EXAMPLE
The owner of land in fee simple makes an agreement with some builders (B) such that the builders acquire by virtue of the agreement an equitable interest in the land. As a result of this agreement, P, the purchaser, would have discovered, had he inspected the land, that much building activity was taking place upon it. This puts P on inquiry about the nature of B's rights, and P is therefore fixed with constructive notice of the builders' equitable interest, and made to take subject to the agreement. This aspect of land transfer does not go away, though successive attempts at the reform or rationalisation of the land transfer process have tried to shift the duties (or risks) of purchasers away from such investigations of "fact" towards documentary or bureaucratically organised registration-based modes of protection of interests and claims.

Investigation of the title deeds
We have already seen that the law at different times laid down minimum periods for searching through the title deeds in order for the purchaser to get good title. As he looks through these conveyances, he may come across other documents which indicate that there are also equitable interests affecting the land. If we return to the example on p.211, above, C, who acquired the land 20 years ago, may have entered into a restrictive covenant in favour of his neighbour X. This is an equitable interest, as we have seen, and X will be able to enforce it against P if P has actual notice of the covenant because he came across it when looking through the title deeds. But if P has not discovered it, or has shut his eyes to its existence, then he will be taken to have constructive notice of the covenant if he would have discovered it had he searched the title deeds properly (*i.e.* as a reasonable purchaser).

The same principles applied in the case of other equitable interests which we have already discussed. Thus, in searching through the title deeds, P might discover that a trust had been created at some point, and this should lead him to inquire whether the beneficial interests behind that trust still affected the title. Similarly, he might discover that V made a previous estate contract if he came across some memorandum in the title deeds to put him on inquiry.

It was questions of this sort—technical questions, conveyancers' questions—which established the "agenda of reform" to which, shortly, we turn. We must first outline the relationship between the recognition of a range of ancillary rights and the process of transfer management.

LEASES AND THE TRANSFER OF TITLE

We have indicated above how a lease of land could itself be the object of a transfer of title. Leases became things which people bought and sold, as well as things to be checked out when a superior title was transferred. We have already outlined that aspect of leases which was, and is, relatively peculiar, namely that leases tend to contain ongoing covenants relating to the use of the property. In legal terms, the transfer of leases—the "assignment of leases" as lawyers call it—is largely a matter of ensuring that the covenants contained in the lease bind (and benefit) the person who takes an assignment of the lease. As between landlord and tenant, covenants remain enforceable if they "touch and concern the land" or if they have reference to the subject-matter of the lease. Here the position of tenants derived from common law and that of landlords from statute, in each case from long ago. We have outlined above (see pp.156–157) recent statutory changes in the position here.

LAND TRANSFER AND THE CREATION OR TRANSFER OF RIGHTS ANCILLARY TO TITLE

The discussion to this point has centred upon the interplay of fragmentation of title and the management of land transfer by lawyers. We have focused upon the problems of ascertaining the quality of title and the nature of the incumbrances upon that title. But one can look at this process the other way round: what exactly did a purchaser get when he bought an estate in land?

How much of what belonged to the vendor passed with the conveyance? At one level, this problem was elementary and easily dealt with at the contract stage: what fixtures would pass with the transfer of title?

The general rule was that anything which was fixed or attached to the land was treated as being part of the land, and so passed with a conveyance of title unless the contract contained express stipulations to contrary effect. Conversely, anything not attached could be removed by the vendor on completion since it was still a chattel. It was for conveyancers to ascertain, during the transfer negotiations, what the contracting parties' intentions were regarding items such as machinery bolted to the ground for the purposes of use but in fact regarded by the seller as moveables which he would take away with him. Ornaments were also the source of complexity in adjudication. The courts took the view that on the one hand large pictures fixed to a wall "for their better enjoyment" retained their chattel character, while pictures or sculptures which came to form part of an overall architectural design became part of the land whether or not they were actually attached to it. However peripheral such matters may seem today, they were once real issues on the transfer and break-up of landed estates, as the law reports reveal. Even in modern conditions, however, there is still room for doubt—unless the contract resolves this explicitly—about the rights of vendors and purchasers regarding, for example, electrical light-fittings, shelving, door-handles, fireplace surrounds and so on.

The main source of complexity here is rather the recognition by English law of proprietary rights ancillary to title, examined in the previous chapter. Leaving aside prescriptive rights, the creation of land obligations was commonly linked to the transfer of title and to the subdivision of large parcels of land in particular. Where land was divided up for residential development, or where an outlying portion of an agricultural estate was sold off to raise money, the question whether obligations should be attached to one or other of the parcels of land arose. In the case of covenants, the question had to be addressed explicitly; in the case of easements, as we see in a moment, it could also arise as a matter of (retrospective) imposition.

The principal mechanism for making rights and obligations run with the land is called "annexation" by lawyers. The word expresses the materialist or reifying way in which conveyancers have tended to think about rights and obligations. Where the benefit and burden of an easement or a restrictive covenant, or the benefit of a positive covenant, is annexed to the land, it thereafter "runs" with the land. This was of course literally true under the title-deed system, provided that a copy of the easement or covenant was made. Such an easement or covenant is treated as a thing because one can literally ask where it—the relevant document—is; and if it cannot be produced it cannot be enforced. So if the owner of a large parcel conveyed an outlying part to a purchaser, taking a restrictive covenant from him to use the land for residential purposes only, or granting an easement over the vendor's retained land, the easement or covenant would live on in the title deeds of the purchaser. The vendor, in such circumstances, would need to keep a copy, if only to prevent fraud in the future, and this copy would form part of the vendor's subsequent title deeds. Clearly, in such a system, future division of either parcel of land could necessitate complex arrangements regarding rights to production of the relevant pieces of paper and parchment.

How does annexation occur? Again, the answer is in the use of the correct formula, one devised by lawyers to indicate both that the benefit of the covenant was not personal to the covenantee and was taken in order to benefit the land. If the benefit of a restrictive covenant was not annexed, equity permitted the covenantee to pass on the benefit on a sale of the land by assignment, that is, the conveyance on sale would expressly refer to the covenant and contain express words of assignment: another formula again.

Easements could also raise by implication. After a conveyance of title on the sale of an outlying part, the question could arise whether the grant or reservation of any easements should be implied into a conveyance even if there was nothing said expressly. Here the courts did come to formulate a number of principles.

The basis for implying easements into transfers of title has recently been said to be the intention of the parties to the transfer. This has been broken down into three alternative formulations: the common intention of the parties, necessity, and what is known as the rule in *Wheeldon v Burrows* (1879).[36] The first two justifications for implying easements into a transfer of title require little comment. The circumstances will usually speak for themselves. Because, however, the basis underpinning the implication of easements is the intention of the parties to the transaction and not some public policy promoting the better utilisation of land, the implication of an easement can always be prevented by an express stipulation excluding it, even if the effect of such an exclusion is to render the land in question completely inaccessible to human beings because it is completely surrounded by land owned by other people.

The third basis for implying easements, formulated in *Wheeldon v Burrows*, implies into a conveyance as easements any rights which were continuous and apparent at the time of the conveyance which are necessary for the reasonable enjoyment of the land.

Finally, s.62 of the Law of Property Act 1925 is sometimes treated in the books as a fourth method of implying easements into transfers of title. This section writes into every transfer what are sometimes called the "general words". The section does not imply easements into a transfer so much as save words by writing them in by force of statute (a point to which we return in the next chapter). As with most such statutory provisions, it is subject to a contrary intention being expressed in the conveyance, which means that it both saves words and focuses the minds of the lawyers of the parties on whether they wish to exclude anything from passing along with the transfer of title.

10

THE MECHANICS OF LAND
TRANSFER: THE 1925 REFORMS
AND BEYOND

The process of land transfer in England is now regulated by what is commonly regarded as the finest flower of codification *à l'anglaise*, the 1925 code of property legislation, as subsequently amended. Major changes are introduced by the Trusts of Land and Appointment of Trustees Act 1996, and, most recently, by the Land Registration Act 2002, which came into effect in 2003. The code operated as a caesura in 1925 and continues to do so; it causes a certain rupture with the past. Several reasons for this can be suggested. First the code is extremely long and complicated, and in its early years required a considerable effort to master. There was pressure to give particular sections some fixed meaning. In a general climate of supposed slavish adherence to precedent (1930s–1950s), there were strong incentives to follow previous interpretations, regardless of whether they were right or wrong (that is, irrespective of whether or not they conformed with the received conveyancing wisdom of the nineteenth century). Secondly, the legislation was in some respects the victim of its own success; inasmuch as it ironed out technical problems which had vexed nineteenth-century lawyers, the past came to seem a terrain best left undisturbed, the province of antique collectors, not practical men. Thirdly, coming to more modern times, by the 1950s practising lawyers had little direct experience of the pre-1926 years, and were encouraged in their happy ignorance by the most influential textbook writers (Anderson, 1984). Finally, the world of real property seemed to have changed. How could the learning of the nineteenth century provide guidance on the scope of the Rent Acts, or in disputes among the families of owner-occupiers?

What sort of animal was the 1925 code? It resembled what had gone before. It was a bundle of particulars, containing no general definitions of *dominium*, usufructs, servitudes or hypothecs, of the kind familiar to civilians. It was a body of particular rules of a particular kind. They were conveyancing rules—rules for regulating the transfer of title to land—as well as procedural rules governing legal relationships where land was, to put the matter generally, in "multiple ownership". Not that these rules were, or are, unimportant. Generations of lawyers have treated them with the utmost respect, even reverence, because the main substance of our law of real property (at least, that part of it which matters to lawyers in their day-to-day activities) is in these rules. The rules are a sort of highway code, the rules of the road telling lawyers how to go about their business, the dos and don'ts of making wills, leases, trusts, of buying and selling houses.

Some of the most important rules (in a practical sense) amount to this: if you transfer title to a house to someone, you will be taken to have transferred to that person (along with the house) this, that and the other (say, the hedges, ditches and fences that are reputed to be part of that piece of land) unless you have expressly stated in your transfer that they are not being transferred. Such provisions are called "word-saving" clauses because that is what they do: they simplify the preparation of the relevant legal instruments. They cut down on the paperwork. And dealing with "paperwork"—interpreting the meaning of words used in legal documents—is in large measure how the English law of real property has grown up. If you use this word but omit that word, you are taken to have done this but not that. So next time round, a lawyer whose client wants to do both this and that must ensure that he uses this word and that word. As will be discussed below, this remains the case even as paper documents gradually become electronic documents. The new electronic media available to land lawyers (and other kinds of lawyers) do not remove either the legacy of the past or the resulting burden of interpretation, whatever the objectives of the framers of the most recent legislative initiatives.

The effectiveness of such a system always depended ultimately upon the adequacy of information flows between the people who prepared the documents and the people who interpreted them in the event of a dispute about meaning. Of course, given that lawyers everywhere have a reputation for splitting hairs, such a system tended towards overkill: verbal inflation resulted. Legal instruments became longer and longer. More and more words, representing every conceivable shade of meaning, were included, in case the omission of any one should prove fatal later on. One important function of conveyancing statutes such as the 1925 code was to bring these verbal formulae into the statutory text, impose them upon all private instruments by force of law, unless those preparing the instrument wished to exclude something (which in most cases they would not).

Beyond that, the 1925 code was an elaborate reworking of the old law on settlements and trusts of land. It addressed, almost completely successfully, nineteenth-century problems in order to make the transfer of title to land subjected to complex settlements more straightforward. Until recently, this has had to serve as the legal framework in the very different world of widespread mortgage-financed owner-occupation. English property law, then, as codified in 1925, did not consist of a definitive statement of property rights and their incidents, but rather a set of rules focused on the procedures and mechanisms of land transfer. This deposited a new, generalised ideological centrepiece into legal culture, created, it would seem, by academic lawyers but adopted, in more recent years, by practitioners and judges. This is "the policy of 1925" which is said, in general but humdrum terms, to consist of the "simplification and facilitation of conveyancing", or, in more glamorous but old-fashioned language, "free trade in land". That this became an ideological centrepiece of *legal* culture must be stressed, because it is only marginally connected with more general political ideologies relating to the merits or demerits of private property rights. In brief, "the policy of 1925" in legal discourse was targeted at adjudication: it functioned as a mode of legitimating those interpretations or applications of the 1925 code which "simplified" or "facilitated" conveyancing—*i.e.* land transfer—and of delegitimating those which pulled in the direction of greater complexity. In other words, as an ideological theme it was very much concerned with the office work of lawyers (and of solicitors in particular), with the paperwork they would or would not have to do in the preparation of land transfer documentation.

For our purposes, the main statutes are: the Settled Land Act 1925 (SLA); the Law of Property Act 1925 (LPA); the Land Charges Act 1925 (now Land Charges Act 1972, (LCA)); and the Land Registration Act 1925 (LRA), the last now replaced by the Land Registration Act 2002. The first three of these Acts changed a few substantive rules and modified some aspects of the traditional conveyancing practices of transfer by title deed, the general character of which was outlined in the previous chapter. The LRA introduced a new system of conveyancing, which we now call registered conveyancing. This was intended to speed up and simplify the process of land transfer by making it easier for purchasers to investigate the title they were buying and to find out whether there were subsidiary rights burdening the land they were buying (like restrictive covenants and easements). The traditional conveyancing procedures (which today we call unregistered conveyancing) were thought to be too cumbersome despite the streamlining introduced by the LPA and the LCA, and the advocates of registered conveyancing hoped that it would rapidly supersede the old title deed system. In fact the process moved slowly and compulsory registration of new transactions across the whole of England and Wales was only achieved in 1990, so when the LRA 2002 was enacted there were still substantial numbers of unregistered titles. These will presumably continue to survive under the LRA 2002 until the land concerned is next subject to transaction. (For the practical logic of registration and its relation to what it sought to supersede, see now Pottage, 1995). Finally, important changes have been made to the SLA and the LPA by the TLATA 1996. These are also outlined below.

Arguably, the LRA 2002 continues "the policy of 1925" at the same time as it acknowledges that there have been profound changes to the social, political and technological contexts of that policy. Obviously it is too soon to know how successful the new Act will be, or from what different perspectives the question of success or failure will be evaluated given that the Act anticipates (perhaps despite itself) a regime of "dematerialised" conveyancing which make even the "new" 2002 scheme appear too restrictive and outmoded.

As was noted in previous chapters, this legislation made considerable inroads into the conceptual framework of property law, especially so far as the distinction between legal and equitable rights is concerned. But since the underlying rationale of these modifications is explicable only in terms of the management by lawyers of land transfer, detailed exploration of these changes has been postponed until this point. The key targets of the 1925 legislation were, for present purposes, twofold: to overcome the fragmentation of title to land (see Chapter 4, above) and to reform the mechanics of land transfer (see Chapter 9, above). Before these are outlined, we must enter an important qualification concerning the character of what follows.

Until the pioneering work of Avner Offer (1977, 1981), very little research had been published on the real history of the 1925 legislation. Of course, an esoteric, largely orally transmitted knowledge of sorts survived well into the century among lawyers, especially among some members of the Chancery Bar, and (in fragmented form) versions of this sometimes found their way into judicial decisions. This kind of knowledge was inevitably destined to die out, and it largely has. Its death has been fuelled by the non-historical focus of the first principal textbook written for students of the post-1925 era, Cheshire's *The Modern Law of Real Property* (see Anderson, 1984). Outside Oxford at least, Cheshire was displaced as the canonical textbook in the 1950s by Megarry and Wade's *The Law of Real Property*, which, despite a certain penchant for antiquarianism, did not significantly alter this emphasis. Gray's *Elements of Land Law* has sought through a number of editions to present a modern face to the subject-matter (if less provocatively than in the earlier Gray and Symes, *Real Property and Real People*), and the 2002 Land Registration Act will presumably give renewed vigour to the academic project of generating 'modern' frameworks for the understanding of land law.

Not least through the quite massive body of textbook commentary, the legislation and its judicial interpretations have acquired a second history of their own, which in a sense stands between us and the origins of the legislation. Moreover, to the lawyers or law student of today, a case from the 1930s already seems in every sense historical. What can be the relevance in such circumstances of concerning oneself with nineteenth-century history?

Knowing which conveyancer was responsible for which section is interesting, but it may not much help the student who is struggling to work out what the section means, or why, in a larger sense, it is there. But a more general, perhaps vaguer, sense of the past, some impression or "feel" of the world of those who wrote these statutes, still has a role to play. Inevitably, the contours of this world are written in the recesses of these statutes, and these are the contours of the draftsmen's experience of their own past, because most of the time, when people seek to make the future, they cannot but fabricate it from the materials they have inherited. As we shall see, the new regime of registered conveyancing, even in its latest form as electronic registered conveyancing, or "e-conveyancing", does not escape the truth of this generalisation. The historical sense can help us to gain access to the meaning of these like any other texts. And it can also help us gain perspective on the difference between the present and the past, and on the way in which the difference between present and past is conjured up in individual judgments or in new legislative initiatives. Lawyers in whatever context have a tendency to abolish the past (history is regarded as a dustbin), to pretend that the gulf between past and present does not exist, or to work with over-simplified models of continuity and change. Arguably, these approaches make the handling of the 1925 legislation more difficult than is necessary precisely because they oversimplify the question of history. This is true even of the most recent evolutions of the 1925 project. For example, the 2002 Land Registration Act is often presented in terms of notions of social—and especially technological—change which oversimplify the co-evolution of legal codes, professional practices, and real estate markets.

Offer located the starting point of the movement for conveyancing reform in the late nineteenth century, but the detailed part of his study begins in 1910. His principal sources were the materials deposited in the Public Record Office (PRO), which enabled him to reconstruct a picture of the exchanges between the principal legal and political actors of the period during which the main legislative proposals were being thrashed out. The interpretation Offer places upon this material is that what was going on was little short of a conspiracy in which the leading conveyancing lawyers succeeded in hijacking the plans of those Land Registry officials and politicians seeking far-reaching reform, with a view to preserving intact the solicitors' monopoly on conveyancing (and thus the considerable material rewards which were derived from the conveyancing income).

In an important new study, Stuart Anderson (1992) has taken issue with Offer's interpretation. Anderson takes the inquiry much further back, so as to draw the history of the 1925 reforms securely into the nineteenth-century history of conveyancing reform. Even if the author writing in the *Edinburgh Review* quoted in the previous chapter proclaimed himself to be a lonely voice in 1821, by the end of that decade, Parliament had set Commissioners to work on the reform of the law of real property and voluminous reports were produced in due course. The statute book of the nineteenth century is littered with Acts concerned with this or that particular aspect of conveyancing practice. What Anderson highlights is the extent to which the reform of conveyancing was a continuing preoccupation of a specialised group of lawyers throughout much of the nineteenth century. In the form in which it finally emerged, large parts of the 1925 legislation were more—much more—of the same. The reforms sought to be comprehensive, but ended up being comprehensive by being detailed and particularistic. The legislation contained its generalities to be sure—including those selected for discussion here, the new regime for strict settlements and tenancies in common—but even here, the SLA ran to 117 pages, which made it longer than the LRA, which weighed in at 106 pages. (The LPA was a bloated 203 pages.) Among other things, of course, this is indicative of the priorities of those who successfully piloted through the version of the code with which we now have to live.

Anderson's study supplements the PRO material with a close examination of the professional press—the *Solicitors' Journal* and the *Law Times*. This enables him to suggest that the motives and concerns which underlay not just the 1925 reforms but the wider movement for conveyancing reform which spanned much of the nineteenth century were more complex and diffuse than Offer had suggested. In place of Offer's conspiratorial picture, Anderson presents one in which lawyers can be found occupying more or less all possible positions in the conflicts and debates.

This study broadly confirms the suspicion that in the end there was no Grand Plan which we can wrap up and label "the Policy of 1925". Given the range of actors, interests and concerns in play, and the time over which the various bills laid before Parliament stretch (wherever one begins the story), it is clear that the final product was an amalgam of several plans, some grander than others, a conclusion at which any reader of the legislation will quickly arrive. Even the idea that the legislation should introduce a "universal curtain" (which would confine equitable interests behind trusts and conceal them from purchasers) could not secure agreement, though Anderson's view is that this became the (practical) law after the legislation was passed, even though the legislation did not enact it (1992, p.313).

But there is a larger question, which critics raised at the time: why could there not be a fundamental overhaul of the land law, a proper codification, instead of something so "short on principle and long on facile devices" (Anderson, 1992, p.293)? Far more innovative and "modern" schemes in this area as in others like social policy had been developed and implemented for parts of the Empire, so why could not the same be done in the heart of the Empire itself? *Plus ça change*: the 1996 Act, which modifies a number of the structural features of the 1925 scheme, again does so on a piecemeal and particularistic basis. (Its vast array of schedules, some of which contain important substantive provisions, is symptomatic of this.)

The same is true of the Land Registration Act 2002, which is considerably shorter than the 1925 original and ostensibly more radical in its approach than any of the earlier "post-1925" reforms. Of course, the most "radical" of the 2002 reforms seek to adjust the procedure of registration to developments outside the sphere of practice and adjudication. The programme of "e-conveyancing" arises from the progressive infiltration of legal practice by information technologies. The idea of "dematerialising" the register, and managing transactions in land through a combination of email and electronic document modification and transfer, would only be practicable in a world in which internet trading and electronic information are gradually becoming entirely conventional (though it is apposite here to notice the anxieties that have accompanied the "dematerialisation" of shares). For these reasons, we might still ask whether or when a radical reconstruction of the concepts and mechanics of the conveyancing project is likely to occur.

SETTLEMENTS, TRUSTS AND THE PROBLEM OF TITLE

Three interrelated objectives fuelled the schemes of reform which culminated in the 1925 code. The first aim was to simplify the problem of the power of dealing with land held in multiple ownership by means of settlements and trusts of one kind or another—powers relating to sale, the execution of mortgages and land management in particular. The general strategy here was to concentrate such powers into the hands of a smaller number of people than had been possible under the old law, thereby facilitating decision-making with regard to the exercise of these powers. Secondly, it was necessary to build in safeguards to protect those with interests in the land who would not under this scheme or for other reasons (such as incapacity owing to infancy or, more generally, because the interests were future interests) be in a position to control the exercise of these powers. Thirdly, it was necessary to provide fairly strong safeguards for third parties—purchasers and mortgagees—

dealing with land held under settlements and trusts. The elaborateness of the 1925 code derived in large measure from trying to secure all these objectives simultaneously. The manner and style in which the code solved these problems inevitably owed much to nineteenth-century conveyancing practice and the normative assumptions which underwrote it.

Almost none of these changes were aimed at interfering with the substance of property distribution and intergenerational transmission within families, the focus (as we have seen above) of so much of the labour of conveyancers over many centuries. So far as was consistent with securing the objectives of rationalising the management of land transfer, the substantive rights of enjoyment—the practical meaning of having an interest in land—were left alone.

The key to the strategy was to force settlements and trusts into two models whose basic design was drawn from existing (nineteenth-century) practice, but each of which required certain refinements if the full range of objectives outlined above was to be met. The first—and at the time more important of these—was the new Settled Land Act settlement, the framework for which was set out in the SLA 1925. The second model was the trust for sale of land, set out in less detail, and with much incorporation by reference from the SLA so far as the powers of trustees for sale were concerned, in the LPA 1925. The principal new use to which the model of the trust of sale was to be put (since the device itself was not in any way new) was to solve the transfer of title problems associated with tenancies in common of the legal estate.

The design of these models displayed much ingenuity. In particular, it trod a fine line between inflexible imposition of the two models on all settlements and trusts, on the one hand, and permitting continued leeway to the lawyers of settlors and testators to customise their own additions of opt-out clauses (for example, consent requirements attached to the exercise of powers) to take account of the peculiarities of individual family circumstances, and which would override to some extent the logic of the general model. But changes in the practical character of wealth-holding and land-ownership, most specifically the decline of the traditional strict settlement and the rise of owner-occupation, have rendered some parts of the model moribund, other parts artificial, and further parts more than a little inconvenient from a legal point of view. These factors lie behind the replacement in the 1996 Act of the two models of 1925 by a single and, in principle, simpler model of the "trust of land".

A. The reform of the strict settlement: the Settled Land Acts 1882–
1925 and the 1996 changes

The 1925 reforms focussed here on giving the tenant for life an unfettered power of sale over the land, the main idea being to make it easier to deal commercially with settled land. The earlier 1882 Act had been limited to this change; the 1925 scheme went further by stipulating that the legal fee simple absolute in possession had to be vested in the tenant for life. To follow this scheme through, it was necessary in addition to cease to recognise at law any other freehold estates in land.

So, after 1925, lesser freehold estates (life estates, entail) and all future estates (remainders, reversions) can exist only in equity behind a trust. The planning of inheritance could continue, but now without fragmenting the title. Finally, if the tenant for life was to be given effective control over the title, the protection of the interests of the family needed to be considered. This was to be done by ensuring that purchase monies were not paid to the tenant for life on a sale but to separate, independent trustees known as "Trustees of the Settlement", and a purchaser who obtained a receipt from these trustees was safe against subsequent claims of other family members entitled under the settlement.

In practical terms, these changes meant that traditional "estate planning" through the use of entails and primogeniture could continue, including the periodic process of resettlement discussed above, although now all beneficial claims on the family estates would be hived off behind a trust.

External factors led to the quite rapid decline of the Settled Land Act settlement. Owners of urban ground rents or agricultural estates increasingly shifted their assets into discretionary trusts. This was largely for tax-avoidance reasons, and specifically with a view to minimising exposure to estate duty, or "death duties" as the tax was commonly known. This tax regime, first introduced in 1894, involved a charge to the settled estate on the death of the tenant for life which was calculated as if the tenant for life had died as an absolute owner of the settled estates. Instead of taking the value of the life interest of the deceased, along with his other assets, as the basis for computing the tax payable by his estate on his death, the capital value of the settled estate in which the life interest had subsisted was also included in the assessment of estate duty, and if the personal estate of the tenant for life was insufficient to meet the tax liability, the settlement itself could be made to pay. Given that this tax regime was progressive, in that the larger the assets the higher the rate of tax payable, and the fact that these rates were themselves steadily increased from the 1920s onwards, the wealthier families when and where possible moved their assets into discretionary trusts under which the former tenant for life had no fixed interest on which the estate duty regime could bite on his death. As one conveyancer observed in 1960:

> "At the present time the strong-rooms of all of us are bristling with discretionary trusts. For the last ten or fifteen years we have been constantly advising testators and settlors . . . to rely on these trusts, the machinery of which was quite unfamiliar to most of us before the war. In many cases we are ourselves the trustees, often coupled with an accountant, which seems to be the ideal combination for trusts of this sort . . . the time will soon be upon us when we shall be involved in the exercise of numerous discretions, raising problems of which we scarcely thought when we light-heartedly let loose on our clients the new learning of tax planning."[37]

In other cases, families sold up completely and moved abroad (a trend already visible in the nineteenth century: see Cannadine 1992, pp.429–443). In the years after the Second World War, country houses and their contents were increasingly handed over to the Treasury under complex arrangements with, among others, the National Trust, in lieu of death duties (see generally Sayer, 1993). More modest landed families sold up in many cases when they could—in terms of the state of the market and in terms of when the time was right from a genealogical viewpoint. In some cases, no doubt, this involved shifting their assets into what were, in one form or another, in reality trusts of land of a type which the 1996 legislation accommodates.

One important consequence of this general pattern of decline and regrouping of traditional landed elites has been the steady disappearance of the entail. For some families it became inappropriate, especially in the light of the large number of deaths of young male heirs from these elites in the two World Wars; for many more it simply became too costly for tax reasons which we have presented in simplified form here.

In the light of these changes, entails are abolished for the future by the 1996 Act: any attempt to create a new entailed interest operates to give an absolute interest to the recipient beneficiary, nor can an entail be created by a declaration of trust

(TLATA 1996, Schedule 1(5)). In general terms, however, the abolition of entailed interests is prospective only, so that existing settlements are preserved (s.2 and, for the avoidance of doubt, s.25(4)) and this includes alterations made to existing settlements, except where these alterations explicitly "opt out" of the SLA regime (s.2(3)).

The abolition of the entail gives statutory recognition to a change in *legal* practice that had already taken place. Even so, the *social* practice of primogeniture, among, for example, the hereditary aristocracy, may well continue, and even survive the abolition of the voting rights of hereditary peers in the House of Lords. The shifting of assets into discretionary trusts of various types means that the social reality of primogeniture, to the extent that it survives in the informal inheritance of wealth among the aristocracy, has been decoupled from the technical forms of legal and equitable ownership. In parallel with this, many burdensome assets have been transferred to the National Trust under its Country House scheme—to such a degree that the Trust has been in recent years more preoccupied with the problem of which properties to reject rather than add to its list (Mandler, 1997). Under these schemes, many former owners of these houses remain in residence under various leasehold arrangements, such that many of the social aspects of aristocracy survive the disappearance of their legal underpinning.

B. The trust for sale, the reform of the tenancy in common and the 1996 changes

As a mode of settling land and predetermining inheritance, the tenancy in common was less ambitious regarding the future (it involved only minimal planning, whereas strict settlements involved rigid planning and prioritising of family claims); but it was much more troublesome in its effect on the state of the title. Tenancy in common was a mode of parcelling rental income from an estate, of sharing it out between a number of people concurrently entitled. Over time, each share could become subdivided. The title could always be dealt with on the market by all such tenants acting together; but over time: (i) a purchaser inspecting the title might be unsure whether he had the aggregate of the right individuals; (ii) some of these individuals might be infants; (iii) some of the shares might be encumbered by mortgages; (iv) some of the "shareholders" might be recalcitrant and even the smallest would have, in effect, a veto over dealing with the title.

It is essential to recall that this was the *rentier's* settlement *par excellence*. It was simply a way of distributing rental income among a family. Its functional character provides the key to the way the reformers dealt with its defects, as they appeared to conveyancers.

(1) The legal tenancy in common was abolished so that serious fragmentation of title ceased. The sharing out of money derived from land was now to be achieved through equity, *i.e.* equitable tenants in common operating behind a trust.

(2) But how was the legal title (the fee simple in possession) to be held? In this form of settlement, there was no real equivalent to the tenant for life (the head of the family) of the strict settlement. But since genealogical seniority played no fundamental part in the rationale of the tenancy in common, and since a trust could be used to protect the claims of the "shareholders", the problem could be resolved in an arbitrary way: where a will or conveyance tried to create a legal tenancy in common, up to the first four persons named would hold the title as legal "joint tenants" on a "statutory trust for sale" for all the persons named as equitable tenants in common. This requires us to examine more closely (a) the joint tenancy and (b) the (statutory) trust for sale.

(3) In the 1925 scheme, the joint tenancy became the only permitted form of concurrent ownership in respect of the legal title. Its advantage, from a conveyancing point of view, concerns what happens on the death of a joint tenant: as we noted in Chapter 4, his or her interest simply disappears or is engulfed by those of the surviving joint tenants. Since only estates held in common could be transmitted by inheritance, joint tenants sometimes tried to convert their joint tenancies into tenancies in common. This is called "severance". After 1925, it is impossible to sever a joint tenancy of the legal estate; it can happen only in equity, behind the trust.

(4) Given the original nature of the tenancy in common, a special statutory framework was required to regulate the relations between the "shareholders" once their substantial entitlements were to be pushed away from the title and behind a trust. This was found in the trust for sale. A trust was imposed by statute (the "statutory trust for sale") whose nature was modelled on a pre-existing device, the "express" trust for sale, which was well established by the nineteenth century.

For example, someone owning four or five houses which were rented out might, in his will, leave them to trustees on trust for sale, the proceeds of sale to be divided equally among his children and, pending sale, the rental income to be similarly apportioned. This provided the model. In place of the legal tenancy in common a statutory trust for sale would arise. Pending sale, the income from the property would be payable to the equitable tenants in common by virtue of those interests, and, on sale, the proceeds divided between them. If the "shareholders" were in disagreement over the desirability of a sale, the court was given a discretion to say yes or no (s.30 of the LPA 1925). The precise powers of the trustees, broadly modelled on those of the SLA tenant for life, were also established by statute (in the LPA 1925).

The 1996 Act, somewhat in the spirit of Lord Birkenhead, who, piloting the 1922 Law of Property Bill through the House of Lords in his capacity as Lord Chancellor, claimed that it "established some contact with sanity in dealing with land" (quoted in Campbell, 1991, p.486), modifies aspects of the statutory law to bring it more closely into line with current judicial practice and with the new underlying socio-economic realities which have generated the problems which the courts have had to solve.

In a loose sense, the trust for sale is abolished and replaced with a trust of land. More precisely, the basic distinction between express and statutory or imposed trusts remains important for understanding the new arrangements.

(1) Under the 1996 Act it is still possible for settlors and testators to create expressly a trust for sale, as in the past, and there will inevitably be circumstances in the future where it will be convenient to employ this mechanism. In such cases, the changes made by the 1996 Act are relatively minor in practical terms. First, s.4 provides that in all cases of such express trusts for sale, whether created before or after the Act, a power for the trustees to postpone sale indefinitely is implied into the trust, even where the trust documents provide to the contrary (though this is without prejudice to any pre-1997 liability which trustees may have incurred).

Secondly, the "doctrine of conversion" is abolished by s.3 except for wills made by testators who died before 1997. This is another "sanity" provision: since a trust for sale traditionally imposed a duty on trustees to convert the trust assets (from land into personalty, or sometimes personalty into land), the application of the maxim "Equity looks on as done what ought to be done" to the trust property meant that the subject-matter of such trusts was usually regarded not as what it was at the outset but as what it would be when the required conversion had taken place. So land held under a trust for sale was regarded by equity as personalty. This sometimes caused inconvenience; it certainly involved a potential pitfall for unwary solicitors; now it is done away with and land held on trust for sale will be treated as land for all relevant purposes as long as it remains land.

(2) The statutory trust for sale of land is abolished and replaced by a simple statutory trust of land without any duty to sell, and this applies whether the circumstances giving rise to the imposition of the trust occur before or after 1997 (s.5 and Sch.2). Once such a trust is imposed, the 1996 Act then sets out a statutory framework to govern the relationship of trustees and beneficiaries, the "functions" of trustees as they are now called, and the procedures through which disputes between affected parties are to be channelled, including enhanced powers for the courts in adjudicating these disputes. As with the 1925 scheme, one important difference between express and statutory trusts in this context is that the statutory provisions necessarily apply automatically in the case of trusts imposed by statute, whereas trusts expressly created under the shadow of the statute as it were usually have more scope to opt out of particular statutory provisions. In Chapter 6, we summarised these provisions so far as the rights of beneficiaries and the obligations and functions of trustees are concerned. In this chapter, we now need to draw out briefly why the 1925 scheme had become artificial and sometimes inconvenient.

The statutory trust for sale, as we have seen, was primarily designed to solve the conveyancing problems of the old legal tenancy in common. While the expectation was that post-1925 conveyancers would use express trusts for sale as the shell for creating tenancies in common, the statutory trust for sale was necessary as a fall-back or default device wherever conveyancers had so drafted documents that their effect in law unless modified by statutory imposition would have been to give rise to a legal tenancy in common. Since the 1950s, however, this rather peripheral device turned out, almost by accident, to be of central importance in the legal framework regulating co-owned and occupied residential property. This was because of the modern development of implied trusts and equities discussed above in Chapter six. Where such a trust arose under the "general principles" of equity, the courts came to hold that it came within this part of the 1925 scheme for dealing with settlements, so that the equitable shares took effect behind a statutory trust for sale, and the relationship between the parties was to be governed by the statutory machinery.[38]

At very least, this made the legal framework of the practical relationship of the parties artificial. A home, which at some stage had been acquired and/or enjoyed as a joint venture, was formally held on a trust for sale. Was the existence of this trust, imposed by statute as interpreted by the courts, relevant in disputes about sale or possession? In essence, the courts came to be confronted by two types of situation—"real" trusts for sale where sale of the land was the reason for creating the trust in the first place, and "artificial" trusts for sale which arose solely by virtue of the statutory scheme, a scheme whose constituent elements regarding powers, sale, rights to occupation and so on often diverged sharply from the informal understandings of the parties regarding their mutual rights and responsibilities. As we have indicated, the courts accommodated many of these new realities, but at the cost of straining the statute or of adding an increasingly complicated gloss to it, through which the uninitiated manoeuvred at their peril. In abolishing the statutory trust for sale, the 1996 Act removes at a stroke these kinds of artificial questions.

(3) The 1996 Act also tidies away an awkward feature of the 1925 code which reared its head occasionally as at least a theoretical problem. Under the code, wherever an equitable life interest came into possession, whether under a will or an *inter vivos* settlement which did not create an express trust for sale, there was the possibility that the land would fall to be governed by the SLA, with the consequence that the legal title would have to be vested in the holder of the life interest. This would strictly be the case, for example, where a man left his house to his widow for life, and after her death to his daughter absolutely. Here it was not uncommon to make the daughter and the solicitor co-trustees. Unless, however, the solicitor remembered to create an express trust for sale, this would create an SLA settlement, since under the LPA no statutory trust for sale arose in these circumstances. The same problem could arise where some kind of life interest in possession came into being by virtue of an implied equity (*e.g.* proprietary estoppel). Some judges sought, not wholly convincingly, to exclude the SLA here[39]; but it is also a case where *ex hypothesi* there is no express trust for sale and, equally, where nothing in the code imposed a

statutory trust for sale. Section 1(2)(a) of the 1996 Act stipulates that the term "trust of land" includes express, implied, resulting or constructive trusts, and bare trusts. Coupled with the abolition of the SLA settlement for the future, this ensures that all these cases will now come under the new 1996 Act scheme for trusts of land.

C. *The position of purchasers: the two-trustee rule, "overreaching" and notice*

The 1925 reforms, targeted at the fragmentation of title, pushed all the sources of complexity behind trusts. But if purchasers were to be affected by notice of these (now) beneficial interests, the old problems could have recurred in a new form. In particular, a purchaser might have been unwilling to proceed even though the legal title was in good order unless the beneficiaries concurred in the transfer. So it was necessary to devise procedures for circumventing such difficulties.

The broad scheme to eliminate notice of trusts from conveyancing—which underpinned the entire code—was that a purchaser who obtained a receipt for the proceeds of sale from two trustees would not be concerned with the beneficial interests in the land. Those interests, it is usually said, were, in such circumstances, "overreached" into the proceeds of sale, and the land was thereby freed from the claims of the beneficiaries. Who these trustees would be would differ in the case of the two devices for dealing with settlements of land introduced in 1925: in the case of the SLA settlement, the trustees of the settlement; in the case of the statutory trust for sale, the trustees for sale. Most of the difficult questions relating to the position of purchasers of land held on trust are left untouched by the 1996 Act. Overreaching and the "two-trustee" rule are preserved but, as we have seen, the artificial fiction of the doctrine of conversion has now gone and, it is to be hoped, all the redundant complexity which came with it.

However, as outlined in Chapter 6 above, the 1996 Act has introduced a range of new consents to transactions which will always apply in the case of statutory trusts of land and which will also apply unless expressly excluded in express trusts. In these cases, the 1996 Act provides that, where the exercise of any "function" by trustees of land is made subject to the consent of more than two people, a purchaser is safe if at least two consents are obtained (s.10(1)).

There are some supplementary provisions in s.16 concerned with the protection of purchasers which will apply in the context of unregistered conveyancing (discussed later in this chapter). In broad terms, s.16 protects purchasers from being affected by the failure of trustees to comply with their statutory obligations to consult beneficiaries in respect of a range of transactions, except where purchasers had actual notice of such claims. In registered conveyancing (see pp.248–251, below) the protection both of purchasers and beneficiaries will be achieved through the entry of a "restriction" on the register which is best regarded as an administrative mechanism.

REFORMING THE MECHANICS OF INVESTIGATION OF TITLE

As should now be clear, by the beginning of this century "land-ownership" meant, for most of those people in a position to think about such matters, ownership or shared ownership of a bundle of documents (wills, conveyances on sale, deeds of settlement) of title. Atiyah (1978) has observed—with the law of contract in mind—that common lawyers tend to "reification" in their thinking: they talk about a contract as if it were a "thing" rather than a bundle of rights and correlative obligations. Whether or not his criticism is helpful, his diagnosis is accurate, and it is even more true of the law of property. When lawyers spoke of "the title", they had in mind not some mystical entity like the civil lawyer's *dominium*, but the tangible, messy, and inordinately verbose collection of documents which did not just stand for, represent or prove the title but in every practical sense (and there was no other for the common lawyer) were the title.

The traditional mode of land transfer on sale which went with this mode of constituting title goes by the grand name of "conveyance by private treaty". As we have seen, it was in essence up to the lawyers acting for each side to satisfy themselves, on behalf of their clients, that everything was in order. The main scope for intervention by the courts (and thus the main opportunity in this area for the formulation of some-thing approaching rules of law, *i.e.* public, general rules appli-cable to everyone: judge-made law is necessarily "public law" in that sense) came as a result of disputes arising after exchange of contracts concerning what terms needed to be included in the conveyance in order to fulfil the obligations created by the contract.

Here, as elsewhere, history is just a succession of occurrences which could have been otherwise. Title, its constitution, proof and transfer, could have been, as it was elsewhere, a public, not a private, matter. Land transfer could have been organised by the state; and by the end of the nineteenth century, this had been set in motion, through the establishment of a Registry of Titles, for the County of London. In 1925, this system could have been made available to the country as a whole. That it was not is tribute to the political acumen of the then leaders of the Law Society. The Land Registration Act 1925 did introduce a nation-wide scheme for registration of title and thus state-organised land transfer. But its implementation was to be by administrative action, different geographical areas to be brought within the new system when the Lord Chancellor so determined. Most recently the LRA 1997 has sought to speed up this process, and the Land Registration Act 2002 provides even more incentives for first registration.

Only today are we approaching the time when the whole country is to be governed by the new system. As a transitional measure (one of the longest transitions in our legal history), a modified version of the old system was established in 1925 in the Land Charges Act 1925 (now 1972). The introduction of a "Public" Register of Titles did not involve the creation of a register open to inspection by members of the public. Here, too, the values and assumptions of the old system were carried through into the new. Just as under the title-deed system, the documents of title were in private hands, and access to the information contained in them basically required the permission of their owner, so in the registered system, although the information was held by public officials, they would disclose it only if the owner so permitted. But the advance of registration of title has gradually turned the register into a public document.

The process was officially inaugurated by the Land Registration Act 1988 and reinforced by the 2002 Act, which makes the (electronic) register open to searches by non-practitioners, and which allows title documents to be scanned in to the register and retrieved almost instantaneously. The objective of an open register is one part of a broader governmental commitment to 'freedom of information' (although the Exempt Information Document System provides for parts of documents (such as extracts from leases) to be kept confidential). Applicants may submit an edited version of their transaction to Registry and request that only the edited version be available for public inspection, but the decision is at the discretion of the Registrar. (The full version is available to the police and to Inland

Revenue.) Inevitably, the ease of access to the register, and the practical simplicity of its operation, have raised concerns within the profession about the loss of status of conveyancing, and about the increased threat posed by agencies such as banks and building societies to the traditional conveyancer/client relationship. The shift to electronic conveyancing makes the control of conveyancing by the profession even more precarious. Of course, many of these complaints echo those made as the 1925 reforms were being planned and implemented.

The reformed old system: alphabetical indexation of encumbrances in name of estate owner

The following is a description of how the system works before the full provisions of the LRA 2002 and electronic conveyancing go into effect. Once e-conveyancing is fully operational, the electronic register will replace land certificates and charge certificates, and the role of the Registry will change correspondingly.

The Land Charges Act established a procedure which involved setting up a national Register of Land Charges. In addition, the Act set out a list of the kinds of equitable interests which are registrable. This list includes estate contracts and restrictive covenants.

Someone who has a registrable interest, such as restrictive covenants, is to register the interests against the name of the estate owner who has created the covenant in his favour. The Land Charges Register is simply an alphabetical list of the names of all estate owners against whom interests have been registered. When a purchaser examines the title deeds, he will see the names of all the previous estate owners prior to the seller (through whom the seller traces title). The purchaser must then fill in a form which is sent to the Land Charges Registry asking whether any charges have been entered in the Register against those names. This is known as a search of the Register. If the Registry writes back and informs P of various interests which have been entered, P does in reality have actual notice of those rights, and takes subject to them if he goes ahead with the conveyance.

The basic principle to grasp is that entry of a land charge on the Register constitutes actual notice to the whole world of the existence of that equitable interest, which means that any purchaser will take the title subject to it.

Estate contracts were also brought within the same procedure of registration. Obviously, though, the practical effect of registration may be different as between estate contracts and restrictive covenants. If, through his search, P discovers a restrictive covenant affecting the property, he may still go ahead and take a conveyance. This will depend on why he is buying the property, and the use to which he wishes to put it. If, however, he discovers an estate contract, he is likely to back out of a conveyance, because, if he takes a conveyance of the legal title from the seller, he is unlikely to acquire anything of value, since the estate contract will be enforceable against him.

What if B had the benefit of a restrictive covenant (_i.e._ the right under the old law to enforce it against a purchaser with notice) but had not registered it, so that P's search of the register would not disclose the existence of the covenant? The rule here was that failure to register a registrable interest (such as a restrictive covenant) made it void (_i.e._ of no legal effect) as against a purchaser of the legal estate for money or money's worth. This means that, even though a purchaser has actual notice under the old law of the existence of the restrictive covenant (_e.g._ by investigating the title deeds), the covenant cannot be enforced against the purchaser because it has not been registered.

For present purposes, two problems need to be mentioned. First, if a purchaser fills in a search form and sends it to the Registry, the official certificate which he receives in reply from the Registry is conclusive as to what equitable interests affect the land. So if the Registry is careless and overlooks a charge which has been entered against the name of one of the estate owners mentioned in P's search form, that official certificate from the Registry, because it is conclusive, takes precedence over the fact of registration.

In other words, although registration counts as actual notice to the whole world, a slip in the Registry can lead to a purchaser taking free of a registered interest, because the Registry's certificate to the purchaser cannot be challenged later. This means that if the person with the registered interest suffers loss as a result of the Registry official's mistake, he must sue the Registry, which owes him a duty of care, in the tort of negligence, and recover financial compensation from the Registry for what he has lost.

Secondly, we have seen that the purchaser will only know what names to include on his search form because he has looked at the title deeds and seen the names of the estate owners through whom the seller traces this title. As we have already seen, a purchaser today is obliged to go back when investigating title to a 15–year minimum period. In the example used in the previous chapter (see pp.211–212, above), P was not required, and indeed is not entitled, to see the conveyance from A to B 30 years ago. What if, when A acquired the title, he had entered into a restrictive covenant with X (the vendor), and X registered this covenant against the name of A (the estate owner at the time the covenant was made)? P will have no way of discovering this registration because D is not required to produce the first conveyance from A to B, so that P will have no means of discovering that A ever owned the land he wishes to buy. Because he has no way of discovering this, he will not enter A's name on the search form which he sends off to the Land Charges Registry. At the same time, the covenant has been registered and, as we have seen, the fact of registration constitutes actual notice to the whole world. Thus P is taken to have actual notice of the covenant, and so to be bound by it, even though, because of the rules about how far back a purchaser is entitled to ask for title to be proved, P had no way of finding out about A's existence. In this situation, P will take subject to X's equitable interest, but if P suffers financial loss as a result, he can seek compensation from the State in respect of that loss (see s.25 of the LPA 1969).

REGISTERED CONVEYANCING

The Land Registration Act 2002 in context

The problems discussed above, and the continuing (indeed increasing) need for alienability and certainty in land transactions in the climate of an expanding housing market, led first to registered conveyancing, and then to the recent reform of the Land Registration Act 1925. The essence of the registered conveyancing scheme is to substitute centralised registration procedures for the bundle of private documents by which title had previously been proved and transferred. This remains the case under the new Land Registration Act 2002. The fundamental objective of the LRA 2002 is that ''. . . the register should be a complete and accurate reflection of the state of the title of the land at any given time, so it is possible to investigate title to land on line, and with the absolute minimum of additional enquiries and inspections" (Law Commission Report 271, *Land Registration for the Twenty-first Century: a Conveyancing Revolution*). The three major objects of the Act are first, to create an electronic system for conveyancing ("e-conveyancing"), secondly, to create as far as possible a conclusive register, and thirdly, to continue the project of transparency and information-gathering that began with the Land Registration Act 1988, which made the register into a public document.

All three of these aims are linked. The electronic accessibility of the register and the completeness of the titles it contains function both as a reflection of the property market, and as recognition of the increasing importance of the property market to institutional and private investors. The land registration legislation currently regulates about £2,000 billion worth of property, and the Land Registry is in charge of maintaining and promulgating the figures that allow actors in the property and landholding market to estimate the value of their investments.

The LRA 2002 seeks to complete the register, both by adding information to the titles already held on the register (around 19 million registrations in 2004), and by providing incentives for voluntary first registration. In order to promote certainty within conveyancing transactions, the LRA 2002 reclassifies and reduces the number of "overriding interests", makes shorter leases registrable, reformulates the rules regarding the protection of "minor interests", and radically changes the rules regarding acquisition of title by adverse possession in registered land. The incentives for first registration include two new registrable interests (a franchise, narrowly defined as specific interests originally granted to the Crown, *i.e.* rights to hold a market or a fair; and *profits à prendre*, *i.e.* sporting and fishing rights), and almost foolproof protection against squatters gaining title to registered land. The oft-repeated tag-line of the new legislation is "title by registration rather than registration of title". What this means for the millions of people involved in property transactions, as owners, occupiers (including family members), leaseholders, renters, and actors in the property market, remains to be seen.

In Chapter 6, we discussed the rise of owner-occupation and the way in which the judiciary carved out proprietary rights for homesharers who would not otherwise be entitled to a portion of the "family home". If this was one major legal initiative in the face of changing social structure, the increasing importance of the housing market is now triggering another. It is not yet clear what the effects of ever-increasing investment in property will be, nor how the courts will deal with new forms of tenure and investment structures such as commonhold, "buy-to-let" and "live/work". These may be urban and suburban variations in landholding that do not affect the deep "grounding" of land rights in England that have tied physical (and ideally agrarian) possession to proprietary rights and social status since feudal times. Or, as will be considered below, perhaps the linkages between possession (however it is defined), proprietary rights, and social status are undergoing a transition. In that case, we must contemplate the emerging shape of society as it is being slowly (and in some cases painfully) reflected in the emerging land law, and speculate as to the content of the next set of revisions to the LRA when e-conveyancing is no longer a new or controversial addition to the legislative scheme. The following analysis proceeds by highlighting the changes that the LRA 2002 makes, and concludes by considering what those changes might mean.

At a certain point in time, a transaction involving an old unregistered title would lead to a moment of first registration. Normally, this occurs on the first transaction for value with a title after the geographic area in which the land is situated is designated an area of compulsory registration. On, for example, the sale of an unregistered title in this area, the purchaser would send all the documents of title which he acquired through the transaction in the old way to the Land Registry, where the title would be given a number, the information contained in the documents transferred to index cards, and the documents stamped and returned. From that time on, all dealings with the title would be on the basis of the entries in the Registry, the original documents now ceasing to have any effect in law and becoming no more than quaint relics. The title number is crucial to the way the system works. Information storage and retrieval (*e.g.* for investigation of title) operate with reference to this number.

This was the system put into place by the LRA 1925, and, with some modifications in technical parameters and documents issued, is still followed in the LRA 2002. However, the introduction of "e-conveyancing" requires some discussion.

ELECTRONIC CONVEYANCING

The aim of the LRA 2002 is to "dematerialise" the Registry (Pt VIII, ss.91–95 and Sch.5, LRA 2002). This phrase gives rise to the image of the entire weight of paper that characterised both unregistered and registered conveyancing vanishing into the electronic ether, and indeed, that is the plan. Under an electronic conveyancing regime, documents will be scanned into the register and kept in electronic form, where they can be easily searched without the intervention of the Registrar. For a fee, they can also be sent by email to anyone who requests them. After they are scanned, they will be destroyed (except for pre-registration deeds forwarded to the Registry with an application for first registration). The main title document, the Land or Charge Certificate, will no longer exist. Old certificates will have no further authority. Instead, ownership will be governed by the entries that appear on the register.

The system will work by requiring solicitors and licensed conveyancers to purchase specialised software and install it on office computers. The software purchaser will then be able to connect to an intranet, a secure computer network, dedicated to electronic conveyancing. Conveyancers will then be able to contact each other and exchange all necessary documentation with mortgage lenders, surveyors, and others in the conveyancing process. (Capps, 2002). Some practitioners and commentators have raised questions about the effect of e-conveyancing on the requirements of writing in land transfers, and the accompanying potential for fraud, as well as the related question of the security of digital signatures. Others, although cognisant of these issues, take a more sanguine view, as they see benefits in terms of efficiency and savings in transaction costs. The economic savings to be had include hiring less staff to deal with documents, less need for storage space, and shorter delays in completion and billing. To some extent, however, any discussion of the scheme at this point, before it comes into full effect, can only be descriptive of the statutory provisions and speculative as to the results.

Certainly, in the future, "deeds" will be drawn up, signed, and verified electronically, thus the LRA 2002 foresees the abolition of many of the legal rules that require conveyancing documents to be in writing and signed. Particularly, the rules in s.53 of the LPA 1925 and s.2 of the Law of Property (Miscellaneous Provisions) Act 1989 regarding contracts for the sale of land must be changed. In the LRA 2002, s.91 does not remove the requirement, but it deems compliance with the requirements of writing in the LPA 1925 and the LP(MP)A 1989. The result is that the electronic document is treated as if it is in writing, and where it meets the other criteria in the LRA 2002 (*i.e.*, a "digital signature" applied by an authorised agent), it will be treated as if it were a deed.

However, the requirements of the LRA 2002 are not the entire legislative picture of e-conveyancing. A linked set of statutory provisions exists to make the computer network functional, and to allay the fears regarding security and reliability that generally plague e-commerce. Under s.8 of the Electronic Communications Act 2000, the Law of Property (Electronic Communications) Order inserts a new clause (2A) into the LP(MP)A 1989, authorising the conclusion of land contracts by electronic media. Under this section, the Lord Chancellor may disapply any statutory requirement regulating how a transaction is to be carried out. This means that the writing requirement as we know it may well be phased out over the next few years. Although this represents a major change in land law and conveyancing practice, e-conveyancing brings us into line with the European market more generally. The new e-conveyancing structure will make the transfer of land in England and Wales subject to the European Directives that regulate e-commerce. As Barbara Bogusz points out in her discussion of e-conveyancing: "The Directive on Electronic Commerce and the Directive on Electronic Signatures have both been incorporated into domestic law through the Electronic Communications Act 2000. The implementation of these Directives will have a knock-on effect of improving access to land information to purchasers anywhere within the internal market" (2002, p.566).

The possible results of e-conveyancing, therefore, include greater transparency in dealing with property, both nationally and internationally. As stated earlier, commentators find both good and bad in this. A constant line of negative commentary stresses the "deskilling" of conveyancing as a result of the new law (Kenney, 2002a), and explicit in this concern is the outsourcing of conveyancing jobs to non-lawyers, or at least, to non-traditional providers of legal services. Banks and building societies are poised to enter the conveyancing market as service providers, which may have a genuinely negative effect on the income of members of the profession today.

Moving beyond the economic considerations, conveyancers have occupied a position of power in the disposition of land and landed interests for centuries, based in part on their mastery of a highly specialised language and a complex world of interlocking and cross-referential documents. The ownership structures (the trust, the freehold, the lease, the other estates and interests discussed throughout this book) are ineluctably contained within the form of the documents that embody the structures. In this sense, the implicit and (in some cases) explicit mourning for the lost days of the title deeds and (even) the paper registry represents a very real loss of métier, of scope for professional mastery, and thus, of professional pride and identity. The end result of the e-conveyancing process might be, over the next few decades, to transform conveyancers from nodes of power in the conveyancing system to mere rubber-stampers or indemnifiers for individual, private transactions engaged in by non-lawyers under the aegis of the Registry. We might indeed see a resurgence of "private" conveyancing, if "private" is defined in this sense. From the point of view of the government, and of the "consumer", the issues are different. Accessibility and transparency may well speak to the privileging of a class other than conveyancers. This will be discussed further in light of the provisions of the Act.

LRA 2002 AND LRA 1925: THE OVERALL PICTURE

The new Act retains the position that, as with deeds before 1925, once the information is on the register the value of the documents themselves is superseded by registration. In addition, as in 1925, once a title has become registered in the way just described, future dealings with it are mediated by the Registry. Investigation of title becomes primarily a matter of ascertaining what information is recorded in the Register; and a transfer of title involves forwarding a deed of transfer, drawn up privately between the parties to the transaction, to the Land Registry. The purchaser takes the land subject to the information on the title, including registered charges such as leases and easements, minor interests such as notices and restrictions, and, exceptionally, interests that do not appear on the title but nonetheless operate on the land regardless of the change in ownership ("overriding" interests).

Under the LRA 2002, the actual transfer of title is still effected by the Registry substituting the purchaser's name for that of the vendor as registered proprietor. Presently, information is recorded on index cards filed under the title number in the Registry under three headings or "registers"—the "Property" register, which summarises all the rights that go with the title; the "Charges" register, where incumbrances affecting the title are recorded; and the "Proprietorship" register, where the name of the registered proprietor for the time being is entered along with a statement as to the quality of his title (absolute, good leasehold, qualified or possessory) and any limitations upon his or her freedom to deal with the title. This information is collected together on the "land certificate", which functions as a summary of the state of the title from time to time, and which must be produced for inspection in the majority of transactions and subsequently returned for alteration in the Registry. As stated above, this system is set to change. The Registrar will not issue land or charges certificates. It is not yet clear what exact form the electronic register will take.

Leases

Leases may be given their own title number. "Long" leases (*i.e.* leases with a significant market value in their own right and, in particular, all leases with over 40 years to run) are given their own title number. However, most commercial property falls outside the scope of the present land registration system. Under the current regime, leases with between 21 and 40 years to run can be protected by registration if the Registry approves, or by the entry of a "notice" on the landlord's title, and thus operate as what are called "minor interests". This procedure is described below. Most shop or office premises are let on much shorter terms than 21 years. Leases for under 21 years are kept off the register and are protected as "overriding interests". These, too, are outlined in due course, but for now, it is important to note that much commercial property remains unregistered.

Several issues arise. First, the stated governmental aim to make the register a true "mirror" of land holding in England and Wales fails if short(er) leases are kept off the register. Second, in an increasingly property-driven economy, in which commercial leases play an important part, failure to have this information might have serious implications for governmental policy. Third, "with e-conveyancing on the horizon . . . a fundamentally different and paper-based system would continue to run alongside the new. For e-conveyancing to be truly successful, it is important that this does not happen" (Chamberlain, 2002, p.1097). In addition, the LRA 2002 is committed to balancing strict accuracy against market efficiency and public utility. If every lease (or other interest) regardless of its length or importance appeared on the register, the register would quickly become too detailed and far too long to be useful. The balance struck, therefore, is that a lease of seven years or more now triggers first registration and is entered on the register under its own individual title. Leases of under seven years continue to operate as overriding interests (see below)[40] under Sch.3, para.1 to the Act. Leases of more than three years and less than seven may be entered on the register, although registration is not compulsory (LRA 2002, s.37).

Easements

The benefit of easements is normally entered in the property register and thus forms part of the description of the land to which the titles relates; the burden, correspondingly, is normally noted in the charges register against the title of the servient landowner. However, under the previous regime, if an easement was not registered, it would bind a purchaser of the servient land as an overriding interest. As we shall see, this rule is now different. The aim of transparency, or, put differently, of making the "mirror" of the registry more accurate, means that only legal easements and *profits à prendre* survive in the LRA 2002 as overriding interests. All other easements must be registered if they are to bind a future purchaser. Legal easements can only be created out of registered land by registered disposition, and they will naturally appear on the register. Therefore, the sources of overriding easements in the LRA 2002 are legal easements that arise by implication or by prescription. The only exception to this rule is found in para.3, Sch.3 to the LRA 2002, where legal easements are only overriding if they have been used within the past year before the purchase. A purchaser will be bound by an easement that she did not know about and could not have noticed, but which is in regular use; but will not be bound by the same easement if it had not been used for a year. (Cooke, 2003, Chs 3 and 5).

Minor interests

This is a term introduced by the LRA 1925 and now dropped by the LRA 2002. It is a general category which embraces a range of mechanisms for protecting interests, claims and rights adverse to or encumbrances on a registered title. It does not refer to some distinctive type of property right (as in "legal interest" or "equitable interest"). Rather, the concept of the minor interest remains as a shorthand to remind us to question the status of third party interests on the register. Is the interest we are considering registered, recorded, overriding or unprotected? Can it be overreached? In the 1925 Act, there were four mechanisms: (1) the restriction; (2) the inhibition; (3) the notice; and (4) the caution. To understand the logic of these mechanisms, it is necessary to keep in mind what kind of practical protection a particular type of incumbrance or claim adverse to a title requires if it is to be effectively protected against the owner or prospective purchaser of that title.

Although the LRA 2002 dispenses with inhibitions and cautions,[41] the inhibitions and cautions made before the Act takes effect are still good, and the underlying philosophy of "minor interests" remains to some extent the same. Under the LRA 1925, notices involved the entry of information on the charges register, indicating for example that the title is subject to a restrictive covenant, or that some other adverse interest has been entered against the title. Any prospective purchaser would have been alerted to the existence of such claims, which should be protected by a notice, on investigating the title. The term "notice" here is simply LRA-speak, but, obviously, its affinity with the old system and its terminology continues to lie in the fact that it is intended to provide a purchaser with actual notice of incumbrances which may decisively affect his willingness to proceed with respect to the vendor's title. Restrictions and inhibitions were entered in the proprietorship register and limited the circumstances in which the Registrar permitted the registered proprietor to deal with the title.

The LRA 2002 keeps this scheme fundamentally intact, while to some extent redefining the meaning of notice and restriction. In gross, notices will be used to protect interests in registered land that are intended to bind third parties (*i.e.* a lease or easement). Restrictions will be used to regulate the entry of dealings with registered land onto the register (s.40, LRA 2002). This means that a restriction restricts or prevents the registration of a disposition if the disposition does not comply with the terms of the restriction. The owners of a registered title will be considered to have unlimited powers over the title (*i.e.* for sale) in the absence of a restriction. We will deal with the question of restrictions first, and then discuss notices.

For our purposes, the entry of a restriction on the title can be employed to ensure compliance with the "two-trustee" rule in one of its various forms. For example, a restriction can be used to ensure payment of purchase money to the trustees of the settlement under the SLA, in which case the Registrar will not enter the purchaser as new proprietor unless the restriction has been complied with. Where land was held on trust for sale (express or statutory) a restriction could be entered requiring any disposition of the title to be made by at least two trustees, thereby indirectly ensuring the protection of the purchaser from the beneficial interests behind the trust (details of which were excluded from the register—see LRA 2002, s.33, and below). The 1996 Act broadly followed this approach, and the entry of restrictions continued as the mechanism by which the enhanced rights of beneficiaries *vis-à-vis* their trustees was secured.

Section 34 of the LRA 2002 states that any person claiming to have an interest capable of being the subject matter of a notice (*i.e.* one of the third-party interests listed above), may, subject to the rules, apply to the Registrar for an entry of an agreed or unilateral notice on the register in respect of that interest. Section 34(3)(a) through (c) sets out the circumstances in which the Registrar may approve the application for an agreed notice. In subsections (a) and (b), the registered proprietor of the land has agreed to the notice. In subsection (c), the applicant has satisfied the Registrar that the third party has in fact the interest that forms the basis for the notice (*i.e.* a lease.) Sections 35–36 of the LRA 2002 provide for unilateral notices, a potentially powerful tool for the protection of third-party interests in registered land. Here, the registered proprietor need not agree to the entry of the notice. He or she may move to cancel the notice, and if the beneficiary does not uphold their claim, the Registrar must remove the notice.

Some interests cannot be protected by the entry of a notice on the register (LRA 2002, s.33). Most importantly, these include interests under trusts of land and under SLA settlements. Leases too short to be registrable (leases under three years at present) and restrictive covenants in leases are other important exceptions. However, the LRA 2002 promotes other interests to the status of proprietary rights that now can be protected by notice. Section 115 states that a right of pre-emption can now be a proprietary right in registered land, and thus be protected by a notice on the register or function as an overriding interest through actual occupation (see below). Section 116 states that two new interests can now be protected by notice on the register: the "equity by estoppel" and the "mere equity." This means that the right of a claimant under a proprietary estoppel may now be asserted against the new proprietor of the property before the court has resolved the claimant's equitable interest. This makes a huge difference to the resolution of claims. Rather than the litigation occurring in a two (or more) step process, in which the claimant first petitions the court for resolution of whether she or he has a proprietary right, and then asserts that right against the new proprietor of the land, the case can be heard in full in one sitting. The claimant asks for relief from the present proprietor, who would then have a claim (or not) against the erstwhile seller.

Overriding interests

The registered conveyancing scheme was designed to render obsolete the practices of investigation and proof of title associated with the old documentary system. In broad terms—and subject to the general 1925 strategy regarding trusts of land— registration was seen as a functional equivalent of or improvement upon private documents. In this sense, the register was intended to be a mirror of the title. But it was never intended that the register should be comprehensive. Short-term or trivial information, or information which would have been apparent, in accordance with normal pre-1926 conveyancing practice, on inspecting the land, was to be excluded from the register. (There seems to have been a clear desire to prevent the register from becoming over-cluttered in the way that private documentary titles had in the past.)

So the scheme carried over from the old system the practice of inspection of the land, broadly making those rights, often non-documentary in origin, which would previously have been so discoverable, enforceable without entry on the register. In LRA-speak, such rights are called overriding interests, and were listed in s.70 of the LRA 1925.

The LRA 1925, s.70, begins:

"All registered land shall, unless under the provision of this Act the contrary is expressed on the register, be deemed to be subject to such of the following overriding interests as may be for the time being subsisting in reference thereto, and such interests shall not be treated as incumbrances within the meaning of this Act . . .".

Then follows a list of items, of varying practical importance, not normally discoverable from the old paper title. Many though not all of these kinds of rights, were already heading, fairly rapidly, for the dustbin of history; they were included in the scheme "just in case". The two sections, however, that gave courts both the most trouble and the most opportunity to "stretch" the overriding interest exception were s.70(1)(g), which was used to give occupiers rights in the "family home"; and section s.70(1)(f)[44], which provided for the rights of adverse possessors vis-à-vis the (new) registered proprietor.

The Law Commission considered the questions raised by overriding interests and the change in home-sharer arrangements, as well as the expansion of s.70(1)(g) (discussed below) at great length in the two Reports it published before the LRA 2002 was promulgated. There is no simple summary of the many arguments made regarding these topics, although they can be traced in Law Commission Reports 254 and 271[45], and in the plethora of commentaries on land registration reform over the past five years. Suffice to say that, instead of definitively closing the section 70 loophole, as might be expected in an Act which seeks to provide a better mirror of title, the Law Commission instead proposed a tighter regime of overriding interests, and made adverse possession of registered land almost impossible.

The question that remains is, why leave any overriding interests? Why not take the opportunity to put an end to doctrine of notice once and for all? The only possible answer is that the English land law is not yet ready to "see" land as purely reducible to the symbolic cipher of money. Although the purpose of the Act is to make the property market accessible through legal and informational transparency, the fundamental notion of land and landed interests continues to include, in some sense, soil, ground or roof—structural conditions for human interaction and survival. We can see this if we look first at the requirements of s.70(1)(g) and (f), and then at the Schedules, which, along with ss.29 and 30, define "overriding interests" for the new legislation. For our purposes, these are Sch.1 "Unregistered Interests Which Override First Registration", Sch.3 "Unregistered Interests Which Override Registered Dispositions of the Act", and, as we are considering adverse possession at this point in the analysis, Sch.6, "Registration of Adverse Possessor".

Section 70(1)(g) LRA 1925 and Schs 1 and 3 LRA 2002

The category of overriding interest which has caused the most difficulty in modern conditions is that set out in s.70(1)(g):

> "The rights of every person in actual occupation of the land or in receipt of the rents and profits thereof, save where

enquiry is made of such person and the rights are not disclosed".

With what in mind was s.70(1)(g) designed? The answer seems to be connected with the pre-1925 decision in *Hunt v Luck* (1901)[44] and to be related to the somewhat similar provision contained in LPA 1925, s.14: "Part I of this Act shall not prejudicially affect the interests of any person in possession or in actual occupation of land to which he may be entitled in right of such possession or occupation".

In *Hunt v Luck*, a widow brought an action in the Chancery Division claiming to be entitled to a number of houses in Wimbledon which had belonged to her husband. Two conveyances existed, dating from 1896, two years before his death, by which he apparently transferred these properties to X, who used the conveyances as security for a loan he then raised. These documents of title were, consequently, in the possession of the mortgagees and it was against them that the widow brought her action; X had since died and his heir did not make an appearance. The widow failed to persuade the court that the conveyances could be set aside as forgeries or because of her husband's incapacity. This left only the argument that there never had been a genuine sale, that the purchase price had never in fact been paid (although one of the conveyances was expressed to be made in consideration of £12,000, and receipt of this sum was expressly acknowledged), and that the mortgagees were fixed with notice of her husband's rights at the time of the mortgage transaction, and of the fact that X, the mortgagor, had no interest in the property.

The houses were occupied by, for the most part, weekly tenants, who paid their rent to a local estate agent. For about two years after the 1896 conveyances, this agent had paid over these rents to the husband. After his death, the agent paid them to X until X also died. (After that, presumably, the agent held on to the collected rents while the dispute was sorted out.) The widow's argument was that the mortgagees, when investigating the title which was to provide security for the loan they were proposing to make, should have asked the tenants who received the rents they paid, and that, on finding out that the rents were paid to an estate agent, the mortgagees should have gone on to ask—at very least, because he was an estate agent—on whose behalf he was collecting the rents.

The judge concluded that "(1) A tenant's occupation is notice of all that tenant's rights, but not of his lessor's title or rights; (2)

actual knowledge that the rents are paid by the tenants to some person whose receipt is inconsistent with the title of the vendor is notice of that person's rights" ([1901] 1 Ch. at 51). The judge went on: "Many landlords have agents, and there is nothing inconsistent with the title shewn to the mortgagees . . . in the fact that the rents of the property were collected by a house agent". The mere fact of payment to an agent could not fix a purchaser with notice. But even if such an extension of the requirements could be envisaged, it could not apply on facts like those of *Hunt v Luck*, where, thought the judge, ". . . the mortgagees rely on the husband's signature and receipt, and the plaintiff the widow is attempting to fix them with constructive notice of facts which would make it their duty to distrust and disbelieve that signature" (*ibid.*, pp.51–52).

The judge's view of the merits frames the central point just as sharply ". . . even assuming both parties to the action to be equally innocent, the man [*i.e.* the husband] who has been swindled by too great confidence in his own agent [*i.e.* X] has surely less claim to the assistance of a court of equity than a purchaser for value who gets the legal estate, and pays his money without actual notice [*i.e.* the mortgagees]" (*ibid.*, p.48).

What could indicate more clearly the priorities of practical men in whose environment paper titles could not always be suspect, even if it was too much to hope that, in every case, they be above suspicion?

Section 70(1)(g) seems to have been targeted at the (limited) questions addressed by this case (though as drafted, it is far from clear whether it sought to follow or extend the rule enunciated in that case: was "in receipt of rent and profits" to be confined to "notice" of the estate agent or did it extend necessary inquiry to the ultimate recipient of the rents?).

At the core of the issue to which the paragraph is addressed is the question of what observable facts, on inspection of the land, should count as inconsistencies with the title. Before 1925, the title was a paper title: now, it is registered title. But the issue is the same. So what is to count as an inconsistency (as a fact which, once observed, should put the purchaser on inquiry) cannot but be a matter of judicial perception, filtered through sociocultural norms concerning property relations between people. Where a vendor offers a good paper title (or, in LRA terms, is registered as sole proprietor), does the presence of his or her spouse, sibling, lover, child, parent or aged relative suggest anything "inconsistent" with the title? However, this question is in turn subject to a further question. Does it make a difference that the old flexibility available to judges on conveyancing questions has been constrained, perhaps severely, by the enactment of the 1925 code?

This raises first the problem of how the legislation should be interpreted. We have explored at length in this book those features of land ownership in England which explain why contemporary land law is put together in the way it is. But the question is then whether the purposes of the 1925 legislation are relevant to its interpretation today. A long time has passed since its enactment and, as we have seen, many features of the world which its draftsmen took for granted have dissolved. The modern judicial tendency has been to insist that the words of the code should be given their ordinary natural meaning. So, it is now said, with reference to the question of the meaning of s.70(1)(g), that "rights" means property rights and "in actual occupation" is a mere question of fact. So if, today, we ask whether the equitable interests arising behind trusts are overriding interests where the holders of the interests are in occupation of land, and therefore bind purchasers without any requirement that such interests be protected by some form of registration, the answer seems to be that they do, because the interests are "rights", and *ex hypothesi* they fall within the "actual occupation" element of the paragraph.

Whether this result is that intended by the draftsmen is another matter. We saw in Chapter 6 that one consequence of the 1925 strategy was to push into equity most of the fragments of title which prior to the code had taken effect at law. We have also indicated that, for the purposes of processing the new types of dispute which have arisen against the backdrop of the rise of owner-occupation and the informal, extra-legal modes of acquiring the rights which the courts came to recognise, new kinds of equities have come to be formulated by the courts: the new version of implied trust, estoppel and contractual licences. As we have seen, the "equity by estoppel" and the "mere equity" may now be protected by a notice on the register, although interests under trusts and the SLA 1925 are still excluded from the register.

The list of overriding interests in the new LRA 2002 is shorter than that in the LRA 1925, but it has not shrunk to nothing. The framers of the legislation have chosen to leave a dark spot in the "mirror principle", both at first registration (Sch.1 to the new Act) and later (Sch.3). In great part, this has been to protect the interests of people who are often vulnerable, by not being on the legal title, to loss of their proprietary rights (especially a home) or to fraud. Most importantly, the Act continues to privilege actual occupation: as under s.70(1)(g) of the LRA 1925, para.2 of Sch.3 to the new Act states:

> (2) An interest belonging at the time of the disposition to a person in actual occupation, so far as relating to land of which he is in actual occupation, except for—
>
>> (a) an interest under a settlement under the Settled Land Act 1925 (c.18);
>> (b) an interest of a person of whom inquiry was made before the disposition and who failed to disclose the right when he could reasonably have been expected to do so;
>> (c) an interest—
>>
>>> (i) which belongs to a person whose occupation would not have been obvious on a reasonably careful inspection of the land at the time of the disposition, and
>>> (ii) of which the person to whom the disposition is made does not have actual knowledge at that time;
>>
>> (d) a leasehold estate in land granted to take effect in possession after the end of the period of three months beginning with the date of the grant and which has not taken effect in possession at the time of the disposition.

In gross, the same exceptions are stated in Sch.1. A comparison of this list and the old s.70 shows refinement rather than change of the interests that can override first registration and transfer of registered land (both registered estates and registered charges). These shorten and clarify the list of possible overriding interests, but we must consider the extent to which the register can adapt to the shifting patterns of occupation, use, recording and hidden (or "taken for granted") practice that keep the list of overriding interests stable and the register (thus) useful. Courts will not interpret legislation in a vacuum. The list as it exists now is a mirror of this time. The combination of e-conveyancing and new forms of landholding and possibly, the regularisation of new interests in land occupation (the return of grown children to their parents' home, the later age of first home buyers who buy with friends rather than partners, etc.) means that what judicial activism will create in the future, and what sort of overriding interests will be maintained in the next reform of the LRA, cannot be known today.

If the purpose of the reformulation of "overriding interests" was a better balance between which interests must appear on the register and which may not, the reformulation regarding the proprietary rights of squatters has a different agenda. Obviously, such rights as a squatter possessed would not have appeared in the vendor's paper title, and indeed, as we have seen at p.67 above, many years might elapse before any documentation relating to the squatter's title came into existence. Under s.70(1)(f), the LRA scheme accommodated itself to these practical realities, providing additionally that a "successful" squatter (*i.e.* one who had, through possession of the land adverse to the superior title for the requisite period, barred the assertability of that title's rights *vis-à-vis* his own) could seek rectification of the register and have his name entered as proprietor instead.

The LRA 2002 takes an entirely different view of acquiring proprietary rights over registered land by mere occupation. The Practice Guide "Adverse possession of registered land under the new provisions of the Land Registration Act 2002", issued by the Land Registry and available online,[45] states in its introduction:

> "Under the law as it existed prior to Land Registration Act 2002, a person who had no documentary title could, in some circumstances, acquire title to registered land by adverse possession for a minimum period of 12 years under the Limitation Act 1980. However, the doctrine of adverse possession did not fit easily with the fundamental concept of indefeasibility of title which underlies the system of land registration. It is registration, not possession, that vests the legal estate in the owner and that person's ownership is apparent from the register".

Immediately, we have several issues to consider. The emphasis on "title by registration, not registration of title" is evident. What does this mean for the classical English emphasis on possession as the basis of land rights? The law is undergoing a paradigm shift in favour of (1) the registered proprietor of land,

and (2) registration itself. Although this may seem obvious and non-controversial, there are some points of uneasiness that arise when the administrative and the substantive merge in this way. Looking more closely at this, we see that registration is also centralisation. Schedule 6 to the LRA 2002 begins in para.1(1) with: "(1) A person may apply to the registrar to be registered as the proprietor of a registered estate in land if he has been in adverse possession of the estate for the period of ten years ending on the date of the application". The rest of the paragraph clarifies the other conditions under which someone may apply to the Registrar to be registered as the proprietor of land that they have been occupying. The entire regime now turns on the Registrar's management of the claim to registration. Under the LRA 2002, a squatter may apply to the Registrar to be registered after 10 years of adverse possession. Once any application is lodged (a decision made by the Registrar in accordance with para.1), the registered proprietor will be notified of the application. In the majority of cases, she or he will be given the opportunity to object to it. If an objection is made, then the application will automatically be denied. The registered proprietor then has two more years in which to take steps to deal with the squatter (either by ejecting him or her or otherwise regularising the squatter's position). If the squatter remains in adverse possession after two years, he or she will be entitled to be registered as the new proprietor. At that point, the Registrar will register the squatter's title as a new title.

The scheme overall, therefore, operates as the gathering and dissemination of land *rights* from a centralised source. This is the most important difference between the system previously in place, in which rights were acquired "on the ground" so to speak and were *then* registered, and the new system in which rights are acquired substantively *through* registration. Arguably, the effect of this is to take a significant step away from the traditional emphasis on possession as defining some (never all) fundamental rights in land. If this is true, what then replaces the multi-faceted and constantly shifting figure of possession in the English land law? Possession has served as a usefully interstitial concept during times of social and legal transition, grounding rights in the family home and in other people's land when the value(s) of these "properties" shift according to cultural or economic changes. If possession becomes destabilised as an argument (or even metaphor) available to the land law—as may be happening in the case of registered land—will the same sorts of social engineering that the courts have engaged in until now still be possible? Or will judicial activism—through the medium of statutory interpretation—attach to other figures? We return to this question at the end of the chapter.

Fraud and non-registration

Any legal system of adjudication of disputes arising out of land transfer can anticipate disputes which are grounded in the claim that someone has acted badly. What should a court do, for example, if it is faced with a collusive transaction in which title is transferred to a purchaser so as to defeat the rights of someone who has an interest which is not protected by registration when it needs to be, and where both vendor and purchaser know of this fact? Should the purchaser succeed if he pleads that the interest in question is void against him for non-registration under the statute? It is often said that to force the purchaser to take subject to the interest despite the statute because he knew of its existence is to reintroduce the doctrine of notice which the requirement of registration sought to eliminate.[46] Such an argument rather overstates the issue. The LRA, as we have seen, set out to replace paper titles with registered titles, and the information retrievable from them (and thus "constructive notice") with information retrievable from registers. Merely to say that someone who actually knows of an interest and engages in a transaction clearly designed to take advantage of the statute—especially in a non-commercial context—should be deprived of the benefit of the statute is not to reintroduce all the baggage of constructive notice from the past.[47] Indeed, cases of this sort in the past were commonly regarded as instances where it was not possible to formulate general rules, precisely because it turned on the judge's impression of the individual facts of the case whether, in all the circumstances, the purchaser had behaved so badly that the court should intervene. So pervasive, however, is the theme of "certainty" in both academic and judicial legal discourse that it is necessary to direct some general remarks to this question in the concluding chapter.

PROBLEMS OF LEGAL AND SOCIAL CHANGE

Nearly 80 years after the enactment of the legislation, it is perhaps not surprising that the law cannot be found by looking only at the statute. While it may be excessive to claim that "the 1925 legislation was already out of date in 1925" (Pottage, 1995, p.400), it is certainly true that conveyancing practice and the assumptions underpinning it have changed significantly in the last 80 years, in part because of changes in the social context, but also, and perhaps as importantly, because of changes in the practices of the management of land transfer. At the core of these changes in practice is a shift of emphasis between the contract stage and the completion stage of the transfer process. In the nineteenth century, the principal emphasis was usually upon the situation post-contract; the purchaser's solicitor was to focus on whether the title being offered conformed to what was promised in the contract, and therefore the conveyance marked an acceptance, following a post-contract period of suspicion and inquiry, that what was promised in the contract could be, and was being, delivered. Slowly but relentlessly, the shift across to registration as the routine basis for proof of and existence of title has altered the emphasis at work here (see Pottage, 1995). In most transactions, the contract has assumed primacy of place, and once it is concluded, the completion and registration stages follow almost as of course. (This has also introduced new anxieties which are rarely taken very seriously—the *scintilla temporis* between the execution of the deed of transfer and the registration of the new proprietor but these must be left aside here, except to note that, to some extent the courts have sought to adjust the interpretation of the legislative framework to these perceptions of changes in practices.)

Secondly, the question of its historical origins, discussed above, provides very little guidance on how today's disputes should be approached and solved. This is partly a result of the imperfections of the legislation itself. But it is also a consequence, inevitably, of drifts and changes in the underlying realities in the world to which the law is to be applied. These include changes in conveyancing and Land Registry practice. To take an example which may seem very specific, but which in fact has considerable practical implications: what is the relevant time for the scheme of overriding interests to take effect? Is it when the transfer document is completed between the parties, or is it when the ownership of title is changed in the Land Registry? Faced with a dispute which turned in part on this question, one judge observed:

> "One does not expect . . . conveyancing absurdities from the pens of the skilled parliamentary draftsmen who implemented Lord Birkenhead's great scheme for the reform of

English real property law embodied in the 1925 legislation, but even they may have occasionally expressed their complex interlocking concepts in forms of words which do not precisely fit every case. If the choice is between accepting a conveyancing absurdity on the one hand and straining or even modifying the draftsmen's language to avoid it on the other, I have no doubt that the latter alternative is to be preferred".[48]

This illustrates the position of lawyers and the courts before the new scheme: conventional piety towards the perfection of 1925, recognition of the impossibility of legislative omniscience, and largely pragmatic decision-making with reference to an assessment of conveyancing realities to the extent that the court understands them. It is, however, far from clear that the new legislation has succeeded in simplifying the legal framework. We may be in the realm that many of the piecemeal proposals put forward by the Law Commission in the last two decades, some of which have passed into law, have seemed to indicate. However well intended, the new legislation may hold out the prospect of further, rather than reduced, complexity. Incremental change by judicial decision-making on a case-by-case basis seems inherently uncertain and more than a little arbitrary as the 1925 legislation itself fades into the mists of the past. But the alternatives in 2002 may be even worse. The questions that the new Act raises turn on a fundamental shift in the balance of power between the government, the conveyancing profession, and the increasingly investment-astute public. However, this new balance does not materially affect the condition of the non-computer-literate portion of the population; nor, strangely, does it maintain the "agrarian ideal" that has underpinned much of English landholding. Instead, we are in the world that Jeremy Rifkin proposes in *The Age of Access*: a world in which a new elite technologically sophisticated, mobile class is privileged by a government that is engaged in a feat of social engineering. This is the same point made by Christopher Lasch and others. The rise of an unrooted elite changes the very structure of community as well as the greater notion of "society." The new LRA heightens and facilitates these changes.

11

CONCLUSION

The categories of English land law have, to a large extent, ceased to mirror social relations in the way they once did. No doubt one can say that the reason for this is that land, by contrast with other things whose existence seems quite natural in our world, has been around as long as people and therefore as long as human thought. And land has often been thought of as different. In the medieval and early modern periods, philosophers and theologians debated the relative merits of land and moveables—especially money—so far as the relationship between virtue or the good life and the ownership of property was concerned. In the eighteenth century, the analysis of wealth and where it came from divided over whether it was land or moveable property which was the fundamental source of wealth. In the nineteenth century, the rather overenthusiastic Henry George could observe that "The real and natural distinction is between things which are the produce of labour and things which are the gratuitous offerings of nature . . . between wealth and land" (n.d., p.239) from which it followed that "Let the parchments be ever so many, or possession ever so long, natural justice can recognise no right in one man to the possession and enjoyment of land that is not equally the right of all his fellows. Though his titles have been acquiesced in by generation after generation, to the landed estates of the Duke of Westminster the poorest child that is born in London today has as much right as his eldest son" (*ibid.*, p.241). In the same period, George Brodrick argued for the abolition of life estates in land though not in personal property. As he put it, "The policy of prohibiting life-estates in land, without prohibiting the corresponding life-interests in personalty, must stand or fall by the peculiar nature, claims and obligations of Real Property" (1881, p.345). "Not a Session", he wrote, "elapses in which Parliament does not affirm the principle that land is a thing sui generis, over which the state may and ought to assume a control far more stringent than it would be politic to assume, but not than it might rightfully assume, over other kinds of property" (*ibid.*).

What happened in the 1920s, as we have seen, was the preservation of a special legal regime for the transfer of title to land. Quite a lot of the baggage of the past was simply scrapped, and this baggage, for the most part, has been ignored in this book. But elements of the past did remain, and we have tried to give some idea of the antecedents of these elements. Whether what happened in 1925 was radical or not is a matter of perspective. What is barely arguable is the consequence of what happened. Because life estates and entails were not abolished in their entirety but were relocated into the realm of equity and lodged by force of statute behind trusts, rather a lot of baggage has survived, albeit in modified form. And so the 1925 legislation, or land law more generally, has become, in many respects, a corpus of learning whose intelligibility, and possibly whose very time, lies in some respects in the past. In many ways this has been true of land law for many centuries. And it has also been the case that one of the primary skills of English lawyers lies in adapting the moribund to the needs of the present and land law exemplifies this very well.

But this involves a cost. In a working paper, the Law Commission observed that "it is virtually impossible to draft a mortgage deed that gives a layman any idea of the consequences of entering a mortgage" (1986, p.4) and that the English law of mortgages "has never been subjected to systematic statutory reform, and over several centuries of gradual evolution it has acquired a multi-layered structure that is historically fascinating but inappropriately and sometimes unnecessarily complicated" (*ibid.*, p.1).

This is true of more than mortgages. In particular, almost every aspect of the law relating to the acquisition, ownership, occupation and transfer of residential property—in other words, of those parts of land law which affect most ordinary people—is "unnecessarily complicated". Lawyers, of course, can muddle through as they have always done. Weber was probably right when he wrote, early in this century, that:

"The formularies of the conveyancers . . . may be quite unintelligible to the layman, as . . . is the case in England. Yet, he can understand the basic character of the English way of legal thinking, he can identify with it and, above all, he can make his peace with it by retaining once and for all a solicitor as his legal father-confessor for all contingencies of life, as is indeed done by practically every English businessman" (tr. 1978, p.891).

But it is doubtful that many of today's owner-occupiers and their families retain such confessors. Nor, if the law was more accessible, is there any reason why they should.

It is easy to complain in this vein. It is much more difficult, as we shall repeat, to formulate what should be done. Certainly nothing of that sort can be attempted here. We conclude rather by gathering together the main features of what has been discussed in this book: the nature of English formalism and the problem of the new informality and its relation to the tradition.

ENGLISH FORMALISM

The energies of conveyancers have always gone into how to get things done for a client. When a conveyancer drafts a will, settlement, lease or restrictive covenant (or rummages through precedent books or standard forms or files on his hard disk to find something suitable), the ultimate objective is to mediate the intention of this client. Of course, he must tell the client that there are certain things you cannot do, or can do only with great difficulty or risk. But the lawyer's principal task is to find out what the client wants to do, and then to discover the appropriate legal formulae to express in legal language what can usually be said more simply in the language of social or business life. Parliamentary draftsmen do exactly the same thing.

But if this is to be possible, it requires a relatively stable set of interpretive expectations. If judges keep changing their minds about what all these formulae mean, lawyers will not know where they are, will lack confidence as to the future effect of the documents they prepare. This may partly explain why, in times past when the communication network of law was much less systematised than it is now, judges took so seriously, or made such heavy weather of, the task of construction.

One final point about English formalism must be emphasised. It is about stylisation. The ideal—which in the nature of things can never be realised—would be to have a formula to meet every wish of every client. Obviously, in the social world, new things are always happening. Old formulae prove insufficient to meet what people want to do. New ones have to be invented, usually by modifying old ones, and the process begins again.

Given this formalist tradition, "private law" really amounts to engendering a state of affairs in which owners of property can make the law concerning their property within the limits set by the public, general law (as in the perpetuity rules). A lease of a building, for example, gives the law to that building. The parties—usually the lessor—make the rules; the courts, if there is a dispute, are there to provide stable interpretations of that law as expressed in the formulae, and to provide, through their auxiliary agencies, the coercive back-up if need be.

Conveyancers can go on doing things for a long time without anyone other than themselves noticing. The longer they go on doing something, a professional view as to its nature grows up. Then, for whatever reason, there is a dispute which results in the matter receiving judicial scrutiny. Private litigation costs money and always has. It is relatively rare, in property matters as in others, for people to litigate for the sake of establishing or "developing" the law. Most private litigation grows out of a conflict of interests in the social world; legal disputation is simply how that conflict is fielded in court and during the run-up to such proceedings in the wrangling between lawyers. A challenge to a lawyer's practice, then, mounted in court, is nearly always just a means, an instrument once again, for the pursuit of the matter at hand.

Unlike most ordinary contracts, many land transactions have effects which stretch over long periods of time. For example, a question can arise in litigation concerning the effect today of a covenant made many years ago. Suppose then that a covenant is made, say, 100 years ago, and the appropriate formula of the time is used to annex the benefit so it will run with the land in the future. Years later, part of the land is sold off. Then the question arises in court: after the sale, does the seller or the buyer have the right to enforce the covenant? How should we assess whatever decision is arrived at by a judge?

(1) How can we tell if the judge is right or wrong? If the question has come up for decision before, and the judge has followed that decision, we would usually say he has done what he should. The older that decision was, the more justified the judge is today in following it, for reasons we will shortly see.

(2) If our judge's decision is new—that is, the question has been decided for the first time—how then do we evaluate it? First, we can ask whether it is in accordance with conveyancing opinion. Even assuming that contemporary opinion on the point is unanimous—which it sometimes is not—there is still a further

question: is it contemporary opinion which is relevant, or conveyancing opinion at the time the covenant was made? The latter is, of course, really an historical question, and neither judges nor conveyancers are primarily historians. In the end it must be contemporary opinion which will prevail, even if such opinion, on points like this, might lay emphasis on whatever happens to be the received wisdom among today's conveyancers about the practices of the past, rather than a serious answer to a serious historian's question. If the judge has followed this opinion in giving his decision, all is well. Indeed, he ought to find reasons if he wishes to depart from this opinion. The question, after all, as so often, is pre-eminently a conveyancer's question: what is the effect of a particular verbal formula?

(3) What policy reasons might a judge put forward for departing from conveyancing opinion on this kind of question? Today, of course, people argue about whether restrictive covenants, as the principal form of private land-use control, should continue to operate in an era of public law planning regulation. But it is hardly open to a judge to adopt such a reason for his decision, when people have conducted their affairs on the basis that such covenants will be effective and when such covenants have received judicial recognition for so long. And very few judges indeed would see it as their role to decide a case on such a basis. There is, however, another policy reason which is not always spelt out. We could call it "in-house" policy. Maybe because it is in-house, it is often overlooked by law students and legal commentators alike. This is where a judge feels that his— or more generally, judicial—time is being wasted on empty questions. In such circumstances, a judge may be tempted to decide a case so as to stop litigation in the future on similar questions. However, on points where conveyancing opinion is relatively settled, a judge who flies in the face of it is likely to generate rather than stem the flood of litigation.

(4) A judge who has gone against conveyancing opinion without the support of existing judicial authority can fairly be said to have changed the rules. Now no one knows how many covenants there are. The only "control" over them, apart from judicial willingness or unwillingness to enforce them, is at the point of their production: in particular, conveyancers' know-how. So if our judge has gone against prevailing opinion, he has changed the rule retrospectively. It is possible, though no one knows for sure, because we work in conditions of high uncertainty (which is why conveyancing opinion is so important), that

"out there" are thousands of covenants whose writers used the particular annexation formula, whose legal effect our hypothetical judge has now changed. All of these covenants, contrary to expectation, would now be unenforceable as a result of the decision of the judge. Most people would probably say, intuitively, that there is something not right about that.

(5) However, in terms of the future, the judge's decision has a largely technical effect. A new formula will be created by conveyancers for the standard forms, precedent books and advice manuals. This will only happen, of course, if conveyancers find out about the decision. One can hardly overemphasise the importance for grasping the degree of systematisation of the legal system of thinking of it as a communication network.

NON-FORMALISM

Where there is formalism, we are likely to encounter its opposite, at least in an environment in which, as is the case in England, people have better things to do than spend their time in the offices of, or on the telephone to, their lawyer, if they have one at all. Yet the English approach to land law and to trusts largely presupposed a familiarity, in every sense of the word, with your lawyer, who was literally your *chargé d'affaires*.

Where people arrange their affairs without the assistance of lawyers, it is obviously the case that lawyers will get involved in trying to make legal sense of the relationship only in the event of a dispute of some kind. But there is nothing new about the need to make sense of informal arrangements, about the need for the interpretation of facts rather than documents, in the adjudicative process. The tenancy at will, outlined in Chapter 7, provides one example, and disputes over the liability to pay rates or over the eligibility to vote, when the franchise was restricted by a property qualification, provide other examples of when courts were called upon to determine the "true legal nature" of an informal arrangement which lawyers had not been able—and would not have expected to have been called upon—to pin down in advance by formalising it.

These were not the kinds of matters which taxed the draftsmen of the 1925 code to any great extent, because, more or less by definition, they were marginal to the principal concerns of conveyancers. Their conveyancing implications were peripheral to what was at issue in 1925, since they amounted to little more than the familiar, routine matter of finding a place in the new schemes for the old practices of inspection of the land outlined in Chapter 9. The development of the new residential "equities", precipitated by the rise of owner-occupation, which we sketched in Chapter 6 and whose conveyancing implications were outlined in Chapter 10, has thrown up what seems, in one sense, to be a quite new set of problems. They threaten to disrupt the unconscious design of English property law, because most of these equities—even the contractual licence as it has come to be formulated in the residential context—import some notion of trust. And trust brings us back to the domain of English formalism.

Informality and its consequences, so far as trusts were concerned, arose against the backdrop of the formalism already considered. The normative expectations appropriate to that formalist and formulaic tradition could be brought into play in the adjudication of disputes. This was true in two obvious respects. First, long practice could itself generate normative expectations. The contents of formal instruments prepared by lawyers in relation to property not only became standardised as part and parcel of the formulaic tradition, but became "typified" or "paradigmatic". Judges who had been conveyancers would have a set of ideas about how people of property ought to arrange their affairs, and even those who had not practised as conveyancers would have received similar advice in the management of their own personal affairs, and this good sense would be reinforced by counsel in the courtroom.

Secondly, formalism and the expectations generated by it serve as the backdrop for adjudication in the sense that lawyers and judges come to typify the circumstances in which they expect people to organise their affairs with their assistance, through their instrumentality. The more reasonable it seems to lawyers to expect that people will invoke their assistance to arrange their affairs in a formal way, especially concerning the disposition of their property, the more justifiable it seems to impose strict limits on the circumstances in which the courts will afford assistance to those whose claims are without a formal basis.

What then is not new is judges drawing upon non-legal normative resources—however these are generated—in the course of resolving disputes between parties whose relations, from a legal point of view, are informal. What is new today is not directly attributable to the judiciary, but to the wider social world with whose conflicts they have to deal from time to time, in which the formalism of lawyers has in large measure disappeared.

This is the range of social relationships which arise informally against the backdrop of owner-occupation. Because these relationships concern property, and do not just appear on its margins, lawyers are supposed to have answers to basic questions to do with people's rights in such situations. The reason why it is difficult to give clear answers when these are sought in the event of a dispute is not least because not even any backdrop of formal legal practice exists to provide a typified point of reference. Instead, these are just diffuse sets of social norms which may in any event, in a modern society, be very divergent.

For some, the solution lies in more legislation: to codify in some way rights of occupation. How far this would help is not clear. But most difficult of all is to work out what criteria should stand as a measure for whatever is proposed. It is not very difficult in principle to work out a conveyancing regime which is less abstruse than the one which we use today. What is difficult is to decide, and to decide how to decide, where to place the priorities, how to allocate the risks. Whose values are to determine any new scheme which might be proposed?

Legislative solutions necessarily tend to generalise one particular set of values, and are exposed to the further problem that it is not always possible to legislate for every contingency. Judicial solutions are more flexible but are, correspondingly, somewhat haphazard (both because courts are largely passive so far as the inflow of disputes is concerned, and because judicial case-by-case decision-making involves a degree of arbitrariness). A "return" to private ordering, the approach which is perhaps closest to the traditions of property law, may hold some attractions, especially in a multicultural society in which agreement on basic values can no longer be taken for granted by legislatures or by courts. But to make private ordering a substantial policy instrument, careful attention needs to be given to the problem of unfairness, as well as to the broader culture shift which would be required to make the legal formalisation of relationships more commonplace and routine than the property case law suggests it is at present. The assumption in the past, which in large measure is still assumed today, was that lawyers are required for such legal formalisation of relationships to take place, and that therefore the problem of formalisation is intimately connected with the problem of access to legal services. We should not conclude leaving this assumption unchallenged: in the future, it may well become routine to form legally binding relationships without using lawyers as intermediaries (*cf.* Susskind, 1998).

NOTES

1. *Mabo v Queensland (No. 2)* (1992) 175 C.L.R. 1; *Wik Peoples v Queensland* (1996) 187 C.L.R. 1.
2. A notable exception is Lawson and Rudden, 1982.
3. See the prefaces to Williams, 1848; Goodeve, 1887.
4. For the Justinian codification, see Honoré, 1978; for the influence of the Roman textbook, the *Institutes*, see Kelley, 1979; for the ways in which modern civilian systems departed from the Roman example, see Jolowicz, 1957; on codification and property, see Straskosch, 1967.
5. *Westdeutsche Landesbank Girozentrale v Islington London Borough Council* [1996] 2 All E.R. 961 at 970.
6. See *South Staffordshire Water Co. v Sharman* [1896] 2 Q.B. 44; *City of London Corporation v Appleyard* [1963] 1 W.L.R. 982; *Parker v British Airways Board* [1982] 1 All E.R. 834.
7. *Asher v Whitlock* (1865) L.R. 1 Q.B. 1.
8. Critchley, 1978, usefully summarises the general issues; for the problems of "feudalism" as an analytical tool for the understanding of the Middle Ages, see Brown, 1974. See also essays in Hudson, 1996.
9. For references, see note 1, above.
10. See Bean, 1968 and *cf.* Milsom, 1981.
11. *Earl of Oxford's* Case (1616).
12. *Duke of Somerset v Cookson* 3 P.W. 390.
13. Lord Loughborough C., *Fells v Read* 3 V. 71.
14. *Maddison v Alderson* (1883) 8 App. Cas. 467.
15. *Midland Bank plc v Cooke* [1995] 4 All E.R. 562 at 567, *per* Waite L.J.
16. *ibid.* at 575, *per* Waite L.J.
17. *Springette v Defoe* [1992] F.L.R. 388.
18. *Midland Bank plc v Cooke* [1995] 4 All E.R. 562 at 575, *per* Waite L.J.
19. *ibid.* at 574, *per* Waite L.J.
20. *Bull v Bull* [1955] 1 Q.B. 234; *Jones v Challenger* [1961] 1 Q.B. 176; Murphy and Clark, 1983, pp.61–68.
21. This is the underlying logic of the so-called "rule in *Saunders v Vautier*" (1841) 4 Beav. 115, which is, in a narrow sense,

limited to the right of adult beneficiaries to override income accumulation trusts.

[22] *Barclays Bank plc v O'Brien* [1993] 4 All E.R. 417.

[23] *Lace v Chantler* [1944] K.B. 368; *cf. Ashburn Anstalt v Arnold* [1989] Ch. 1.

[24] The precise requirements here, originally codified in ss.52 and 54 of the Law of Property Act 1925, have now been made more complicated by the "reform" introduced in s.1 of the Law of Property (Miscellaneous Provisions) Act 1989.

[25] For what follows, see especially Horn, 1980; Beckett, 1986.

[26] For what follows, see Dennis, 1984; Daunton, 1983; and note Swenarton and Taylor, 1985.

[27] See *Street v Mountford* [1985] 2 W.L.R. 877; *cf. Antoniades v Villiers* [1990] 1 A.C. 417.

[28] *Expert Clothing v Hillgate House* [1985] 3 W.L.R. 359.

[29] See *Billson v Residential Apartments Ltd* [1992] 1 A.C. 494.

[30] *National Carriers Ltd v Panalpina (Northern) Ltd* [1981] 2 W.L.R. 45.

[31] Leasehold Reform Act 1967; now see Leasehold Reform, Housing and Urban Development Act 1993.

[32] See *Walsh v Lonsdale* (1882) 21 Ch.D. 91; *Manchester Brewery v Coombs* [1901] 2 Ch. 608.

[33] See *Rhone v Stephens* [1994] 2 All E.R. 65.

[34] Another means, of uncertain scope, is suggested in the judgments in *Halsall v Brizell* (1957) Ch. 169 and *E.R. Ives Investment Ltd v High* (1967) 2 Q.B. 379.

[35] For a discussion of the broader issues here, see Pottage, 1994.

[36] 12 Ch.D. 31.

[37] JPL, "How Discreet Are You?" [1960] *Solicitors Journal* 553.

[38] *Bull v Bull* (note 20, above).

[39] *cf. Binions v Evans* [1972] Ch. 359.

[40] Before the LRA 2002, this was governed by the LRA 1925, s.70(1)(k): "Leases for any term or interest not exceeding twenty-one years, granted at a rent without taking a fine". As we have seen, the landlord-tenant relationship can come into existence in two ways—by a deed or purely verbally, *i.e.* with or without paper. If the relationship is fixed to last for more than three years, a deed must be used. Informal tenancies were of a shorter duration: commonly from week to week for working-class housing and year to year for agricultural tenancies. Middle-class residential lettings were commonly for two or three years under seal. The intention of this paragraph was to exclude these latter from the register, since in practice the

existence of such tenancies would be apparent on inspecting the land, and the extent of the tenant's rights ascertainable from the lease itself.

[41] A caution is just that: a warning, rather than a notice, a direct communication, to the inquiring purchaser. Here we are concerned with what is known as the "caution against dealings" with the registered title. It works as follows. (1) The person with a claim against the title which is capable of protection under s.54 of the LRA 1925 must make a statutory declaration outlining the nature of his claim. (2) This is sent to the Registry and a caution is entered against the title. (3) This entitles the cautioner to be notified of any proposed dealing with the title. (4) When this occurs, he then has 14 days to enter an objection. (5) Equally, the registered proprietor can apply to have the caution removed (as where a prospective purchaser discovers the caution during his inquiries and indicates that he will not continue until the caution is removed); the cautioner will be notified and has 14 days to make his case. It is primarily for the Land Registrar to decide, in accordance with the LRA and the Land Registry Rules, what course of action is appropriate in such circumstances, though his discretion is ultimately subject to the jurisdiction of the Chancery Division of the High Court.

[42] "Subject to the provisions of this Act, rights acquired or in the course of being acquired under the Limitation Acts."

[43] Law Commission, *Land Registration for the Twenty-First Century* (Law Com. Rep., 1998); Law Commission, *Land Registration for the Twenty-First Century: A Conveyancing Revolution* (Law Com. Rep., 2001).

[44] [1901] 1 Ch. 45.

[45] *www.landreg.gov.uk/publications/practice_guides*

[46] *cf. Peffer v Rigg* [1977] 1 W.L.R. 285 and *Midland Bank Trust Co. v Green* [1981] A.C. 513.

[47] *cf.* in this context *Barclays Bank v O'Brien* [1993] 4 All E.R. 417.

[48] Lord Bridge of Harwich in *Abbey National Building Society v Cann* [1990] 2 W.L.R. 833 at 838.

BIBLIOGRAPHICAL REFERENCES

Anderson, J. Stuart (1984), "Land Law Texts and the Explanation of 1925" 37 *Current Legal Problems* 63–84.

Anderson, J. Stuart (1992), *Lawyers and the Making of English Land Law 1832–1940* (Oxford: Clarendon Press).

Arendt, Hannah (1958), *The Human Condition* (Chicago: Chicago University Press).

Ariès, Philippe (1983), In *The Hour of our Death*, tr. Helen Weaver (Harmondsworth: Peregrine).

Atiyah, P.S. (1978). "Contracts, Promises and the Law of Obligations" 94 *Law Quarterly Review* 193–223.

Barrell, John (1980), *The Dark Side of the Landscape: The Rural Poor in English Painting 1730–1840* (Cambridge: Cambridge University Press).

Bean, J.M.W. (1968), *The Decline of English Feudalism* (Manchester: University of Manchester Press).

Beaune, Colette (1991), The *Birth of an Ideology: Myths and Symbols of Nation in Late-Medieval France*, tr. Susan Ross Huston, ed. Fredric L. Cheyette (Berkeley: University of California Press).

Beckett, J.V. (1986), *The Aristocracy of England 1660–1914* (Oxford: Basil Blackwell).

Beckett, John (1994), *The Rise and Fall of the Grenvilles: Dukes of Buckingham and Chandos, 1710 to 1921* (Manchester: Manchester University Press).

Berle, Adolf A. and Means, Gardiner C. (1932), *The Modern Corporation and Private Property* (New York: Macmillan).

Blackburn, Colin (1845), *A Treatise on the Effect of the Contract of Sale on the Legal Rights of Property and Possession in Goods, Wares and Merchandise* (London: William Benning).

Bodmer, Walter and McKie, Robin (1995), *The Book of Man: The Quest to Discover our Genetic Heritage* (London: Abacus).

Bogusz, Barbara (2002), "Bringing Land Registration into the Twenty-First Century—The Land Registration Act 2002", 65 Modern Law Review 556–567.

Boniface, Priscilla and Fowler, Peter J. (1993), *Heritage and Tourism in the "Global Village"* (London: Routledge).

Bourdieu, Pierre (1977), *Outline of a Theory of Practice*, tr. Richard Nice (Cambridge: Cambridge University Press).

Brewer, John and Porter, Roy (eds) (1993), *Consumption and the World of Goods* (London: Routledge).

Brodrick, George C. (1881), *English Land and English Landlords* (London: Cassel, Petter, Galpin).

Brown, E.A.R. (1974), "The Tyranny of a Construct: Feudalism and Historians of Medieval Europe", 79 *American Historical Review*, 1063–1088.

Bullen, Edward (1899), *The Law of Distress*, 2nd ed. by Cyril Dodd and T.J. Bullen (London: Butterworth).

Campbell, John (1991), *F.E. Smith: First Earl of Birkenhead* (London: Pimlico).

Cannadine, David (1977), "Aristocratic Indebtedness in the Nineteenth Century: The Case Re-opened" 30 *Economic History Review*, 2nd ser., 624–650.

Cannadine, David (1992), *The Decline and Fall of the British Aristocracy* (London: Picador).

Chandler, Alfred D. and Daems, Herman (eds) (1980), *Managerial Hierarchies* (Cambridge, Mass.: MIT Press).

Capps, Deveral (2002), "Conveyancing in the 21st Century: An Outline of Electronic Conveyancing and Electronic Signatures", Conveyancer and Property Lawyer September/October, 443–445.

Chamberlain, Linda (2002), "The Land Registration Act 2002: a 'Conveyancing Revolution'—Part I", 152 New Law Journal 1093–1095.

Cheshire, G.C. (1925), *The Modern Law of Real Property* (London: Butterworths).

Clanchy, M.T. (1979), *From Memory to Written Record* (London: Edward Arnold).

Clark, J.C.D. (1985), *English Society 1688–1832* (Cambridge: Cambridge University Press).

Clark, J.C.D. (1986), *Revolution and Rebellion* (Cambridge: Cambridge University Press).

Clarke, David N. (2002) "The Enactment of Commonhold — Problems, Principles and Perspectives", Conveyancer and Property Lawyer, July/August 349–386, 351.

Clastres, Pierre (1977), Society against the State, tr. Robert Hurley (Oxford: Basil Blackwell).

Clay, Christopher (1968), "Marriage, Inheritance and the Rise of Large Estates in England, 1660–1815" 21 *Economic History Review*, 2nd ser., 503–518.

Cooke, Elizabeth (2003), The New Law of Land Registration (Oxford and Portland, Oregon: Hart).

Coombes, Annie E. (1991), "Ethnography and the Formation of National and Cultural Identities" in Susan Hiller (ed.), *The Myth of Primitivism: Perspectives on Art* (London: Routledge), 189–214.

Corbier, Mireille (1991), "Divorce and Adoption as Roman Familial Strategies" in Beryl Rawson (ed.), *Marriage, Divorce and Children in Ancient Rome* (Oxford: Clarendon Press), 47–78.

Critchley, John (1978), *Feudalism* (London: George Allen and Unwin).

Daunton, M.J. (1983), *House and Home in the Victorian City* (London: Edward Arnold).

Daunton, M.J. (1987), *A Property-Owning Democracy? Housing in Britain* (London: Faber and Faber).

Daunton, M.J. (1995), *Progress and Poverty: An Economic and Social History of Britain 1700–1850* (Oxford: Oxford University Press).

Davidoff, Leonore and Hall, Catherine (1987), *Family Fortunes: Men and Women of the English Middle Class 1780–1850* (London: Hutchinson).

Dennis, Richard (1984), *English Industrial Cities of the Nineteenth Century* (Cambridge: Cambridge University Press).

Dixon, Martin (2003), "The Reform of Property Law and the Land Registration Act 2002: A Risk Assessment" Conveyancer and Property Lawyer, March/April 136–156.

Durkheim, Emile (1984), *The Division of Labour in Society*, tr. W.D. Halls (London: Macmillan).

Edinburgh Review (1821) [C.H. Bellenden Ker].

Ekelund, Robert B. and Tollison, Robert D. (1981), *Mercantilism as a Rent-Seeking Society* (College Station: Texas A. and M. University Press).

Evans, David (1993), *Sexual Citizenship: The Material Construction of Sexualities* (London: Routledge).

Evans, Eric J. (1976), *The Contentious Tithe* (London: Routledge and Kegan Paul).

Fiss, Owen (1984), "Against Settlement" 93 *Yale Law Journal*, 1073–1090.

Freyer, Tony (1992), *Regulating Big Business: Antitrust in Great Britain and America 1880–1990* (Cambridge: Cambridge University Press).

Fukuyama, Francis (1992), *The End of History and the Last Man* (Harmondsworth: Penguin).

Gatrell, V.A.C. (1994), *The Hanging Tree: Execution and the English People 1770–1868* (Oxford: Oxford University Press).

George, Henry (n.d.), *Progress and Poverty* (London: J.M. Dent).

Glendon, Mary Ann (1991), *Rights Talk: The Impoverishment of Political Discourse* (New York: Free Press).

Godwin, William (1985), *Enquiry Concerning Political Justice, 1797* ed. (Harmondsworth: Penguin).

Goodeve, L.A. (1887), *The Modern Law of Personal Property* (London: W. Maxwell).

Goody, Jack (1983), *The Development of the Family and Marriage in Europe* (Cambridge: Cambridge University Press).

Gray, Kevin (1987), *Elements of Land Law* (London: Butterworths).

Gray, Kevin and Symes, Pamela (1981), *Real Property and Real People: Principles of Land Law* (London: Butterworths).

Greenfield, Susan (1996), *The Return of Cultural Treasures*, 2nd ed. (Cambridge: Cambridge University Press).

Gudeman, Stephen (1986), *Economics As Culture* (London: Routledge and Kegan Paul).

Gurevich, A.J. (1985), *Categories of Medieval Culture*, tr. G.L. Campbell (London: Routledge and Kegan Paul).

Handler, Richard (1988), "On Having a Culture" in *Stocking*, ed., 1988, 192–217.

Haraway, Donna (1997), *Modest_Witness@Second_Millennium. FemaleMan©_Meets_OncoMouse™* (London: Verso).

Harpum, Charles (2002), "Leases under the Land Registration Act 2002", Landlord & Tenant Review 6(3), 51–54.

Hayek, F.A. (1944), *The Road to Serfdom* (London: Routledge and Kegan Paul).

Hegel, G.W.F. (1991), *Elements of the Philosophy of Right, 1820*, ed. Allen W. Wood (Cambridge: Cambridge University Press).

Hewitt, E.P. and Richardson, J.B. (1928), *White and Tudor's Leading Cases in Equity*, 9th ed., vol. 2 (London: Sweet and Maxwell).

Honoré, Tony (1978), *Tribonian* (London: Duckworth).

Honoré, Tony (1982), *The Quest for Security: Employees, Tenants, Wives* (London: Stevens).

Hopkins, Keith (1983), *Death and Renewal* (Cambridge: Cambridge University Press).

Horn, Pamela (1980), *The Rural World 1780–1850* (London: Hutchinson).

Hudson, John (ed.) (1996), *The History of English Law: Centenary Essays on "Pollock and Maitland"* [89 Proceedings of the British Academy] (Oxford: Oxford University Press).

Hunt, Alan (1997), *Governance of the Consuming Passions: A History of Sumptuary Law* (London: Macmillan).

John, Michael (1989), *Politics and the Law in Late Nineteenth-Century Germany: The Origins of the Civil Code* (Oxford: Oxford University Press).

Jolowicz, H.F. (1957), *Roman Foundations of Modern Law* (Oxford: Clarendon Press).

Jones, Steve (1994), *The Language of the Genes: Biology, History and the Evolutionary Future* (London: Flamingo).

Kant, Immanuel (1965), *The Metaphysical Elements of Justice*, 1797, tr. John Ladd (Indianapolis: Bobbs-Merrill).

Kelley, Donald R (1979), "Gaius Noster: Substructures of Western Social Thought" 84 American Historical Review 619–648.

Kenney, Phillip H. (2002a), "Editorial: A Kaleidoscope of Change", Conveyancer and Property Lawyer September/October 431–433.

Kenney, Phillip H. (2002b), "Land Registration Rules O.K.", Conveyancer and Property Lawyer November/December, 518–522.

Korman, Sharon (1996), *The Right of Conquest: The Acquisition of Territory by Force in International Law and Practice* (Oxford: Oxford University Press).

Lasch, Christopher (1991), *The True and Only Heaven* (New York: W.W. Norton).

Lasch, Christopher (1995), *The Revolt of the Elites and the Betrayal of Democracy* (New York: W.W. Norton).

Law Commission (1986), Land Mortgages, Working Paper No. 99 (London: HMSO).

Lawson, F.H. and Rudden, B. (1982), *The Law of Property*, 2nd ed. (Oxford: Clarendon Press).

Lee, R.B. and Devore, I. (eds) (1968), *Man the Hunter* (Chicago: Aldine).

Lévi-Strauss, Claude (1969), *The Elementary Structures of Kinship*, 2nd ed. (Boston: Beacon Press).

Locke, John (1924), *Two Treatises of Government*, 1690 (London: J.M. Dent).

Lowenthal, David (1996), *The Heritage Crusade and the Spoils of History* (London: Viking).

Lumley, Robert (ed.) (1988), *The Museum Time-Machine: Putting Cultures on Display* (London: Routledge).

Macfarlane, Alan (1978), *The Origins of English Individualism* (Oxford: Basil Blackwell).

Maine, Henry (1917), *Ancient Law* (London: Dent).

Maitland, F.W. (1909), *Equity and the Forms of Action* (Cambridge: Cambridge University Press).

Mandler, Peter (1997), *The Fall and Rise of the Stately Home* (New Haven: Yale University Press).

Marx, Karl (1975), "On the Jewish Question", 1844, tr. Clemens Dutt, in Karl Marx and Frederick Engels, *Collected Works*, vol. 3 (London: Lawrence and Wishart), 146–174.

Marx, Karl (1974), *Capital*, vol. 3, 1894, ed. F. Engels (London: Lawrence and Wishart).

Mauss, Marcel (1969), *The Gift*, 1925, tr. Ian Cunnison (London: Routledge and Kegan Paul).

Megarry, R.E. and Wade H.W.R. (1959), *The Law of Real Property* (London: Stevens).

Milsom, S.F.C. (1981), *Historical Foundations of the Common Law* (London: Butterworths).

Milsom, S.F.C. (1996), "'Pollock and Maitland': A Lawyer's Retrospect" 89 *Proceedings of the British Academy* 243–259; also in Hudson, 1996.

Murphy, W.T. and Clark, Hilary (1983), *The Family Home* (London: Sweet and Maxwell).

Neeson, J.M. (1993), "An Eighteenth-Century Peasantry" in John Rule and Robert Malcomson (eds), *Protest and Survival: Essays for E.P. Thompson* (London: Merlin Press), 24–59.

Northrup, David (1978), *Trade Without Rulers* (Oxford: Oxford University Press).

Oakley, Francis (1984), *Omnipotence, Covenant and Order* (London: Cornell University Press).

Offer, Avner (1977), "Origins of the Law of Property Acts 1920–1925" 40 *Modern Law Review* 505–522.

Offer, Avner (1981), *Property and Politics 1870–1914* (Cambridge: Cambridge University Press).

Parry, J. and Bloch, M. (eds) (1987), *Money and the Morality of Exchange* (Cambridge: Cambridge University Press).

Pennington, Kenneth (1993), *The Prince and the Law 1200–1600: Sovereignty and Rights in the Western Legal Tradition* (Berkeley: University of California Press).

Perkin, Harold (1992), "The Enterprise Culture in Historical Perspective" in Paul Heelas and Paul Moms (eds), *The Values of the Enterprise Culture* (London: Routledge), 36–60.

Pocock, J.G.A. (1989), *Politics, Language and Time: Essays on Political Thought and History* (Chicago: Chicago University Press).

Pollack, Robert (1994), *Signs of Life: The Language and Meanings of DNA* (Harmondsworth: Penguin).

Pottage, Alain (1994), "The Measure of Land", 57 *Modern Law Review* 361.

Pottage, Alain (1995), "The Originality of Registration" 15 *Oxford Journal of Legal Studies*, 371–401.

Rabinow, Paul (1996), *Making PCR: A Story of Biotechnology* (Chicago: Chicago University Press).

Reynolds, Susan (1994), *Fiefs and Vassals* (Oxford: Oxford University Press).

Richardson, Ruth (1989), *Death, Dissection and the Destitute* (Harmondsworth: Penguin).

Rifkin, Jeremy (2000), *The Age of Access* (Harmondsworth: Penguin).

Rose, Mark (1993), *Authors and Owners: The Invention of Copyright* (Cambridge, Mass.: Harvard University Press).

Ross, Michael (1996), *Planning and the Heritage*, 2nd ed. (London: E & FN Spon).

Russo, Enzo and Cove, David (1998), *Genetic Engineering: Dreams and Nightmares* (Oxford: Oxford University Press).

Ryan, Alan (1984), *Property and Political Theory* (Oxford: Basil Blackwell).

Samuel, Raphael (1994), *Theatres of Memory* (London: Verso).

Sayer, Michael (1993), *The Disintegration of a Heritage: Country Houses and their Collections 1979–1992*, ed. Hugh Massingberd (Norwich: Michael Wilby).

Schama, Simon (1987), *The Embarrassment of Riches* (London: Fontana).

Shell, Marc (1993), *Money, Language and Thought* (Baltimore: John Hopkins University Press).

Sherman, Daniel J. and Rogoff, Irit (eds) (1994), *Museum Culture: Histories, Discourses, Spectacles* (London: Routledge).

Simpson, A.W.B. (1961), *An Introduction to the History of the Land Law* (Oxford: Oxford University Press).

Snell, Edmund H.T. (1908), *The Principles of Equity*, 15th ed. by Archibald Brown (London: Stevens and Haynes).

Spring, Eileen (1993), *Law, Land and Family: Aristocratic Inheritance in England, 1300 to 1800* (Chapel Hill: University of North Carolina Press).

Stocking, George W. Jr (ed.) (1988), *Objects and Others: Essays on Museums and Material Culture* (Madison: University of Wisconsin Press).

Strakosch, Henry E. (1967), *State Absolutism, and the Rule of Law* (Sydney: Sydney University Press).

Sugarman, David and Warrington, Ronnie (1996), "Land Law, Citizenship, and the Invention of "Englishness": The Strange

World of the Equity of Redemption" in John Brewer and Susan Staves (eds), *Early Modern Conceptions of Property* (London: Routledge), 111–143.

Sugden, E.B. (1858), *A Handy Book on Property Law*, 5th ed. (Edinburgh).

Susskind, Richard (1998), *The Future of Law*, rev. ed. (Oxford: Oxford University Press).

Swenarton, Mark and Taylor, Sandra (1985), "The Scale and Nature of the Growth of Owner-occupation in Britain between the Wars" 38 *Economic History Review*, 2nd ser., 373–392.

Sykes, Christopher Simon (1982), *Black Sheep* (London: Chatto and Windus).

Thompson, E.P.(1991), *Customs in Common* (London: Merlin).

Thompson, F.M.L. (1955), "The End of a Great Estate", 8 *Economic History Review*, 2nd ser., 36–52.

Tully, J. (1993), *An Approach to Political Philosophy: Locke in Contexts* (Cambridge: Cambridge University Press).

Twiss, Horace (1846), *The Public and Private Life of Lord Chancellor Eldon*, 3rd ed., 2 vols (London: John Murray).

Vergo, Peter (ed.) (1989), *The New Museology* (London: Reaktion Books).

Walsh, Kevin (1992), *The Representation of the Past: Museums and Heritage in the Post-Modern World* (London: Routledge).

Weber, Max (1978), *Economy and Society*, eds. Guenther Roth and Claus Wittich; tr. Ephraim Fischoff *et al.* (Berkeley: University of California Press).

Wilkie, Tom (1994), *Perilous Knowledge: The Human Genome Project and its Implications* (London: Faber and Faber).

Williams, Joshua (1848), *Principles of the Law of Personal Property Intended for The Use of Students in Conveyancing*, 3rd ed., 1856 (London: H. Sweet).

Williams, Joshua (1848), *Principles of the Law of Personal Property*, *etc.*, 18th ed., 1926 by T. Cyprian Williams (London: Sweet & Maxwell).

Williams, Raymond (1975), The *Country and the City* (London: Paladin).

Williams, T. Cyprian (1922), *Vendor and Purchaser*, 3rd ed. by T. Cyprian Williams and John M. Lightwood, 2 vols (London: Sweet and Maxwell).

Wilson, Peter J. (1988), *The Domestication of the Human Species* (New York: Yale University Press).

Woodburn, J.C. (1972), "Ecology, Nomadic Movement and the Composition of the Local Group among Hunters and

Gatherers: An East African Example and Its Implications", in Peter J. Ucko *et al.* (eds), *Man, Settlement and Urbanism* (London: Duckworth).

Yelling, J.A. (1977), *Common Field and Enclosure in England 1450–1850* (London: Macmillan).

INDEX